Jesus, Paul and the People of God

A Theological Dialogue with N. T. Wright

EDITED BY

Nicholas Perrin and Richard B. Hays

Originally published in the United States of America in 2011
by InterVarsity Press, P.O. Box 1400, Downers Grove, IL60515-1426

First published in Great Britain in 2011

Society for Promoting Christian Knowledge
36 Causton Street
London SW1P 4ST
www.spckpublishing.co.uk

British Library Cataloguing-in-Publication Data
A catalogue record for this book is available from the British Library

ISBN 978–0–281–06213–3

1 3 5 7 9 10 8 6 4 2

Printed in Great Britain by MPG Books Group

Produced on paper from sustainable forests

Contents

Introduction

NICHOLAS PERRIN

IN THE INTRODUCTION TO HIS 1914 English translation of Albert Schweitzer's first book on Jesus, *The Mystery of the Kingdom of God*,
Walter Lowrie writes:

> Obviously it was not the weakness of the book, but rather its strong
> originality and in particular the trenchant way in which it demolished
> the "liberal life of Jesus" which accounts for the passive hostility with
> which it was greeted. In fact it contained more than could be readily
> digested either by a liberal or a conservative mind. . . . The reception
> accorded to Schweitzer's work does not seem creditable. It was met by
> something like a conspiracy of silence.[1]

As best as we can tell, Lowrie was right. Schweitzer's breathtaking
account of an apocalyptic historical Jesus, presented in both *Mystery of
the Kingdom* and *The Quest of the Historical Jesus* (1910 [1906]), had met
with mixed reviews from both liberal and conservative peers. And,
generally speaking, where one did not find mixed reviews, there was an
icy silence. Even with his *Paul and His Interpreters* (1911), a compara-
tively restrained work which sought to emphasize the apocalyptic and
mystical side of the apostle to the Gentiles, Schweitzer would not get a
much better reception. In fact, the liberal scholar Ernst von Dobschütz
was so scandalized by Schweitzer's "thoroughgoing eschatology" that
for a time he even dedicated himself wholly to refuting the position,

---

[1]Walter Lowrie, introduction to Albert Schweitzer, *The Mystery of the Kingdom of God: The Secret of
Jesus' Messiahship and Passion*, trans. Walter Lowrie (New York: Dodd, Mead, 1914), pp. 18-19.

converting his personal animus into a kind of international lecture road show.[2] Today, one may be forgiven for wondering whether Schweitzer ever regarded his hard-hitting experience as a young scholar to be a kind of mental preparation for his later experience of World War I. As in modern-day warfare, so in the academic guild: stick your head too far above the trench and you *will* undoubtedly draw fire from opposing lines.

But when it came to Schweitzer's accounts of Jesus and Paul, matters were even more complicated than one might expect in a typical war. For in this regard, as Lowrie also rightly points out, Schweitzer faced not one but two opposing lines: a conservative trench manned by those who were accustomed to reading Jesus and Paul according the Biblicist tradition, and on the other side a counterpart which did not take kindly to calls to surrender its much-loved liberal lives of Jesus and Paul. This is not to say that no one across the theological spectrum saw promising glimmers of hope in Schweitzer's account—some certainly did. For respondents on both sides, Schweitzer's conclusions made for a handy sledgehammer capable of destroying the icons of the opposing theological positions. But even here there was a nagging ambivalence, for even the most fervent iconoclast had to recognize that the hammer of an apocalyptic Jesus and mystical Paul swung both ways: conservative and liberal icons alike would have to pay the price—and that was a cost too dear. Nor did it help matters that at the time Schweitzer's argument resisted any categorization within easily recognizable schools of thought. In this sense the Alsatian was neither fish nor fowl, and paid his own price accordingly. Transcending the categories and camps of his own day, he fell victim to his own daring and originality.

When I consider the life and writings of my friend N. T. (Tom) Wright, I am struck by certain comparisons and contrasts with the life and work of Schweitzer. First, there is a relatively obvious comparison in relation to their respective portraits of Jesus and Paul. By his own acknowledgment, Bishop Wright offers us a Jesus that bears a certain

---

[2]Walter P. Weaver notes: "Dobschütz came to England as a kind of emissary to attempt to discredit Schweitzer" (*The Historical Jesus in the Twentieth Century: 1900-1950* [Harrisburg, Penn.: Trinity Press International, 1999], p. 31).

family semblance to the Jesus of Schweitzer. To recall a memorable metaphor from *Jesus and the Victory of God*, Schweitzer and Wright share the same *Autobahn*. Likewise, for Schweitzer as for Wright, mystical union with Christ is central to their mutual understanding of the apostle Paul. While Schweitzer and Wright are far from two peas in a pod, they nonetheless share certain basic views on Jesus and Paul.

There is a further point of comparison between Tom Wright and Albert Schweitzer: both figures in their own time managed to defy conventional templates of "conservative" or "liberal." In the case of Schweitzer, Lowrie is undoubtedly right that both conservatives and liberals had trouble "digesting" him. In the case of Wright, his work too has resisted such labels as "conservative" or "liberal," even as he has been simultaneously invoked and dismissed by both. Perhaps, indeed, this fact makes for one of the most compelling yet finally intangible evidences that Tom Wright, in his accounts of Jesus and Paul, is onto *something*. In any case, Wright and Schweitzer have shared a mutual determination to remain as historians unhindered by the constraints of theological tradition. Of course neither writer is simply interested in history for history's sake; they both have theological interests. But in their respective studies of Jesus and Paul, both in their own way insist on keeping theology off the stage, even if it was found to be waiting in the wings all along. Or as Bishop Tom puts it elsewhere in this volume, it's a matter of Scripture "setting the questions rather than establishing the answers." Quite apart from personal judgments as to the merits of this approach or even its possibility (as shall become clear in the following pages, certain contributors to this volume raise their own doubts on this score), it is impossible to deny a certain verve and freshness that comes of it. Apart from such new and bold ways of looking at the historical Jesus and the historical Paul, theology itself runs the risk of becoming either hopelessly abstract or desperately stale. When the bread of theological conversations begins to harden on the shelf, both the church and the academy— whether they know it or not, whether they like it or not—find themselves looking to the occasional Schweitzer or Wright to provide a fresh batch of yeast. New yeast yields new bread, which delivers us from our soon-to-be-petrified ways of thinking and speaking.

Having mentioned several points of comparison between Albert
Schweitzer and Tom Wright, I might now add a final commonality: a
certain reception of silence. To be clear, this does not mean in the first
instance that the academy has ignored Tom Wright outright. Quite
clearly, it has not.[3] In contemplating the sum total of all the books written on Jesus and Paul in the last twenty years, one would be hard-
pressed to think of a name that comes up more in the indexes than
"Wright, N. T." Nor is this to say that Bishop Wright's works have been
met with the degree of hostility that Schweitzer faced. While Tom's
positions and conclusions have not gone unopposed, he has garnered
plenty of sympathizers and fans in the academy and in the church—
among both leaders and lay audiences. Although N. T. Wright is not a
household name the way, say, Michael Jordan is, he comes as close to
household name status as any biblical scholar or theologian in the business today. Still, there is a *kind* of silence that has attended Wright up
to this point: a theological silence. Over the past two decades or so
quite a bit has been written on whether or not Tom has gotten history
right, but precious little has been said as to if and how all this translates
into Christian theology. It was in order to close this gap that this book
was conceived. It is not enough to admire the bread on the shelf: it must
be broken, shared and tasted. It has been said somewhere that there is
no better place to do such things than among friends, friends who are
also dialogue partners.

The present volume, *Jesus, Paul and the People of God*, represents the
proceedings of the nineteenth annual Wheaton Theology Conference,
which took place at Wheaton College on April 16-17, 2010. For this
conference my coeditor Richard Hays and I invited a range of scholars
who not only were able to speak theologically to Tom's writing but who
also happened to be his personal friends. In this sense the book you are
about to read is a kind of *Festschrift*. At the same time, whereas contributions to *Festschriften* often prove to be quite tangential to the honoree's main contributions and interests, we intended this conference and

---

[3]One might consider, by way of example, *Jesus and the Restoration of Israel: A Critical Assessment
of N. T. Wright's* Jesus and the Victory of God, ed. Carey C. Newman (Downers Grove, Ill.:
InterVarsity Press; Carlisle, U.K.: Paternoster, 1999).

its resulting volume to speak directly to what we as participants saw as some of the most important talking points of Tom's writings on Jesus and Paul. Naturally, this also means that our essayists have points of disagreement—sometimes fundamental disagreement—with Bishop Tom. Although Richard and I are aware that "fundamental disagreement" is not normally associated with a *festlich* experience, we also believe that the highest honor that can be paid any scholar is not undiluted applause, which in the end amounts to empty flattery, but a sympathetic and critical assessment. Our essays were written both out of our fondness for Tom as a friend and out of deep respect for him as a scholar. He deserves nothing less than both our hearty praise and reflective engagement. Our common goal throughout was to relate Tom's history of Jesus and Paul to the church, that is, as the title indicates, the "people of God." For the layperson, the pastor or the scholar who asks, "What difference does Wright's reading of Jesus and Paul make *on the ground level?*" we hope that this book provides some answers—as well as the beginnings of some important conversations.

The volume is broken down into two parts: the first half dealing with the historical Jesus and the second half, the historical Paul. In both parts we include papers from four presenters, each followed by a response from Tom, and then finally a separate essay in which he takes up broader questions regarding Jesus or Paul, as the case may be.[4] The first essay of part one, by Marianne Meye Thompson, is titled *"Jesus and the Victory of God Meets the Gospel of John."* Here Marianne notes the ways in which Wright's *Jesus and the Victory of God* falls in line with a longstanding tradition of historical Jesus scholarship bypassing John in favor of the Synoptic Gospels. Yet matters do not stop there. For she also argues that there are important points at which John's Jesus substantially overlaps with Wright's Jesus (in a way that the Synoptic presentation does not); there are also points—or certainly one significant point in particular—at which John's account militates against Tom's. Thompson's putting the Fourth Evangelist into dialogue with Wright's most well-known account of the historical Jesus raises a number of in-

---

[4]The third paper is actually coauthored and copresented, thus making in this case, five authors for the four Jesus essays.

triguing issues on both a historical and theological level.

In the next essay, "Knowing Jesus: Story, History and the Question of Truth," Richard Hays resumes a conversation begun at a Society of Biblical Literature meeting in Boston in 2008. At that meeting Wright took Hays to task for his role in coediting (with Beverly Gaventa) a volume titled *Seeking the Identity of Jesus*.[5] As Richard reflects on that moment, he finds himself discovering a long-hidden fault line between his own Barthian understanding of faith and history, on the one side, and Tom's, on the other. The thrust of his essay is to bring the dividing line into clearer light. In so doing Hays assesses Wright's approach to the historical Jesus in *Jesus and the Victory of God* and finds the project posting both gains and losses. Hays's focus is not so much on the Jesus that Wright finally offers but on the methodological route by which he summons this Jesus (granted, the two concerns cannot finally be separated). Closing on an interesting twist, Richard submits that Tom is perhaps much closer to Barth than the bishop himself may be aware.

In "'Outside of a Small Circle of Friends': Jesus and the Justice of God," coauthors Sylvia Keesmaat and Brian Walsh get some help from singer-songwriter Phil Ochs and present their paper in dialogic format. Together they commend Wright's Jesus inasmuch as he speaks to the plight of the poor. Nevertheless they feel that Tom "pulls back" when it comes to sufficiently treating Jesus' socioeconomic critique: more can and should be said regarding Jesus' polemic against this particular systemic sin. Following their own distinctive reading of certain Jesus materials, our coauthors advance specific suggestions as to how Jesus' teachings, rightly understood, might apply today, especially in light of the economic turndown of the last several years.

The last participant paper in part one is my own, "Jesus' Eschatology and Kingdom Ethics: Ever the Twain Shall Meet." Here I explore how Wright's eschatology, at least as attributed to Jesus in *Jesus and the Victory of God*, continues much along the same lines of his *Doktorvater*, George Caird, who understood the Galilean as directing his eschato-

---

[5]Beverly Roberts Gaventa and Richard B. Hays, *Seeking the Identity of Jesus: A Pilgrimage* (Grand Rapids: Eerdmans, 2008).

logical pronouncements on a national as opposed to individual level. After exploring a number of theological dividends yielded up by this eschatological framework and the larger argument of the volume as a whole, I propose modifying Wright's position so as to allow for a more thorough retrieval of both corporate *and* personal ethics in the message of Jesus, grounded, respectively on a corporate and personal eschatology of resurrection. Apart from a convergence of the individual and the collective, the spirit of the post-Bultmann line, so I argue, will in the end come back to haunt the house of Jesus studies.

At the close of the first part of the volume, Wright offers his own ruminations in "Whence and Whither Historical Jesus Studies in the Life of the Church?" Implicitly engaging with the first four papers on various levels, Tom's essay begins by offering a semi-autobiographical reflection on the primacy of history in our investigation of Jesus. On a related note, Wright then goes on to speak to how the controlling categories of "divine" and "human" have unhelpfully served to flatten out the story of Jesus. Finally, Tom wishes to bring together that which has been put asunder: kingdom and cross, and then cross and resurrection. For Bishop Tom, the future of Jesus study requires a steadfast refusal to atomize, either on a theological or methodological level, the revealed story of Jesus. Although the essay is rather lengthy (roughly double the length of other essays contained in this volume), I believe it wonderfully encapsulates some of the leading motifs of Tom's thinking.

In part two the volume turns to the apostle Paul. We begin with Edith Humphrey's essay "Glimpsing the Glory: Paul's Gospel, Righteousness and the Beautiful Feet of N. T. Wright." Following a treatment of Bishop Tom's understanding of gospel and the righteousness of God, which includes her own exegesis of 2 Corinthians 5:21 (a verse for which Wright has offered his own ingenious and well-known exegesis), Edith turns to his handling of apocalyptic language. Finding cause for both praise and complaint, she commends Tom for steering clear of both rigid literalism and undue skepticism, but expresses dissatisfaction for his neglecting to interpret apocalyptic images typologically, that is, "as pointers to heavenly or future realities interconnected with our own

lives." The difficulties she finds in Wright's handing of the eschatological discourse and the ascension becomes a case in point. Along
these lines Humphrey calls on Wright to interpret with a keener awareness of the broader communion, the early church fathers and the Eastern church in particular.

Moving from the ancient East to the postmodern West, Jeremy
Begbie's "The Shape of Things to Come? Wright Amidst Emerging
Ecclesiologies" begins by asking why a grassroots, anti-establishment
movement like the emerging church should be so attracted to such a
"powerful figurehead in an ancient [top-down] institution" as we find
in Tom Wright? The answer in large part, Jeremy offers, lies in Tom's
articulation of Pauline ecclesiology, a rendering which is characteristically integral, eschatological, cosmically situated, material and improvisatory. At the same time there are certain aspects of Wright's ecclesiology that the emerging church has thus far overlooked—much to its
own peril. While, according to Begbie, the movement stands to gain
much from a closer reading of Wright, he also ponders in closing just
what it may have to teach Bishop Tom.

In his provocatively titled essay "Did St. Paul Go to Heaven When
He Died?" Markus Bockmuehl focuses on Tom's famous description of
resurrection: "life after life after death." After citing important points
of mutual agreement and points where credit is due, Markus questions
Tom's "conviction that an affirmation of the bodily resurrection necessitates a denial of the traditional Christian belief that the faithful 'go to
heaven' when they die." Bockmuehl argues, first, that Paul's writings
speak both to a future bodily resurrection and the deceased believer's
immediate and everlasting entry into the presence of the risen Christ;
second, that postapostolic Christianity also shared the view that this
"abiding heavenly presence with Christ is compatible with being resurrected bodily when God creates his undivided new heaven and earth."
The essay suggests that Wright's eschatology would be better served by
giving appropriate emphasis to "heaven," that is, the intermediate state,
and further recognition to the fact that in resurrected existence the
distinction between "heaven" and "earth" is rendered moot.

Kevin Vanhoozer's contribution, "Wrighting the Wrongs of the Reformation: The State of the Union with Christ and St. Paul and Protestant Soteriology," is a cleverly written, lighthearted piece dealing with what has been for many a rather heavy subject. Vanhoozer begins by contemplating what he sees as the most controversial aspect of Tom's work, namely, the "pitting [of] one half of the Protestant principle *(sola scriptura)* against the other (God's gracious justification of sinners by the merit of Christ alone through faith alone)." From here Kevin explores whether there might be some meeting ground after all between Wright and some of his Reformed critics. In the end he proposes that such a bridge between the two camps may well present itself in the conceptual merging of "union in Christ" and imputation: filial adoption. He closes with a plea that both sides of the debate engage in less diatribe and more dialogue.

Just as Tom offers his own response at the end of each of the four Jesus essays, he does the same with Paul. We also give him the last word in his "Whence and Whither Pauline Studies in the Life of the Church?" Speaking to his evolving thinking within the context of his own life and intellectual journey, Tom argues that for Paul the central symbol is the unified family in Christ. God calls us into this family not "to take us out of the world but to qualify us to be God's putting-right people for the world." This leads to a discussion of the task of Christian theology, the rethinking of monotheism, election and eschatology along Christological lines. All three considerations point in the same direction: "In Christ you are reconciled, and here's how it might work out. *This* life, *this* community, here, now, is where it matters." The present essay gives us a welcome teaser for Wright's forthcoming and much-anticipated volume on Paul.

So closes out both the book and the event, what during this past spring proved to be a wonderful and even celebratory dialogue. It was—and remains—a dialogue made possible not because all involved willingly deferred to some vaguely defined consensus, but, quite the contrary, because our honoree, Tom Wright, has spent his career willing to look at things differently. Here again one can hardly resist a final, instructive comparison with Albert Schweitzer. I close my introduction with the closing of another book, titled *Albert Schweitzer, Musician.* Tom

himself put me on this tome one morning while we were sitting in his
study in Westminster Abbey. Here the author, Michael Murray, seeks to
summarize the life and thought of Schweitzer by introducing and then
quoting from his subject's words as recorded in his autobiography:

> If, then, the chief beauty of Schweitzer's prose lies in the contrast be-
> tween density of thought and transparency of medium, let chapter and
> book come to an end with a statement of that conviction which in-
> formed not only his literary art but his musical, not only his art but his
> life:
>
> "With the spirit of the age I am in complete disagreement, because it
> is filled with disdain for thinking. That such is its attitude is to some
> extent explicable by the fact that thought has never yet reached the goal
> which it must set before itself. Time after time it was convinced that it
> had clearly established a world-view which was in accordance with
> knowledge and ethically satisfactory. But time after time the truth came
> out that it had not succeeded.
>
> "Doubts, therefore, could well arise as to whether thinking would
> ever be capable of answering current questions about the world and our
> relation to it in such a way that we could give meaning and a content to
> our lives.
>
> "But today in addition to that neglect of thought there is also preva-
> lent mistrust of it. The organized political, social, and religious organi-
> zations of our time are at work to induce the individual man not to
> arrive at his convictions of his own thinking but to make his own such
> conviction as they keep ready made for him. Any man who thinks for
> himself and at the same time is spiritually free, is to them something
> inconvenient and even uncanny. He does not offer sufficient guarantee
> that he will merge himself in their organization in the way they wish."[6]

Writing with density of thought yet clarity of medium, confronting worldviews which are neither in accordance with knowledge nor
fully ethically satisfactory, drawing steadfastly on Scripture to answer
"current questions about the world and our relation to it in such a way
that we could give meaning and a content to our lives," Tom Wright

---

[6]Michael Murray, *Albert Schweitzer, Musician* (Aldergate, U.K.: Scolar Press, 1994), p. 90. Quotation from Albert Schweitzer's *Out of My Life and Thought: An Autobiography* (1933; reprint,
New York: Holt, 1990), pp. 254-55.

leaves us—as any great writer should—with as many questions as answers. True, to some he remains "uncanny" or "inconvenient," for he grants no prior guarantees that he will conform his own conclusions to any particular theological or ideological agenda. But I believe that God has called Tom to nothing less. I know I speak for Richard and all the contributors of this volume when I say that we rejoice in Tom's exemplary insistence on arriving at his own hard-earned convictions. We are grateful for God's gift to the academy, to the church and to us in sending us N. T. Wright. May the celebration begin in the pages that follow.

PART ONE

JESUS AND THE PEOPLE OF GOD

1

Jesus and the Victory of God Meets the Gospel of John

MARIANNE MEYE THOMPSON

JESUS AND THE VICTORY OF GOD, N. T. WRIGHT's biggest book on Jesus—although neither his only book on Jesus nor his biggest book overall—has already been the subject of a full-length "critical assessment," published by InterVarsity Press.[1] So far as I can tell, none of the contributors to that volume offers any substantive comment on the topic of the Gospel of John in *Jesus and the Victory of God* (*JVG*). And so the organizers of this conference apparently deemed that it was time for *JVG* to meet the Gospel of John. I pondered briefly whether the topic— "*Jesus and the Victory of God* meets the Gospel of John"—had in view the clash of the titans, where the two parties would "meet" to determine a winner, or whether what was anticipated was the long-awaited introduction of two parties, heretofore inexplicably unacquainted. Either of these sorts of meetings would frankly be more interesting than the third option—a committee meeting—in which these two titans would meet to hammer out some sort of compromise document that robbed each of their genius and spirit and left no one eager for more.

Assuming that what we are after is a conversation, and neither a showdown nor a compromise, I have divided my paper into three main

---

[1]*Jesus and the Restoration of Israel: A Critical Assessment of N. T. Wright's* Jesus and the Victory of God, ed. Carey C. Newman (Downers Grove, Ill.: InterVarsity Press; Carlisle, U.K.: Paternoster, 1999).

parts. First, I will discuss the issue of the relative absence of the Gospel of John from the pages of *JVG*, and set that phenomenon in the larger context of the quest for the historical Jesus. Next, drawing on some intriguing comments made by Wright in other writings that would allow John a larger role in studies of Jesus, we will bring John and *JVG* into dialogue at a few points. Here we will see that, on the whole, the Jesus of *JVG* would often be quite at home in the Gospel of John—and vice versa. Finally, I will focus on one particularly noteworthy feature of *JVG*'s presentation of Jesus, namely, the argument that Jesus saw himself as replacing the temple or the temple system. And here I will suggest that John has somewhat more substantive disagreements with *JVG*.

THE GOSPEL OF JOHN IN *JESUS AND THE VICTORY OF GOD*

Let us begin, then, with the role of the Gospel of John in *JVG*. To put not too fine a point on it, in *JVG* Wright does not make use of, quote or discuss passages from the Gospel of John in any way that explicitly determines his conclusions or his portrayal of Jesus. The Gospel of John is not a source, or not explicitly a source, for *JVG* and its depiction of the aims of Jesus. Wright explains the relative absence of John from the discussion with the following comment: "The debate to which I wish to contribute in this book has been conducted almost entirely in terms of the synoptic tradition."[2] In this regard, *JVG* follows in the footsteps of virtually all studies of the historical Jesus since the publication of David Friedrich Strauss's *Life of Jesus: Critically Examined*.[3] Under Strauss's critical scrutiny, the historicity of material in all the Gospels was examined and often found wanting, the Johannine discourses and narratives above all; according to Strauss they lacked verisimilitude and concentrated too much on Jesus himself.[4] The narratives were dogmatically shaped, appealing frequently to supernatural causation for explanations of events in Jesus' life.[5] John simply could not serve as a source for the

---

[2] N. T. Wright, *Jesus and the Victory of God* (Minneapolis: Fortress, 1997), p. xvi.
[3] D. F. Strauss, *The Life of Jesus: Critically Examined*, trans. George Eliot (1846; reprint, Philadelphia: Fortress; London: SCM Press, 1972).
[4] Ibid., pp. 381-87.
[5] Ibid., pp. 390-91.

historical Jesus. Ever since Strauss, the quest of the historical Jesus has been essentially a quest for the Synoptic Jesus.

Jesus and the Victory of God also gives us a portrait of the Synoptic Jesus; that is, the Jesus of the threefold and not fourfold Gospel canon. There are references to John here and there in *JVG*, but while all the references to John in the Scripture index of *JVG* run to just slightly over one column, the references to Luke and to Matthew take up over nine columns each. No space is given in *JVG* to discussion of any distinctly Johannine episode or discourse, as there is, for example, to the parable of the prodigal son, which figures significantly in Wright's reconstruction of Jesus' aims. There are some minor exceptions. In a discussion of Jesus' appearance before Pilate, evidence from John bolsters the historical authenticity of the Gospels' collective portrait of Pilate as "weak, vacillating," and "bullying," and as eager to remain Caesar's friend.[6]

But *JVG* does not differ significantly from other recent studies of Jesus in its overall treatment of John. The ratio of the references of John to the Synoptic Gospels found in *JVG* is about the same as in Dominic Crossan's *The Historical Jesus: The Life of a Mediterranean Jewish Peasant* or E. P. Sanders's *The Historical Figure of Jesus*. Interestingly, in *The New Testament and the People of God*, the ratio of references of Luke to John is about 1:1. In that earlier work Wright treats the Gospel of John in the section titled "Stories in Early Christianity," a section that also includes discussion of each of the three Synoptic Gospels, Paul and Hebrews. Here there are a number of remarks relevant to our current discussion.

First, "everyone knows that John is a very different sort of book to Luke, Matthew and Mark."[7] But, second, when compared to a reconstructed Q source, or to the gospels of *Thomas* or *Peter*, John "comes out at least as much like the Synoptics as unlike."[8] And, third, John's Gospel is "more obviously than the synoptic Gospels . . . a story about Jesus and the Jewish people of his day."[9] Elsewhere, the introduction to *John for Everyone* accounts for the distinctive character of John as follows:

---

[6]Wright, *Jesus and the Victory of God*, pp. 545-47.
[7]N. T. Wright, *The New Testament and the People of God* (Minneapolis: Augsburg Fortress, 1992), p. 410.
[8]Ibid., p. 411.
[9]Ibid., p. 412.

"[John] gives the appearance of being written by someone who was a very close friend of Jesus, and who spent the rest of his life mulling over, more and more deeply, what Jesus had done and said and achieved, praying it through from every angle, and helping others to understand it."[10] It would be promising to probe the relationship of two of these statements about John—namely, that it is more obviously a story about John's own day, and that it is the result of a close friend's long and deep reflection on Jesus' life. If together they accurately capture John's approach, they also suggest that this approach differs significantly from that taken in *JVG*. For John, knowing Jesus would not entail going "back there" but bringing Jesus forward. John presents an understanding of the Jesus who both was and is, and he does so in light of Jesus' life, death and resurrection, through the words and thoughts of the one who bore witness to him.

John's Gospel thus proceeds differently from *JVG*, whose stated purpose is to "answer certain specific questions" about Jesus, namely, what were his aims? In focusing on the question, what were Jesus' aims? *Jesus and the Victory of God* echoes the title and approach of Ben Meyer's *The Aims of Jesus*, itself recalling the section on the aims of Jesus in H. S. Reimarus's posthumously published *Fragments*, a work often designated as signaling the beginning of the quest of the historical Jesus. Reimarus argued that Jesus announced a "speedy worldly deliverance," and that Jesus saw himself as the "worldly deliverer of Israel."[11] But when Jesus failed to deliver Israel, the disciples invented "the new system of a suffering spiritual Savior." Needless to say, Reimarus thought that the answer to the question, What was Jesus up to? would be devastating to Christian faith, since the historical figure of Jesus would be shown to be radically different from the Jesus of the church or the Gospels. The ditch is broad and ugly indeed between Jesus and the Gospels, between what Jesus said and did, and what the church reported him to have said and done: what Jesus intended he did not accomplish, and what the church claimed he accomplished, Jesus himself did not intend. The

---

[10]N. T. Wright, *John for Everyone*, part 1 (London: SPCK, 2002), p. x.

[11]H. S. Reimarus, *Fragments*, ed. Charles H. Talbert, trans. Ralph S. Fraser (Philadelphia: Fortress, 1970), pp. 10, 12.

resurrection of Jesus could equally be shown to be an invention of the church. From beginning to end, Christianity is based on and perpetrates a fraud. If taken seriously, study of the historical Jesus would—or should—destroy the Christian faith.

No wonder that Wright calls Reimarus "the great iconoclast."[12] Reimarus wants the real Jesus of history, the Jesus without dogma, without the church, Jesus *wie er eigentlich gewesen* (as he actually was).[13] In *The Challenge of Jesus*, Wright wrote this about Reimarus:

> Reimarus challenged [Christian dogma] in the name of history. . . . I believe that Reimarus's question was necessary. . . . The fact that Reimarus gave his own question an answer that is historically unsustainable does not mean he did not ask the right questions. Who was Jesus, and what did he accomplish?[14]

Thus Wright takes up the challenge implicit in Reimarus's questions and work, demonstrating what Leander Keck once wrote, "It is not overstating the case to claim that all historical study of Jesus is a critical appropriation of [Reimarus's] view or a debate with it."[15] *Jesus and the Victory of God* is an implicit debate with Reimarus. It takes Reimarus's questions as its agenda, believing it absolutely crucial that Christian faith arise from and be based on "Jesus' mind set, aims and beliefs prior to the crucifixion."[16] We might then also note that in *JVG* the "history" of this "historical Jesus" ends on Good Friday, and his aims are essentially accomplished at that time.

Now, following the publication of *The Resurrection of the Son of God*, surely no one will deny the importance that Wright assigns to the resurrection for understanding early Christian history and theology. Nevertheless, it seems that the "Jesus" presented in *JVG* is still the Jesus without Easter. As E. P. Sanders puts it at the end of *The Historical*

[12]Wright, *Jesus and the Victory of God*, p. 16.

[13]The description of the task of history as recovering *wie es eigentlich gewesen* (as it actually happened) comes from Leopold von Ranke, *Geschichten der romanischen und germanischen Völker von 1494 bis 1535* (Leipzig/Berlin: Reamer, 1824), 1:vi.

[14]N. T. Wright, *The Challenge of Jesus: Rediscovering Who Jesus Was and Is* (Downers Grove, Ill.: InterVarsity Press, 1999), p. 20.

[15]Leander Keck, *A Future for the Historical Jesus: The Place of Jesus in Preaching and Theology* (Nashville: Abingdon, 1971), p. 18.

[16]Wright, *Jesus and the Victory of God*, p. 12.

Figure of Jesus, "The resurrection is not, strictly speaking, part of the story of the historical Jesus, but rather belongs to the aftermath of his life."[17] This may be another reason for the omission of the Gospel of John from *JVG*, as well as from other studies of Jesus: rarely is John regarded as presenting "Jesus' mind set, aims and beliefs prior to the crucifixion"—that, and nothing more.

Instead the Fourth Evangelist arguably presents an account of Jesus that, all the way through, rolls the results of what happened into the causes of those events, and the substance of things that Jesus said and did, along with the acclamations and confessions of Scripture and human witnesses, into Jesus' self-conscious identity. If in the Synoptic Gospels Jesus' identity is slowly unfolded throughout the narrative, to be known cumulatively and vindicated in the resurrection, so that the whole becomes the sum of its parts and more than the sum of those parts, then in John the whole of Jesus' identity already appears in nearly every part of the narrative. In John, Jesus is known from the end. John might well find the project of *JVG*—to know "Jesus' mind set, aims and beliefs prior to the crucifixion"—to be an odd project. It is not, as Sanders puts it, that the resurrection is the aftermath of Jesus' life, but that what happened through the resurrection, and in the aftermath of the resurrection, is simply part of who Jesus is and what his life was all about. To a large extent, this conviction makes the Gospel of John what it is, and Jesus who he is in the Gospel of John. The Jesus who laid down his life is also the Jesus who took it up again, the one who is resurrection and life. If he is not living, then this statement cannot be true. Because there is no Jesus without the resurrection, there is no historical Jesus without the resurrection.

THE JOHANNINE JESUS IN *JESUS AND THE VICTORY OF GOD*
And yet the plot thickens. At the end of *Jesus and the Restoration of Israel*, a collection of essays discussing and responding to *JVG*, Wright includes this reply to Luke Timothy Johnson's question regarding the absence of John from *JVG*:

---

[17]E. P. Sanders, *The Historical Figure of Jesus* (London: Penguin, 1996), p. 276.

My explanation for why John plays little part in the book remains thin (*JVG* xvi), though not as thin as Johnson implies. I was contributing to a complex debate in which the Synoptics were the main subject matter. I do think, however, that to rule John out altogether a priori as a historical source is a mistake. Nobody in the current debate seems to read C. H. Dodd or Percy Gardner-Smith or even J. A. T. Robinson, let alone to engage with them; rather they rest content with century-old shibboleths about the nonhistorical nature of John. If I am even half right about the Jesus of the Synoptic tradition, . . . this old scholarly tradition is ripe for reconsideration.[18]

I suspect that Dodd, Gardner-Smith and Robinson might not be alone in uttering a doubled "amen" to these points. If one must "discard the century-old shibboleths" and reconsider the "nonhistorical nature of John," presumably then one ought to ask what role it should play in reconstructions of the historical Jesus—and how it might have changed or affected the conclusions in *JVG*.

One typical way of taking John into account in the study of Jesus is to gather those bits of data that seem to have the ring of historicity about them and suggest how they might supplement or add to the Synoptic portrait. Archaeological and historical studies have pointed to the degree of accuracy about certain matters of topography and culture evidenced in John. There are features of Jesus' ministry only in John that are sometimes evaluated positively on historical grounds; for example, Jesus' multiple visits or pilgrimages to Jerusalem at the time of the feasts. If we take John's viewpoint here, we might also ask, does the Johannine chronology, with Jesus' multiple visits to Jerusalem, challenge the view—held by Schweitzer and adapted by Wright—that "Jesus went to Jerusalem to die," rather than to work? This position fits admirably with the statement of the Gospel of Luke that "Jesus set his face to go to Jerusalem" (Lk 9:51), because "it is impossible for a prophet to be killed outside of Jerusalem" (Lk 13:33). But John troubles the water a bit in suggesting that Jesus was frequently to be found in Jerusalem and in the temple, and that the threat of death hung over each

---

[18]N.T. Wright, "In Grateful Dialogue," in *Jesus and Restoration of Israel*, ed. Carey C. Newman (Downers Grove, Ill.: InterVarsity Press, 1999), pp. 251-52.

visit (Jn 2:17-23; 5:18; 7:1, 19, 25; 8:37). Perhaps John's picture comple-
ments the Lukan picture: while Jesus regularly went to Jerusalem on
pilgrimage, there was a final occasion when his purposes were different. But John's account raises the question how one knows that Jesus
himself believed his final visit there had a different aim rather than a
different result. Substitute John's framework for Luke's and it is harder
to assign this last visit a distinct motive on Jesus' part.

I return to Wright's comment, "If I am even half right about the Jesus
of the Synoptic tradition, . . . this old scholarly tradition [of the nonhistorical nature of John] is ripe for reconsideration." I gather that the point
here is not to find yet more bits of historical information in the Gospel
of John, but that "the Jesus of the Synoptic tradition," indeed, the Jesus
of *JVG*, forces a reconsideration of the "historicity" of Jesus in John. The
overall picture of Jesus and of the exercise of his vocation in *JVG* stands
so near to John's Jesus as to invite a reevaluation of the historical character of the witness of the Gospel of John. At this point allow me to recall
briefly the main contours of the portrait of Jesus in *JVG*.

Jesus is a prophet who not only announced but enacted the kingdom
of God, by which is meant the return of YHWH to Zion; the real end
of Israel's exile; the forgiveness of Israel's sin; the reconstitution of Israel around Jesus who, together with his movement, constituted a new
or alternative temple; a concomitant call to faith centered on him and
not in Torah and temple; and the fulfillment of God's promise to the
Gentiles. The end of exile and the "rebuilding" of the temple indicate
the Messiah has come at last and that the new age, Israel's redemption,
the resurrection from the dead, is coming into being. In order to accomplish his ends, Jesus gave himself to death on the cross, and allowed
evil to do its worst, and so to be the means by which God would finally
deal with evil. Most pithily summarized, "Jesus believed he had to do
and be, for Israel and the world, that which according to scripture only
YHWH himself could do and be."[19]

What would the Gospel of John say to such a reconstruction? Another doubled amen? The Jesus of *JVG*, who "believed he had to do and

---

[19]Wright, *Jesus and the Victory of God*, p. 653.

be, for Israel and the world, that which according to scripture only YHWH himself could do and be," is the Johannine Jesus who acts and speaks only as the Father tells him to, who claims his Father's prerogatives to heal on the Sabbath and to judge, and who does the work of God in giving life and raising the dead. While using different language and concepts, *JVG* and the Gospel of John nevertheless make very similar, if not identical, judgments about the identity and mission of Jesus. One might say that in spite of the absence of John from *JVG*, in its pages we are meeting the Johannine Jesus again for the first time.

Not surprisingly, then, in the passage from *JVG* that I quoted earlier, Wright suggests that we might take seriously the work of J. A. T. Robinson, presumably referring to Robinson's posthumously published book, *The Priority of John*—a title that, quite deliberately, flies in the face of "orthodox" judgments, such as those of Clement of Alexandria and others, of the so-called posteriority of John. Robinson does not necessarily mean to argue, nor does he believe that he needs to argue, that John was written or published before the other Gospels. He is referring not to "temporal" priority but rather to a "'procedural' priority," which he characterizes as "beginning with John and asking how his picture, however near to the source (and my answer would be: very near, yet also in its fullness the outcome of profound theological maturity), sheds original and not merely reflected, light on everything else."[20] Robinson's view—that John is at once "very near" to the historical source, and yet simultaneously the "outcome of profound theological reflection"—is very nearly the position that Wright proposed in the introduction to *John for Everyone*.

Yet, for Robinson, the "priority of John" does not pertain solely to the Gospel's chronology or other things such as we might assign to the category of probable "historical information." Elsewhere Robinson quotes T. E. Pollard's judgment that John, as he writes his Gospel, is saying in effect, "This is what Jesus was really like; we did not realize it then, but now we know it."[21] John retells the story of Jesus in such a way

---

[20]J. A. T. Robinson, *The Priority of John*, ed. J. F. Coakley (London: SCM, 1985), p. 5.

[21]Ibid., p. 362, quoting at length from an address of T. E. Pollard, delivered at Knox Theological Hall, Dunedin, 1964, and published in a privately circulated journal for ministers of the

that it answers certain questions more explicitly than the other Gospels do, "Who then is this? What was he up to? And why did he die?" As noted earlier, for John, the answers to these questions are seen from the end of the story, looking back. As Sir Edwyn Hoskyns once wrote, John wishes to show that "what Jesus is to the faith of the true Christian believer, He was in the flesh."[22]

We might take as an example of this "Johannine shape" of Jesus in *JVG* the portrayal of Jesus' death. The conclusions that emerge from *JVG* about Jesus' aims, self-understanding and the purpose of his death find deep resonance with the Johannine formulations of these same points. In some cases the wording of *JVG* could have been taken from the pages of the Gospel of John. In John, the regathering and unification of God's people constitute a particular feature of what Jesus' death accomplishes. As the good shepherd, Jesus willingly gives his life in order to keep the sheep from being scattered by wolves and abandoned by hirelings (Jn 10:11-18). Caiaphas, the high priest, unknowingly prophesies that Jesus must die in order "to gather into one the dispersed children of God" (Jn 11:52). Jesus is the grain of wheat that must fall into the earth and die in order to bear much fruit (Jn 12:24). When Jesus is lifted up, he will "draw all people to [him]self" (Jn 12:32). Finally, anticipating his death, Jesus prays that his disciples may be one people (Jn 17:21). In John, Jesus' death and resurrection effect the regathering of the dispersed children of God. We have in John an interpretation of Jesus' death that simultaneously bears the distinct stamp of Johannine theology, but fixes him firmly within the so-called restoration eschatology central to the delineation of Jesus' aims in the Third Quest and in *JVG*. There is, however, one major difference: for the Gospel of John, the gathering together of God's people happens both after and as a result of Jesus' death and resurrection.

None of the passages just noted from John is discussed in *JVG*. Again, given the avowed intention to conduct the debate about the historical Jesus in Synoptic terms, this omission is entirely explicable. But it does leave one with a number of questions: do we omit the Fourth Gospel in

---

Presbyterian Church in New Zealand (*Forum* 16, no. 6 [1964]: 2-9).
[22]E. C. Hoskyns, *The Fourth Gospel*, ed. F. N. Davey (London: Faber & Faber, 1956), p. 35.

such discussions because it would somehow be taken to compromise any historical reconstruction? If John and *JVG* often make strikingly similar judgments about Jesus' mission and accomplishments, what shall we conclude about either one? And does John's approach to understanding Jesus suggest that we ought to rethink how Jesus is known "historically"?

Arguably John and *JVG* have been shaped by similar forces: on the one hand the traditions and accounts of Jesus' life and on the other, early Christian confessions about him. Again, this can be illustrated by a glance at the interpretation of the death of Jesus given in John and in *JVG*. The Gospel of John is the only Gospel that speaks of the death of Jesus in terms of love, be it the love of God for the world (Jn 3:16) or the love of Jesus for his own (Jn 13:1, 34-35; 15:13). Of course, Paul speaks of the death of Jesus in these terms as well, when he writes of "the Son of God, who loved me and gave himself for me" (Gal 2:20). In probing Jesus' motives in giving his life, Wright cites Ben Meyer's moving discussion from *The Aims of Jesus:*

> What, in the end, made Jesus operate in this way, what energized his incorporating death into his mission, his facing it and going to meet it? . . . It is above all *in the tradition generated by Jesus* that we discover what made him operate in the way he did, what made him epitomize his life in the single act of going to his death: He "loved me and handed himself over for me" . . . "having loved his own who were in the world, he loved them to the end."[23]

Wright attributes this understanding of Jesus' death to the earliest Christians.[24] This seems to be one of the few places in *JVG* where the interpretation of the early church becomes a lens through which the aims of Jesus are explicitly brought into focus. In other words, here the Gospel of John, or at least John alongside Paul, does not so much serve to provide historical information about Jesus to be added to the Synoptic treasury, but rather catalyzes a certain reading of the Synoptic materials, a reading that reveals "what Jesus was really like; we did not realize it then, but now we know it."

---

[23]Ben F. Meyer, *The Aims of Jesus* (London: SCM, 1979), pp. 252-53 (emphasis added).
[24]Wright, *Jesus and the Victory of God*, p. 607.

But what do we mean when we speak of "what Jesus was really like"? The Gospel of John itself clearly recognizes that there are other ways to tell the story of Jesus; indeed, the Gospel is shot through with the divisions that arise over differing assessments of him (Jn 1:10-13; 6:66; 7:26-42; 9:34). Partly for these reasons, John insists on the importance of the Beloved Disciple's "testimony." It is clear that those who had such differing assessments often witnessed the same deeds, heard the same words and "read" Jesus within the same context. The "naked history" does not answer the crucial questions about who Jesus was and is. It was within the context of the early gathering of Jesus' immediate disciples and those they taught, a community that was inspired by the Spirit, and that read the Scriptures as a witness to the Risen One, that the fullness of Jesus' identity and the significance of his words and deeds came to be articulated. Or, to repeat an earlier quotation, "[John] gives the appearance of being written by someone who was a very close friend of Jesus, and who spent the rest of his life mulling over, more and more deeply, what Jesus had done and said and achieved, praying it through from every angle, and helping others to understand it."[25] Is it possible to tell the story of Jesus any other way? If so, what story is one telling?

JOHN AND *JESUS AND THE VICTORY OF GOD* IN DIALOGUE: TEMPLE AND FORGIVENESS OF SINS

In the last part of this paper, then, I want to turn to one key feature of Wright's presentation of Jesus, namely, his understanding of Jesus in relationship to the temple and the forgiveness of sins. Especially since the publication of E. P. Sanders's *Jesus and Judaism* in 1985, Jesus' "action in the temple" has played an increasingly important role in studies of Jesus, including *JVG*, that are part of the so-called Third Quest. Wright argues that with the action in the temple on the occasion of Jesus' final visit to Jerusalem, Jesus intended to symbolize the imminent destruction of the temple—God's judgment at the hands of the Romans, because the "temple and its hierarchy had become hopelessly corrupt."[26] But Jesus' action in Jerusalem during that final week is not

---

[25]Wright, *John for Everyone*, p. x.
[26]Wright, *Jesus and the Victory of God*, pp. 417, 317.

an isolated incident but rather the fitting climax to his challenge to the whole temple system. Indeed, throughout his ministry, Jesus acted "as if he is simply bypassing the Temple system altogether."[27] Although he did not "condemn" the temple and its worship,[28] in offering forgiveness for sins outside the temple, Jesus was presenting himself, or himself and his followers, as an alternative to the temple, even as a new temple. "All that the temple stood for" was now available through Jesus and his movement. Worshiping in the temple was not inherently wrong, but it was on its way to being redundant. In thus bypassing the temple, Jesus was in effect reconstituting Israel around himself.

The Gospel of John raises a number of questions for this reconstruction. John is the only canonical Gospel to identify Jesus explicitly as a temple. This identification occurs in connection with Jesus' "cleansing" of the temple in John 2:13-22, and Jesus' subsequent challenge, "Destroy this temple; and in three days I will raise it up." John is also the only Gospel to juxtapose the cleansing of the temple with a word about destruction. However, here it is important to note that Jesus' action in the temple and the word about destruction refer to two different temples. Jesus' action in the temple has as its goal the purification of his Father's house, but the saying about the destruction of the temple applies to Jesus himself. That is to say, there is one temple that must be purged from the trappings of buying and selling so that it can indeed be the temple, the house of God; there is another temple that will be destroyed and raised up again. This other temple is Jesus himself.

The Gospel of John is the only Gospel that gives a positive hint of the restoration of a temple. The Evangelist explains that in speaking of the destruction of the temple, "he spoke of the temple of his body." In the setting in John, Jesus is standing in the courts of the Jerusalem temple, and the natural way to take his words is to assume that he means, "If you destroy this building, I will raise it up in three days." It is precisely this understanding that the editorial comment corrects: Jesus was not speaking of a miraculous act he would perform if the Jerusalem temple were leveled, but of what he would do in the event of his own death; that

---

[27]Ibid., p. 130.
[28]Ibid., p. 416.

is to say, in John the entire saying about destruction has to do with Jesus' crucifixion and resurrection. Jesus is not understood to say, "If the Jerusalem temple is destroyed, I will replace it." Rather, the narrator informs us that Jesus was speaking of another temple altogether, namely, one that was destroyed about the year 30, not the year 70.[29]

Jesus' intent to purify the temple recalls the accounts of the deaths of the Maccabean martyrs. The deaths of the martyrs purified the homeland and the temple, as the faithful who died "became a ransom for the sin of our nation," an "atoning sacrifice," that spared others from death (2 Macc 7:36-38; 4 Macc 6:27-30; 17:20-24). The deaths of the faithful were understood to purify the temple, the very temple the Maccabees and others zealously fought to reclaim and restore. But the fact that such atonement could be effected outside the temple system did not imply a replacement of the temple or the temple system. Within the Gospels, one might think that the actions and identity of John the Baptist who, at least in Luke's account, is of priestly descent, baptizes for the forgiveness of sins, and practices ritual ablution of some sort, would have raised the question about "bypassing the temple" much more acutely than did Jesus' ministry. Indeed, according to John, citing Psalm 69:9, it was not Jesus' neglect of or turning from the temple, but his zeal for it that led him to drive out the animals, sellers and moneychangers.

One might also ask whether, following the Hasmonean debacle in which the priestly Hasmonean family usurped royal prerogatives, Jesus who, in the Gospels, is presented as a son of David of the line of Judah, would have ventured to usurp priestly prerogatives to himself. The book of Hebrews, at least, understands Jesus' descent from Judah to be a significant objection to his priesthood, and produces an argument that he is a priest after another order. And while Psalm 110 (the proof for Jesus' priesthood after the order of Melchizedek) is cited by Jesus in the Gospels, it is cited to establish his messianic identity as the one who is David's Lord. The king, the Messiah, was to be a

---

[29]See here Robinson, *Priority of John*, p. 70; Klaus Berger, *Im Anfang War Johannes* (Stuttgart: Quell Verlag, 1997), p. 37, as well as Berger's article, "Neue Argumente für die Frühdatierung des Johannesevangeliums" in *Für und Wider die Priorität des Johannesevangeliums* (Hildesheim: Georg Olms Verlag, 2002).

temple builder, as was David's son of old; not a priest.

In this regard, we might note that John is the only New Testament book to mention the feast of Hanukkah (Jn 10:22) and, on that occasion, Jesus is found in the temple. Hanukkah commemorated the victories of the Maccabees over the Syrian forces of Antiochus IV Epiphanies, and the rebuilding and refurbishing of the altar and temple, at the conclusion of the Maccabean revolt (1 Macc 4:45-61).[30] At this feast, Jesus speaks of himself as the "good shepherd," leading the crowds to demand, "If you are the Messiah, tell us plainly." In the Gospel of John at least, the presence of Jesus in the temple at Hanukkah, and his reference to himself there as a shepherd, perhaps calling to mind the Davidic shepherd of Ezekiel 34 who carries out God's own work of gathering and protecting the sheep, forces the question whether Jesus' intentions are kingly or messianic.

Let me then return to the destruction of the temple. It is hard to imagine how a statement of the temple's coming destruction could be taken as part of an announcement of the end of the exile. If the prophets of old warned that God would judge Jerusalem, its people and its temple through destruction and exile, and if Jesus warns similarly of the upcoming fate of Jerusalem, its people and its temple, his warnings would seem to signal not the end of exile but the beginning of a new exile, or at least to be a sign of God's judgment rather than God's forgiveness. One might compare the jubilation of 2 Maccabees after the restoration of the temple with the lament of 4 Ezra. In 2 Maccabees the restoration of the temple is marked as follows, "Therefore the place itself shared in the misfortunes that befell the nation and afterward participated in its benefits; and what was forsaken in the wrath of the Almighty was restored again in all its glory when the great Lord became reconciled" (2 Macc 5:20). But in 4 Ezra the destruction of the temple is lamented: "Our sanctuary has been laid waste, our altar thrown down, our temple destroyed; our harp has been laid low, our song has

---

[30]A somewhat different account is given in 2 Maccabees, which links Tabernacles and Dedication, and focuses on the cleansing of the temple rather than the altar per se. For an overview of the feast, see James C. VanderKam, "Dedication, Feast of," *Anchor Bible Dictionary*, ed. David Noel Freedman (New York: Doubleday, 1992), 2.123-24.

been silenced, and our rejoicing has been ended; the light of our lamp-
stand has been put out" (4 Ezra 10:19-23). In speaking of the destruction of the temple, John's Gospel also speaks immediately of a restoration, but the other Gospels do not. In fact, the only claim that Jesus
said he would destroy and rebuild the temple was deemed to be false
testimony (Mk 14:58). John's Gospel provides a hope of restoration that
the other Gospels do not. John's understanding seems to be present in
spirit, if not in letter, in *JVG* and indeed seems crucial to its presentation of Jesus as an alternative temple.

Interestingly, while the Gospel of John is the only Gospel to desig-
nate Jesus as a temple, it is at the same time the only Gospel in which
Jesus does not expressly forgive someone's sins. The Gospel does include the scene where the risen Lord, having "breathed" the Holy Spirit
upon the disciples, confers on them the power to forgive each other's
sins (Jn 20:22-23). What is the relationship of this forgiveness to the
temple? Both the power to forgive sin and the identification of Jesus as
a temple are part of John's postresurrection perspective and, in John,
perhaps even part of a post-A.D. 70 viewpoint.

Outside of the Gospel of John, no other early Christian literature
calls Jesus himself "the temple" or "a temple." A number of other New
Testament passages point to the individual believer as the temple of the
Holy Spirit (1 Cor 6:19; cf. *2 Clement* 9.3; *Epistle of Barnabas* 6.15;
16.8-10) or to the church as the temple of God or as God's dwelling
(1 Cor 3:17; 2 Cor 6:16; Eph 2:21; and probably 1 Pet 2:5; cf. Ignatius
Letter to the Ephesians 9.1). In Revelation 21:22, there is no need of a
temple, a symbol of God's presence, a place for God to dwell, because
the Lord God Almighty and the Lamb dwell in the city there. The holy
city is in effect the holy temple of the Lord. It may be that the allusion
to the body of the church in 1 Corinthians assumes prior identification
of Jesus as the temple, and one can perhaps speak of "Jesus and his movement" as an "alternative to the whole temple system." Yet the question
arises why the identification of Jesus as the temple plays so little role in
the rest of early Christian thought if it was central to Jesus' aims and
actions. The answer of the Gospel of John is that the understanding of
Jesus as the temple of God arose after his resurrection. Perhaps it also

arose after the destruction of the Jerusalem temple in A.D. 70. That might also explain why the disciples of Jesus apparently continued to gather in the temple, as the book of Acts shows, and perhaps also why the authority to forgive sins was first conferred by the risen Lord.

CONCLUDING REFLECTIONS

In conclusion, I think that John and *JVG* would get along quite well; at times, even better than the Synoptics and *JVG*. For example, in *JVG* Jesus calls for faith in himself rather than temple or Torah. While Wright writes, "the theme occurs in all strands of synoptic tradition,"[31] we might add that in no Gospel does Jesus more clearly sound the call for faith in him than in John. In *JVG*, the book of Isaiah, with its announcement of the end of exile, the pardon of sin and YHWH's return to Zion, is crucial to understanding Jesus. But while the Gospel of John draws on the same parts of Isaiah as does *JVG*, the Isaianic patterns of divine speech play little or no role in *JVG*. In *JVG*, we read of Israel's history turning its long awaited corner in the ministry of Jesus, so that those who oppose him are the enemies of the true people of God, a statement that reflects Jesus' stinging polemic in John 8—that Jesus' opponents are "children of the devil"—more closely than it does even the diatribes of Matthew 23. And one could go on. These places of agreement between John and *JVG* might suggest that *JVG* has been more influenced by the Fourth Gospel or its theological contribution to the New Testament and early Christian thought than the avowed avoidance of it suggests.

But, finally, the question that John poses to *JVG* is how Jesus is known. Reimarus wanted to discover who Jesus was by entirely rational means—without dogmatic considerations and ecclesiastical control—trusting in rigorous historical work to turn up Jesus *wie er eigentlich gewesen*. Subsequent pursuit of the historical Jesus has followed in his train, and the quest for Jesus has often been linked to two assumptions; first, that one can (and should) find "the historical Jesus behind or in the Gospels," and that, second, recovery of the facts about Jesus, when understood in their proper context, ought to give us a single interpreta-

---

[31]Wright, *Jesus and the Victory of God*, p. 259.

tion of him. But the Gospel of John does not present the Jesus who was understood by all, but rather the Jesus to whom his disciples and, above all, the Beloved Disciple bore witness. We have Jesus as the Beloved Disciple remembered him, Jesus as the church remembered him, as the church bore witness to him. The paucity of data in the Jewish and Roman sources of Jesus' day makes it very clear that unless the memories of Christian disciples had been preserved, we would know as little about Jesus as we do about the Egyptian or Theudas, those revolutionary figures mentioned in the book of Acts—and that at least some would not have reckoned that much of a loss. These ancient Roman and Jewish sources are not primarily interested in Jesus as a political dissident or social critic, but in the figure who generated a movement that lived on into their own day. And that is the Jesus in whom John is interested. This means that to know Jesus, one cannot bypass the memory and witness of those who followed Jesus. Indeed, the Gospel of John might well note that Thomas's error lay not in his empiricist refusal to believe what he could not see, but in his historicist refusal to trust the apostolic witness to Jesus.

The meeting between the Gospel of John and *JVG* may well prove to be long, but I am sure that it will be invigorating. In the preface to *JVG*, Wright writes, "I am aware that there is a large range of mountains still waiting for me; aware, too, that they may offer views, prospects and of course risks yet more breathtaking than the ones I habitually climb. I hope I shall be spared to explore them in due course."[32] Tom, may you enjoy the climb and the views from the summit![33]

Response to Marianne Meye Thompson
N. T. WRIGHT

I enjoyed Marianne's elegant, quizzical piece, and wish I had space to engage it fully. Certainly I believe and hope that clear convergence is possible between the Jesus I have sketched and the Jesus of John's Gospel.

---

[32]Wright, *Jesus and the Victory of God*, p. xvi.
[33]I wish to thank Markus Bockmuehl for his helpful comments on the initial draft of this paper.

That highlights the strangest thing to me in Marianne's paper: her supposition that John and *JVG* part company on the temple theme. I'm not sure I agree with her understanding of the temple incident in John 2: granted that John understands Jesus' cryptic remark to refer to his own body, there is nevertheless, throughout the Gospel, considerable emphasis on Jesus as the temple's replacement. I think particularly—I was surprised that Marianne didn't draw this out—of the prologue itself, with its temple resonant climax: the word became flesh, *kai esk™n¢sen en h™min*, "and *tabernacled* in our midst." The result, again as in the temple: "we beheld his glory." Throughout the Gospel, Jesus goes again and again to Jerusalem, keeping the great festivals and drawing their meaning on to himself. And when Caiaphas warns that if Jesus goes on like this the Romans may come and take away "our place and our nation," we should not miss the point.

I do think, then, that *JVG* and John converge when it comes to Jesus-as-temple upstaging the Jerusalem temple. And since I think that is the clue to John's incarnational Christology, then yes, *JVG* does arrive—by a quite different route—at something like the Johannine solution.

Another convergence would have been good to draw out, concerning Jesus and the kingdom. This may be another sign of the great ecclesial tradition squeezing out canonical material which wasn't wanted by the later church. John's theology of Jesus as the spearhead of God's kingdom climaxes, of course, in the dialogue with Pilate (Jn 18–19). That dialogue is rooted in earlier sayings about the ruler of this world being cast out, having no power over Jesus, and about Jesus having already overcome the world (Jn 12:31; 14:30; 16:33). Jesus' kingdom is not "from" this world (Jn 18:36), but it is *for* this world. And when the Judean leaders tell Pilate that Jesus "made himself the Son of God," the sequel makes it clear that they are not just thinking of incarnational Christology. Twice in what follows they offer Pilate the choice: Jesus or Caesar (Jn 19:7, 12, 15)? They, and Pilate, choose Caesar. John leaves us to draw the conclusion about the political meaning of the unfolding events of cross and resurrection. How might this affect the resonances of "son of God" elsewhere in the Gospel? The divinity of Jesus in John is, I note, a richly Jewish doctrine, rooted in the theology of temple,

Torah and Wisdom in a way that is by no means always true of later Christology.

All of this indicates to me, since Marianne has interestingly brought it up, that Reimarus was correct to explore what the church had managed to marginalize, namely, the question of Jesus and the kingdom, even though he was woefully mistaken in what he concluded about it. Reimarus, of course, couldn't put together the kingdom and the cross, but then nor could the rest of the Great Tradition he was reacting against. John, like the Synoptics, does it effortlessly. Here too I welcome Marianne's nicely turned phrase about meeting the Johannine Jesus again for the first time.

There are many other questions Marianne has raised which I haven't answered here. These things are answered so that it may appear that, were there room enough in the world, I would love to pursue the historical and theological question of John more fully. If and when I do so, I will expect to find rich convergence among the multiple Gospel witnesses.

2

Knowing Jesus

Story, History and the Question of Truth

RICHARD B. HAYS

WE ARE GATHERED HERE TO CELEBRATE the scholarly work of Tom Wright. His prolific writings have reshaped the way many of us read the New Testament. His books have situated Jesus and Paul squarely on the map of Second Temple Judaism, while at the same time showing how a historically particular reading of Jesus and Paul as first-century Jews can enhance Christian theological interpretation. Tom has written extensively for both academy and church, and he has been one of our generation's most effective Christian apologists in a post-Christian culture. He is a devoted servant of the church, and he writes with grace, wit and power. And so this large crowd of friends and appreciative readers has come together to honor Tom Wright and his work.

Yet, at the same time, we have also come to reflect critically upon it. Those two aims (laudatory celebration and critical scrutiny) might seem to conflict, but in fact they do not. The greatest honor that can be shown to a scholar is for his or her work to be engaged deeply and tested rigorously by colleagues. Adulation is for rock stars—but patient, searching, truthful dialogue is for those we love. In the preface to *The New Testament and the People of God*, written eighteen years ago, Tom wrote:

> I frequently tell my students that quite a high proportion of what I say is probably wrong, or at least flawed or skewed in some way which I do not at the moment realize. The only problem is that I do not know

which bits are wrong; if I did I might do something about it. . . . Serious debate and confrontation is the stuff of academic life, and I look forward, not of course without some trepidation, to more of it as a result of this project.[1]

And so the essay that I offer today will seek to honor Tom as a true friend precisely by telling him which bits I think might be wrong. What you are about to hear, then, is the continuation of an unexpectedly challenging conversation between two friends.

For more than twenty-five years Tom Wright and I have been allies in various battles within the field of New Testament studies. The two of us have also been engaged in a long-running, mutually edifying conversation about the interpretation of Scripture; each of us has frequently drawn on the other's writings for inspiration and instruction. I regard Tom not only as an insightful interpreter of the New Testament and an eloquent preacher of the gospel, but as one of my very closest friends.

It therefore came as a shock to me—and I think to him as well—when at the Society of Biblical Literature (SBL) meeting in Boston in 2008, Tom delivered a withering attack on my most recent book project. The book was *Seeking the Identity of Jesus: A Pilgrimage*, coedited by Beverly Roberts Gaventa and me.[2] It was the subject of a review panel at SBL, and Tom had been asked to be one of the respondents. I knew he would find things in the book to criticize; it was, after all, a collection of essays by sixteen different scholars, and I myself disagreed with some of their arguments on various particular points. But I had expected that he would warmly welcome the book's fundamental approach and claims: that Jesus of Nazareth was a first-century Jew whose life and teachings could be understood only within the context of Israel's history and Israel's Scripture; that the identity of Jesus is reliably attested in the canonical Gospels (and not in extracanonical literature such as the various Gnostic gospels); that the Jesus we find in the canonical New Testament is rightly understood in the church's subse-

---

[1]N. T. Wright, *The New Testament and the People of God* (Minneapolis: Fortress, 1992), pp. xvii-xviii.

[2]Beverly Roberts Gaventa and Richard B. Hays, eds., *Seeking the Identity of Jesus: A Pilgrimage* (Grand Rapids: Eerdmans, 2008).

quent confessional traditions—that is, the notion of Jesus as the incarnation of God is not a later fanciful aberration but a faithful construal of the figure we encounter in the Gospels; that after his crucifixion, Jesus was raised from the dead; consequently, he is not only a figure of past history, but he remains a living presence in the community of his people; and finally, that knowing Jesus rightly requires a lifelong process of discipleship, in which we are conformed to the pattern of his life so that we seek to embody God's will in the world—or, to put this last point in a Wrightian idiom: true beliefs about Jesus cannot be separated from praxis that seeks to implement Jesus' kingdom agenda. All this, I expected, would be profoundly congenial to Tom's own scholarly commitments and conclusions.

But instead Tom greeted the book with sharp criticism, chiefly because he saw its approach to seeking Jesus as insufficiently historical. Our "pilgrimage," he said, was overdetermined by dogmatic concerns and theological traditions, and inattentive to the realities of first-century history. Real pilgrims, Tom observed, would get their feet dirty on the dusty roads of ancient Palestine. But this book of essays was instead "a pilgrimage by helicopter," and its authors and editors were "pilgrims with suspiciously clean feet." The result was therefore, in his words, a "pseudo-theological project of non-historical retrieval of Jesus." And much, much more in this vein.[3] A great deal of this critique was, I believe, wide of the mark. But it was delivered with the inimitable wit and dazzling rhetorical fireworks we have all come to admire in Tom's writing.

Now, my purpose in recounting this tale of a surprising showdown at SBL is not to set the stage for a rebuttal or to shift our attention today away from Tom's work to the book I coedited. Instead, my purpose is to set the stage for some reflections about the way in which we might most fruitfully understand the relation between story and history in our effort to grasp the truth about Jesus. Tom's visceral reaction to *Seeking the Identity of Jesus* exposed for both of us a large area of previously undiscovered, or at least unexamined, differences. In our subsequent conversations, I learned, for example, that he regards the theol-

---

[3]These quotations are taken from N. T. Wright, "Pilgrims with Suspiciously Clean Feet," a paper presented at the annual meeting of the SBL, Boston, November 24, 2008.

ogy of Karl Barth as the source of much mischief and error, and that he
is deeply suspicious of the whole Barthian/postliberal project of "narrative theology" associated with the so-called Yale School of theologians
such as Hans Frei and George Lindbeck. On his view, their "intratex-
tual" hermeneutical approaches lead to an escapist denial of critical history and a detachment from the real world of historical events outside
the text of the Bible. I, on the other hand, have been profoundly influenced by Barth and his heirs, and I believe Tom's negative evaluation of
them is based on an unfortunate caricature of their theology. And so,
the blowup in Boston exposed some important fault lines in the alli-
ance between Tom and me. (Perhaps it was a little like the confrontation between Peter and Paul at Antioch: Tom believed I was not walking straight toward the truth of the gospel.) Consequently, this argument
has forced me to go back and reread Tom's work with new questions in
mind to see what I missed before.

The questions concerning us in the present essay are these: How are
we to understand the relation between story and history? What roles, if
any, do the church's scriptural canon and tradition play in New Testament hermeneutics? Is there a legitimate discipline of historical inquiry
that operates outside and apart from that tradition? If so, what claim
does such a discipline have on determining the ways in which Christians
know Jesus? In what ways might the historical study of Jesus play a role
in apologetics or in conversation with non-Christians? And finally, what
is the significance of the resurrection of Jesus for our epistemology?

Of course, to treat such huge questions is impossible in one short
paper. All I can hope to do is offer a few summarizing observations and
proposals. My remarks will proceed in three stages. First, I will sketch
briefly my understanding of the ways in which Tom approaches these
issues of story and history. Second, I will offer some reflections on the
theological gains and losses entailed in Tom's working methodology.
And finally, I will venture some programmatic proposals about where
we might go from here.

APPROACHING JESUS: THE WRIGHT METHODS

The book in which Tom has most fully developed his account of the

figure of Jesus is, of course, *Jesus and the Victory of God* (*JVG*). At the
time of its publication in 1996, I wrote a blurb for the book jacket. That
blurb still expresses accurately my view of the book's significance:

> Tom Wright's bold and brilliant book challenges us to rethink every-
> thing we thought we knew about the Jesus of history. Wright master-
> fully surveys the field of research on Jesus and proposes a fresh account
> of Jesus as a first-century Jewish apocalyptic prophet. . . . The result? A
> portrait of Jesus that situates him firmly "on the ground" in the politics
> of first-century Judaism while integrating the data of the Gospel tradi-
> tions in fresh and surprising ways. Wright's sweeping hypothesis, pre-
> sented in delightfully lucid prose, sets a benchmark for all subsequent
> investigations of the historical Jesus.[4]

But I now want to unpack a little more fully the judgments expressed
in this blurb by analyzing the working methods Tom employs in the
book. Exactly how does he challenge us to rethink our picture of Jesus,
and how does he integrate the data in fresh ways?

One of the book's many virtues is that Tom is deeply reflective about
methodological issues. He does not merely adopt the methods conven-
tionally employed in historical study of the Jesus tradition; instead, he
works out his own approach to the problem. The sophisticated methodological underpinnings of *JVG* are explained at length in his earlier book
The New Testament and the People of God.[5] For the purposes of our present
analysis, I want to highlight seven features of Tom's working method.

***Descriptive observations on Tom Wright's historical methods. 1. Criti-
cal realism.*** In *The New Testament and the People of God*, Tom devotes an
opening chapter to the problem of epistemology. He rejects a naive
historical positivism which supposes that "facts" about the world can be
clearly and objectively discerned by the knower from a position of neu-
trality. But he also rejects a radical postmodernism that treats all knowledge as constructed by the knower and denies the possibility of true
access to a reality external to the self. In place of these rival epistemolo-

---

[4]Richard B. Hays, book jacket endorsement for N. T. Wright, *Jesus and the Victory of God* (Minneapolis: Fortress, 1996).
[5]There is also a helpful brief summary of Wright's approach in M. J. Borg and N. T. Wright, *The
Meaning of Jesus: Two Visions* (San Francisco: HarperSanFrancisco, 1999), pp. 15-27.

gies, Tom opts for "critical realism," an epistemologically chastened
position that recognizes both the role of the human agent's worldview in
shaping perception—like the spectacles he or she wears—and, at the
same time, the reality of the external world perceived by that agent.
Through a process of trial and error, the testing of "fit" between worldview and evidence, the knower can gradually attain a reasonably accurate picture of the real world, including the real world of past history.

   2. Hypothesis and verification. This aspect of Tom's method is one of
the ways in which his approach to Jesus differs radically from most
other studies. In the twentieth century, studies of the historical Jesus
usually sought to apply various criteria that enable the sifting of individual sayings and narrative units in the Gospels, separating the authentic from the inauthentic, assigning various levels of probability to
their claim of historical factuality. The Jesus Seminar's color-coded
edition of the Gospels is the most vivid visual representation of this
methodology. The usual procedure is to extract the residue of "critically
assured" units of tradition and build a picture of Jesus on that basis. But
Tom rejects this whole approach out of hand. Instead, his method aims
at "getting the evidence in." He takes the whole body of (canonical)
traditions about Jesus and tries to develop a hypothesis about the identity of Jesus that will allow for maximum inclusion of the data. In fact,
at no point in almost seven hundred pages of *JVG* does Tom say of any
unit of Gospel material, "Jesus probably didn't say that," or "This is
legendary embellishment." Instead, he tries to make all the pieces of
the puzzle fit together as historically factual elements of his reconstruction. This is one of the reasons that many evangelicals love the book.
Conversely, it is one of the things that causes many New Testament
scholars in the academic guild to regard it with suspicion. The methodology requires initial immersion in the New Testament texts and other
texts that provide insight into Jesus' cultural environment, followed by
a highly intuitive, synthetic leap of induction that generates a master
hypothesis. The master hypothesis is then—perhaps in circular
fashion?—evaluated on the basis of its capacity to explain as much of
the evidence as possible.

   3. Skepticism about form and redaction criticism, and about Synoptic source criticism. A corollary of the previous point is that Tom brackets out any use of the critical methods usually employed by Gospel scholars to distinguish stages of development within the tradition or relations of literary dependence among the three Synoptic Gospels. His reason for this radical methodological decision is simply stated: "If all this worked, and if most scholars agreed about it, it would be fine. But it doesn't, and they don't, and it isn't. Despite frequent claims, a century of research has failed to reach anything like consensus on a single one of the stages in question, let alone on the hypothetical developments in between."[6] Here I must register a slight qualm. On the question of Synoptic literary relationships, something like the method of hypothesis and verification has been in play for a long time, and there is actually a very high degree of consensus among scholars on the priority of the Gospel of Mark, and the conclusion that both Matthew and Luke used Mark as a source. I myself would want to give this hypothesis considerably more weight in a historical reconstruction than Tom wants to allow. Tom's complete embargo on such considerations is another of the factors that has caused some New Testament critics to regard *JVG* as an apologetic tour de force.

4. Extensive use of Second Temple Jewish material. Less distinctive to Tom's methodology, but deeply integral to it, is his broad engagement with Jewish sources from the Second Temple era. These texts and sources allow him to draw the map on which the Jesus of the Gospels is to be located. That map is not the framework of the Christian creedal tradition, or even of the canonical New Testament. Rather it is the "cultural encyclopedia"—the cultural framework of reference—of Jewish religion and culture in the ancient Mediterranean world. The important conversation partners for Tom's interpretation of Jesus are not Irenaeus or the Council of Chalcedon, not even the letter to the Hebrews or 1 Peter. Rather, the key conversation partners are Josephus, the Dead Sea Scrolls, 4 Ezra and so on. (This attention to ancient Jewish sources is one of the characteristic features of what Tom has named "the Third Quest for the historical Jesus.") And here the polarities shift:

---

[6]Ibid., pp. 20-21.

at this point, Tom's method is much more in synch with the priorities
of the academy and less in keeping with the perceptions of the church.
This is certainly one of the points at which his critique of the book
Beverly Gaventa and I edited is most acute: he simply thinks we have
placed the Gospels in an anachronistic "encyclopedia of reception."
(Not his term, but Umberto Eco's.) It should be noted also that Tom is
not merely mining ancient Jewish texts for parallels to this or that saying of Jesus. Rather, he is consistently reading them with an eye to
discerning their worldview, asking about the story they tell about God,
Israel and the world. In this respect Tom's method is more sophisticated and holistic than the work one sometimes finds in the professional journals of the biblical academy.

   5. *Exclusive focus on the Synoptic Gospels*. By design, Tom's account of
Jesus in *JVG* focuses on material found in the three Synoptic Gospels
and excludes John from the picture almost entirely. Tom explains this
methodological decision as a strategic move: since most Gospel scholars tend to regard the Fourth Gospel as later and full of highly theological, unhistorical material, he found it simpler to bracket out John in
hopes of making his reconstruction of Jesus more accessible and credible to other scholars. Here I must register a small note of puzzlement.
Given the radical ways in which Tom disregards scholarly consensus on
other issues, why the sudden scruple here to conform to mainstream
convention? And if his working method seeks to get all the evidence
into the picture, surely the testimony provided by John is a necessary
part of the puzzle, isn't it?[7]

   6. *Inattention to the literary and theological shape of individual Gospels*.
JVG shows little or no interest in the distinctive literary contours of the
individual canonical Gospels, or even in the distinctive theological witness of the individual Evangelists. In my judgment this is a significant
oversight, and I will have more to say about it in what follows.

   7. *Reconstruction of a Jesus behind the canonical Gospels*. Instead of attending to the distinctive portrayals of Jesus in the individual New Testament texts, Tom aims instead at something else: a reconstruction of

---

[7]On the role of the Fourth Gospel in Wright's work, see *"Jesus and the Victory of God* Meets the
Gospel of John"* by Marianne Meye Thompson in the present volume.

the historical figure of Jesus behind the texts, including the construction of an account about Jesus' intentions and his self-understanding. Such an account necessarily involves a considerable amount of inference and speculation, because the Synoptic Gospel writers—with the exception of John, who has been sent out of the classroom for the purpose of Tom's inquiry—actually give us rather little direct access to such information. But Tom regards this sort of "archaeological"[8] process of recovery as an essential part of the work of the historian. So the Gospels themselves become not the focus of attention but the windows through which Tom peers to find a Jesus outside and beyond the Gospels themselves.

Evaluative reflections on Tom Wright's historical methods. These last two points (inattention to the actual Gospels as literary texts and reconstruction of a Jesus behind the texts) seem a little odd given Tom's strong focus on story as a key to understanding Jesus. For example, he writes: "Since (a) stories are a key worldview indicator . . . and (b) a good part of the New Testament consists of stories, of narratives, it might be a good idea to consider how stories might carry, or be vehicles for, authority."[9] But in fact, upon closer examination, we see that the story in Tom's viewfinder is not exactly any of the specific stories actually told by the Evangelists; rather, it is a critically abstracted construct, the master metanarrative of the Bible. It is Israel's grand story of creation, fall, covenant, exile and return. More specifically, it is that metanarrative as told from within the perspective of late Second Temple Judaism's consciousness of "exile" and oppression, accompanied by a passionate hope for Messianic deliverance.

Tom finds the locus classicus of this consciousness in the ardent prayer of Daniel (Dan 9:3-19), but a similar sketch of Israel's metanarrative can be found in the narrative frame of the Gospel of Matthew. Consider, for example, the evocative ending of Matthew's genealogy: "So all the generations from Abraham to David are fourteen generations; and from David to the deportation to Babylon, fourteen generations; and from the deportation to Babylon to the Messiah, fourteen generations" (Mt 1:17). But again, I would note that Tom is not inter-

---

[8]On the use of *archaeological*, see Gaventa and Hays, *Seeking the Identity of Jesus*, p. 5.
[9]Wright, *New Testament and the People of God*, p. 140.

ested (at least not in *JVG*) in Matthew's theology; instead, his interest lies in tracing these ideas back into the mind of Jesus.

And so, in light of the methods he has employed, Tom arrives at the now well-known account of Jesus that he has offered with great passion and rigorous consistency over the past twenty years. Let us recall the key findings: the Jesus of Tom's historical reconstruction is a Jewish eschatological prophet who comes proclaiming the long-awaited coming of God's kingdom, the end of Israel's exile and the return of Yahweh to Zion. Indeed, Jesus is not just proclaiming the return of Yahweh to Zion, he is embodying it, enacting it in such a way that his journey to Jerusalem actually is the long-awaited eschatological coming of Israel's God.

In all this I would suggest that there is at least some unresolved tension between theological and historical perspectives. In *The Meaning of Jesus: Two Visions*, published three years after *JVG*, Tom wants to say that history and theology are complementary; indeed, that both are necessary. And in *JVG* Tom can even assert that theological exegesis can be achieved through the historical study of Jesus.[10] It seems in principle that Tom's exposition of critical realism ought to allow faith an epistemological role, since we cannot avoid reading the evidence through the "spectacles" of our own worldviews. Yet in several weighty passages he seems to suggest that faith can obscure real history, or that hard-nosed history has a certain hermeneutical priority.[11]

One clear example is the passage near the end of *JVG* in which Tom speaks of Jesus' "awareness of vocation" to enact a "symbolic encoding" of the return of YHWH. Tom then distinguishes this claim sharply from Jesus' having a "'supernatural' awareness of himself" as being in some ontological relation to Israel's God. "Jesus did not," Tom writes, "'know that he was God' in the way that one knows one is male or fe-

---

[10]Wright, *Jesus and the Victory of God*, p. 662. Surely this formulation requires more careful exploration and explanation than Wright has so far given it in his work.

[11]That is why Stephen Evans castigates Tom's work as philosophically slanted in the direction of "methodological naturalism" (C. S. Evans, "Methodological Naturalism in Historical Biblical Scholarship," in *Jesus and the Restoration of Israel: A Critical Assessment of N. T. Wright's Jesus and the Victory of God*, ed. C. C. Newman [Downers Grove, Ill.: InterVarsity Press, 1999], pp. 180-205). Evans' criticism is perhaps overdrawn, but I would suggest that he is in fact picking up some signals that really are there in Wright's work.

male, hungry or thirsty, or that one ate an orange an hour ago." Rather, it was a sort of knowledge that can be discovered only by living into it, "like knowing one is loved." This is something very different from what Tom calls, "pseudo-orthodox attempts to make Jesus of Nazareth conscious of being the second person of the Trinity."[12] Christian theological tradition is by and large bracketed out—at least at the explicit level—in Tom's treatment of the evidence.

Or consider this passage on faith and history in *The Meaning of Jesus:* "The Jesus I know in prayer, in the sacraments, in the faces of those in need, is the Jesus I meet in the historical evidence—including the New Testament, of course, but the New Testament read not so much as the church has told me to read it but as I read it with my historical consciousness fully operative."[13] In that formulation, we hear, I think, a Tom Wright speaking who is still carrying the intellectual legacy of the liberal historicism of the First and Second Quests for the historical Jesus, the quests of the nineteenth and twentieth centuries. "The church" here seems to offer chiefly an oppressive and misleading hermeneutical framework that obscures the real Jesus. To discover that real Jesus we must bracket out the church's received traditions about him and reread the New Testament with a fresh (modernist?) historical consciousness. Only then will we truly know Jesus in two ways: through our own experience (prayer, etc.) and in our historical reconstruction. Experience and critical history rescue us from the misreading of Jesus ?/ bequeathed to us by the church. Tom does not always write about Jesus in these terms, but it is one important strand of his working methodology. And this is certainly the Tom Wright who was speaking on that difficult day in Boston.

The bracketing out of the church's theological tradition is also suggested by two other important features of *JVG:* the absence of the Gospel of John in the database used for reconstruction of the historical Jesus, and the deferral of the resurrection to a subsequent volume. Tom might well plead that these deferrals are either strategic or simply necessitated by the large scope of the topics. He did, after all, write an

---

[12]Wright, *Jesus and the Victory of God*, p. 653.
[13]Borg and Wright, *Meaning of Jesus*, p. 26.

even longer subsequent volume on the resurrection! But I would still suggest that the omissions of John and the resurrection from *JVG* are hermeneutically significant. Clearly it makes a huge difference whether or not one reads the Synoptic Gospels in dialogue with John's proclamation that Jesus was the incarnation of the logos or in light of the resurrection as the true climax of the story.[14]

Perhaps I could put my point here simply as a question to Tom: Now that you have worked through the evidence and written a comprehensive study of the resurrection that concludes Jesus really was raised from the dead, should this finding retrospectively affect the content treated in *JVG*? If you were going to revise that volume for a second edition now, almost fifteen years later, would your assessment of the evidence have to be different in light of the findings of *The Resurrection of the Son of God*?

THEOLOGICAL GAINS AND LOSSES IN TOM WRIGHT'S CRITICAL-REALIST HISTORICISM

It is time now to sum up what we have observed and reflect on what is gained and lost in Tom Wright's far-reaching and insightful account of the Jesus of history.

Gains. As *Jesus and the Victory of God* rolls on and the evidence accumulates, page after page, we find that Tom has achieved some impressive results. His construction of Jesus is wide-ranging, eloquent and cohesive. From a theological point of view, here are the major gains that I see:

1. Reading in historical context and depth. Tom narrates a Jesus who for the most part fits intelligibly into the history of Israel in the first century under Roman rule. His identity is thoroughly Jewish, and many of his actions and teachings come freshly into focus within the setting that Tom constructs. The Gospels themselves gain texture and precision when read alongside the extant corpus of ancient Jewish literature hoping for Israel's restoration and renewal.

2. Recovery of the political/pragmatic character of the gospel. The Jesus

---

[14]See R. B. Hays, "Reading Scripture in Light of the Resurrection," in *The Art of Reading Scripture*, ed. E. F. Davis and R. B. Hays (Grand Rapids: Eerdmans, 2003), pp. 216-38.

who steps out of the pages of Tom's book is not an otherworldly, apolitical figure. He fits within a vivid political landscape of pragmatic collaborators, resistance fighters, would-be messiahs and others struggling to sort out the national identity of a people trodden down by pagan powers but always dreaming that God would set them free and bring justice. Against this backdrop Jesus' prophetic proclamation of "the kingdom of God" recovers its properly explosive political meaning. So Tom's work goes a long way to overcome the misguided modernist divide between theology and politics.

3. Positive coherence of the Synoptic story line with Old Testament/Israel. One benefit of Tom's work that is not often enough recognized is that it goes a long way toward resolving the perennial problem of the relation between the Old and New Testaments. The Synoptic Gospels, on Tom's reading, narrate a linear continuation of the story line of Israel's national struggles and hopes. The God who appears clearly in these pages is the God who made covenant with Israel, led them out of slavery in Egypt, gave them a promised land, banished them into exile because of their unfaithfulness, but nevertheless remains faithful to them. The New Testament then becomes, simply but profoundly, the story of God's restoration of his people Israel, and Jesus is "the one to redeem Israel" (Lk 24:21). I say this is a theological gain, though some of Tom's critics protest that his account overstates the salvation-historical continuity between Israel and church, and underplays the radical newness of God's saving action in Christ's death and resurrection. I would like to go on record as saying that, theologically speaking, this is a misguided objection. Rather than diminishing the newness of God's saving action, Tom's account deepens our understanding of the way in which the death and resurrection of Jesus is not simply a matter of saving individuals from their personal guilt; instead, it is the culmination of God's astonishing large-scale plan to restore his covenant people and bring salvation to the whole world.

4. High christology. Perhaps the most surprising theological outcome of Tom's historical construction is the way in which, while working "from below" on the plane of historical events, it unexpectedly opens the door to the development of an exceedingly high christology. Here is

the now-famous concluding passage of Tom's account of Jesus' beliefs
about himself and his mission:

> I propose, *as a matter of history*, that Jesus of Nazareth was conscious of
> a vocation: a vocation, given him by the one he knew as "father," to
> enact in himself what, in Israel's scriptures, God had promised to ac-
> complish all by himself. He would be the pillar of cloud and fire for the
> people of the new exodus. He would embody in himself the returning
> and redeeming action of the covenant God.[15]

If that is what Jesus thought about his own identity, the subsequent
development of the church's worship of him becomes more readily in-
telligible. From a historical point of view, if Jesus was a simple Galilean
prophet and teacher, the church's later claims about his divinity have
always appeared to be nothing other than a theological mistake, the
superimposition of a mythological construct that Jesus himself would
probably have found blasphemous. Not so on Tom's reading. But of
course, while Tom's proposal that Jesus saw himself as embodying the
return of YHWH to Zion is the linchpin of his historical account, it is
also the one feature of his reconstruction that has been seen as most
unpersuasive to most of his colleagues who labor in the vineyard of
"historical Jesus" studies.

5. *Apologetic value*. Finally, from a theological point of view, one
might hope—and I think Tom does hope—that his historical account
of Jesus might have apologetic value and impact. He seeks to give us a
historical narrative that takes in all the evidence and shows that the
Gospels actually do give us a persuasive, coherent picture of what
really happened in the life of Jesus—history *wie es eigentlich gewesen ist*.
To the extent that Tom's construction works as "secular" history, it creates a bridge for dialogue with nonbelievers about Jesus. They can be
invited to cross the bridge, to "come and see" who Jesus was[16] without
first having to surrender their own historical consciousness and worldview. I fear, however, that this apologetic hope is illusory or at least
exaggerated. But Tom's book may in fact serve a slightly different sort

---

[15]Wright, *Jesus and the Victory of God*, p. 653 (emphasis added).
[16]I choose the past tense of the verb "to be" deliberately. By contrast, see L. E. Keck, *Who Is
Jesus? History in Perfect Tense* (Columbia: University of South Carolina Press, 2000).

of apologetic function: it is not a sign for nonbelievers but for believers. It may allow uncertain believers to gain greater confidence about the historical credibility of the story that they already haltingly believe on other grounds.

Losses. The theological gains enumerated here are weighty. But I think a full assessment of *JVG* must also reckon with some factors that should be entered on the debit side of the theological ledger.[17]

1. Voices of the writers disappear. First, as I have suggested already in my descriptive remarks, within Tom's project, the individual voices of the Synoptic Gospel writers disappear. The distinctiveness of the testimony of each individual Gospel witness is lost, or at least drowned out, by Tom's synthetic renarration of his account of Jesus. This is theologically regrettable, and it effectively turns back the clock and loses some of the very significant gains achieved by literary study of the Gospels over the past generation. As a reader of the New Testament I want to hear the complex polyphony of the choir of singers, not just a critically extracted unison melody.

2. Over-systematization. The reference to a "critically extracted" melody points to my second concern: the danger of over-systematization. The question that haunts many readers of *JVG* is whether Tom's synthetic construct is too clever by half, whether it obsessively forces all the evidence into the single mold of the exile and return pattern. The parade example is Tom's interpretation of the parable of the prodigal son as a story about Israel's exile and restoration.[18] No matter how many times I read Tom's elegant treatment of the parable, I simply can't persuade myself that this is what Jesus meant when he told the story. There are two simple reasons for my incredulity.

First, Luke, the one Gospel writer who recounts this parable, does not seem to think it means what Tom thinks it means. He contextualizes it within a controversy between Jesus and the Pharisees and scribes about Jesus' practice of eating with sinners (Lk 15:1-2). In Luke 15 the parable is one of a string of three parables, following the lost sheep and

---

[17]Perhaps some of the objections posed here may be counted as open questions, rather than losses.

[18]Wright, *Jesus and the Victory of God*, pp. 125-31.

the lost coin, about mercy and forgiveness. It requires a couple of tricky hermeneutical dance steps to get to Tom's reading about Israel's new exodus. I think finally he can get there only by assuming that the Jesus of history was really talking about national exile and return, but that Luke himself either failed to understand that theme or suppressed it deliberately. Tom never actually puts it that way, but I think that is the implicit logic of the argument. It seems to me that what Tom really has done is to make a brilliant homiletical move, showing how the parable of the prodigal son could function metaphorically to illustrate his own major theme of Israel's exile and return. But merely to show the aptness of the metaphor is not to demonstrate historically that Jesus used the parable that way.

Second, Tom's reading of the parable is unprecedented in the history of interpretation. He points this out explicitly: "Years of scholarship have produced many commentaries on Luke, and many books on the parables. But none that I have been able to consult has noted the feature which seems to me most striking and obvious."[19] Indeed. Perhaps it is the case, then, that it is not really so "obvious." Perhaps we are dealing here not with a recovery of what Jesus really meant back in the first century but instead with a wonderful flash of poetic insight, the sort of artistic *poi*™*sis* that makes Tom such a fine preacher.

3. The church's confessional tradition. All this raises the question of the relation of Tom's critical reconstruction of Jesus to the church's confessional tradition. He sometimes seems to insist that his account, as historical in character, is independent of that tradition. In the first place I must say that I doubt that. Tom Wright has never come to the New Testament as a neutral historian. His own account of critical realism should serve amply to make the point. He comes to his reading of the Gospels as a believing Christian, formed intellectually and imaginatively by years of participation in the rich liturgical life of the Church of England; even as a Christian trying to think historically, he is engaged in the project of faith seeking understanding. But if that is the case, why not acknowledge that the church's tradition might

---

[19]Ibid., p. 126.

provide aid rather than hindrance in seeking to understand the New Testament's witness about the identity of Jesus? Ben Meyer, one of the important influences on Tom's thinking, puts the point in the following way: it may be "in the *tradition generated by Jesus* that we discover what made him operate in the way he did."[20] Why then not acknowledge more forthrightly, Tom, that your reading of the historical evidence is actually stimulated by the church's orthodox confessional traditions, even if your reading fills in details and makes connections that the tradition has not often made before? Or, conversely, if your reading seems totally unprecedented in the church's whole tradition of reading—as in the case of the prodigal son parable—should that give you pause about whether your interpretation can persuasively claim historical validity? Should you think of it instead as a fresh constructive theological proposal, an exercise in typological reading, analogous (say) to Paul's reading of Christian baptism and the Lord's Supper as prefigured by Israel's exodus experience (1 Cor 10:1-22)?

4. The canon as authoritative for theology. Another theological loss in Tom's project is a loss of clarity about the role of the canon of Scripture as authoritative for theology. (Or at least this is a potential danger in the project.) When we seek to know who Jesus is, how do we do that? Do we look to the narrative representations of Jesus in the canonical fourfold Gospel? Or must we instead read *JVG* to discover Tom Wright's reconstructed metanarrative as the distinctively authoritative construal of Jesus' identity? The problem here is the one long ago identified by Martin Kähler: the critical historian becomes in effect a Fifth Evangelist whose secondary reconstruction becomes the center of authority, perhaps even displacing the very texts it seeks to interpret.[21] One major difference between Tom and many other questers for the historical Jesus (such as Marcus Borg or John Dominic Crossan) is that he certainly does not intend to contradict or supplant the canonical

!?

---

[20]B. F. Meyer, *The Aims of Jesus* (London: SCM, 1979), p. 253, cited in Wright, *New Testament and the People of God*, p. 115 (emphasis added).

[21]Martin Kähler, *The So-Called Historical Jesus and the Historic Biblical Christ* (1896; reprint, Philadelphia: Fortress, 1964).

accounts of Jesus. But at the end of the day the more strongly Tom emphasizes the distinctiveness of his account, the more acute the problem becomes.

5. Narrative identity. Finally, these problems may be restated in terms of the concept of narrative identity: how is identity rendered? Tom seems to locate the identity of Jesus in something like an abstracted pattern—the critically reconstructed story of Jesus as enacting the pattern of return from exile—rather than in the New Testament's specific narrative renderings. Paradoxically, at this point Tom's work bears a striking formal similarity to Hans Frei's classic study *The Identity of Jesus Christ.*[22] Frei of course said nothing about return from exile or restoration of Israel. But he saw Jesus' identity as enacted in a narrative pattern of self-emptying obedience to which the Gospels generally point. And, like Tom Wright, he made no effort to relate his proposed narrative pattern to the actual way the individual Gospels narrate the passion, death and resurrection of Jesus. For Frei, the thing that mattered was a fundamental kerygmatic narrative pattern underlying all the canonical Gospel texts. It seems to me that Tom is actually doing something analogous, but he differs from Frei in insisting that the kerygmatic pattern he identifies was also present in the mind of the historical Jesus, consciously shaping his aims and actions. Against both Frei and Wright, I would like to propose that it is more theologically fruitful for interpretation of Jesus to adhere more closely to the actual specific narratives given us in the canonical Gospels: Matthew, Mark, Luke and John.

WHERE DO WE GO FROM HERE? A THEOLOGICAL ASSESSMENT

First, I would like to arrange a conversation, in the near future, between my friends Tom Wright and Karl Barth. Maybe I could invite both of them to dinner. If they should accept the invitation, here is how I would introduce the dinner-table conversation: "Karl, I want you to listen to this passage from Tom's *Jesus and the Victory of God.*"

---

[22]Hans Frei, *The Identity of Jesus Christ: The Hermeneutical Bases of Dogmatic Theology* (Philadelphia: Fortress, 1975).

Those who have desired to explore and understand the incarnation itself
have regularly missed what is arguably the most central, shocking and
dramatic source material on that subject, which if taken seriously would
ensure that the meaning of the word "god" be again and again rethought
around the actual history of Jesus himself.[23]

"And now, Tom, listen to this passage from Karl's *Church Dogmatics*": "The meaning of his deity—the only true deity in the New Testament sense—cannot be gathered from any notion of supreme, absolute, non-worldly being. It can be learned only from what took place
in Christ."[24]

My point is that Tom and Karl ought to find they have more in common than Tom supposes! They are in full agreement, I think, that the
incarnation forces us to rethink the very meaning of the word *god*, for
in Jesus God is concretely present in a very surprising way. The particularity of incarnation requires a fundamental reconfiguration of our
understanding of God. God is made known precisely in Jesus, not
through general speculation or natural knowledge. Consider the opening of chapter fourteen of Barth's *Church Dogmatics:*

> The atonement is history. To know it, we must know it as such. To think
> of it, we must think of it as such. To speak of it, we must tell it as history.
> To try to grasp it as supra-historical or non-historical truth is not to
> grasp it at all. It is indeed truth, but truth actualised in a history and
> revealed in this history as such—revealed, therefore, as history.[25]

I would think Tom would applaud that! But I think my two friends
Wright and Barth would still find plenty to argue about, because they
still differ on the hermeneutical issue of how we come to know the
truth about this historical figure of Jesus in whom God is embodied.

Second, we need to seek to overcome, with renewed determination,
the pernicious dichotomy between story and history. Tom and I agree
about that. Why, then, have we somehow come to think differently
about the proper way of relating story and history? In pondering this

---

[23]Wright, *Jesus and the Victory of God*, p. 661.
[24]Karl Barth, *Church Dogmatics* IV/1, trans. G. W. Bromiley (Edinburgh: T & T Clark, 1956),
    p. 177.
[25]Ibid., p. 157.

question I stumbled across a particularly telling autobiographical insight offered by Tom in *The Meaning of Jesus:*

> I react against attempts to pull me back into the old split-level world . . .
> with the vigour of one who does not want to be imprisoned again in the
> attic (faith divorced from history) or the dungeon (history divorced from
> faith). This reaction will be understood, perhaps, by those who have
> experienced other liberations, for instance from heavy-handed traditional Protestantism or Catholicism.[26]

This may go some way toward explaining Tom's vehement response to *Seeking the Identity of Jesus:* he perceived it as an attempt to imprison him again in the attic by banishing history and enforcing conformity to some sort of antihistorical disembodied faith

But nothing could be further from the truth. In a significant essay in *Seeking the Identity of Jesus*, the theologian Robert Jenson confronts exactly this issue and asks a provocative question: "But what if the church's dogma were a necessary hermeneutical principal of historical reading, because it describes the true ontology of historical being?"[27] Let me paraphrase that: if it is true that Jesus was the incarnation of the Word, the fleshly embodiment of the one through whom all things were made—and if it is true that he was raised from the dead by the power of God and now reigns over the whole world (whether the world acknowledges it or not)—then it follows that the historical figure of Jesus cannot be rightly known or understood apart from the epistemological insight articulated precisely in the confession that Jesus is Lord—Jesus is the *kyrios*. This is where we ought to begin if we want to know the truth about Jesus.

This is the insight that Tom's whole historical Jesus project doesn't ever quite take on board. The "hypothesis" that Tom seeks to verify by pulling together the evidence of the Synoptics is not a naked inference from uninterpreted data. Rather, the hypothesis that Tom is testing is already encoded in the New Testament texts themselves as proclamatory stories, and already imbedded in Tom's own worldview

---

[26]Borg and Wright, *Meaning of Jesus*, p. 16.
[27]Robert W. Jenson, "Identity, Jesus, and Exegesis," in *Seeking the Identity of Jesus*, p. 50.

by virtue of his lifelong participation in a community that continues
to retell the story. So the hypothesis-verification model can't escape
the hermeneutical circle. Nor should it. Precisely because the church's
dogma names a truth the world does not or cannot know, it rightly
describes the truth about history in a way that secularist history is
bound to miss.

Another way to put this point is to affirm that the resurrection of
Jesus is the epistemological key to understanding the world and therefore the key to all history. If so, any history that does not begin from the
vantage point of the resurrection of Jesus is perforce distorted because
it denies or fails to grasp the true history of the world.

CONCLUSION

The fault line between Tom and me on story and history is broadly
emblematic of a pervasive ambivalence in contemporary evangelical
Christianity. The desire for historical validation of Christian claims
stands in some tension with a deeply felt desire for the postmodern recovery of canon and tradition as the necessary hermeneutical framework for understanding both Scripture and the world. Both Tom and I
want both things, but we have different ways of seeking to integrate
them. On the one hand, Tom insists that without historical investigation of the factuality of the Gospels, the story is vacuous, not least at
the level of concrete action in the world. I insist, on the other hand, that
without the canonical form of the story, we could never get the historical investigation right in the first place.

Throughout these critical reflections on Tom Wright's magisterial
work, I have been seeking to extend a deep conversation between the
two of us—that is to say, between the sort of colleagues whom Paul
calls "fellow-workers belonging to God" (1 Cor 3:9). Ultimately, that
conversation will end, I trust, not like the testy confrontation between
Peter and Paul at Antioch, but more like the meeting in Jerusalem that
led to the mutual recognition of the grace of God given to each, culmi-
nating in the giving of the right hand of *koinɸnia*. In that spirit, may
faith and history unite; may story and history meet and embrace. May
Richard and Tom embrace—and rejoice in the truth.

Response to Richard Hays
N. T. WRIGHT

My fuller response to Richard Hays is contained within my longer essay on Jesus, "Whence and Whither Historical Jesus Studies in the Life of the Church?" in this volume. Here I simply venture a few suggestions, not to resolve the questions but (hopefully) to take the discussion forward.

First, some comments on method. All historical inquiry uses hypothesis and verification, whether or not it recognizes or acknowledges it. The New Quest "criteria," and their nadir in the Jesus Seminar, was an attempt to verify or modify a particular hypothesis about Jesus. As the portrait needed more and more extra hypotheses to sustain it—speculative reconstructions of traditio-historical stages between Jesus and the pre-Gospel traditions—the normal tests for good hypotheses started to come up negative. I advanced my own hypothesis instead. This historical method is not the same thing as skeptical modernism. Post-Enlightenment "historiography" and postliberal dogma-and-story are not the only options.

I have been cautious about the "received methods" of source and form criticism because I think much of the scholarship concerned presupposed the wrong frameworks and asked the wrong questions. But redaction criticism, and more especially composition criticism, certainly matter. We actually have Matthew, Mark, Luke and John, but not Q, Proto-Luke and so on. We can ask sensible questions about what the Evangelists were doing. The section on the Evangelists in *The New Testament and the People of God* was designed as part of the introduction to *Jesus and the Victory of God (JVG)* for just the reasons Richard mentions. I wanted to note their different angles of vision before asking the perfectly proper question about whether what they said about Jesus made sense historically.

Ironically, it is the source and form critics who constructed something "behind" the Gospels. But even if we could actually agree on sources and pre-literary forms, that would reveal nothing much about their historical value. Earlier sources might be more accurate if the spread was a few hundred years, but over a generation or so it's largely irrelevant.

In writing *JVG* I put John to one side for (I imagine) a similar reason to why Richard omits Ephesians and Colossians (not to mention the Pastorals) when writing about Paul. If your opponents insist on playing tennis on a small court, you'd better learn how to keep the ball in play. When I was planning *JVG*, in the late 1980s, I had published next to nothing. Had I brought John into the equation without comprehensive justification, my principal conversation partners would have ignored the book. I am thus attacked by liberals because I included too much of the Synoptics, and by postliberals because I didn't include John. So be it.

Constructing a Jesus "behind the text": many writers encourage their readers to reflect on the presuppositions and intentions of their central characters. When we do that, we are not sneakily setting aside the story they are telling. We are trying to understand it. One good friend commented that I was giving people back the Jesus who had been in their Gospels all along but whom they had not noticed. All readers of the Gospels have a mental picture of who Jesus was, what he was thinking, what he was like. I decided to subject mine to conscious, critical reflection. Jesus could have been an unthinking person who had no game plan or larger purpose, but simply found himself doing and saying various things. The Gospels, though, tell us that he wrestled with questions of vocation and mission, and went off frequently to pray. It is not going behind their backs to inquire what that wrestling was about and what conclusions Jesus came to.

The Great Tradition has seriously and demonstrably distorted the gospels. Eager to explain who "God" really was, the church highlighted Christology; wanting to show that Jesus was divine, it read the Gospels with that as the question; looking for Jesus' divinity, it ignored other central themes such as the kingdom of God. By the fourth century the church was not so eager to discover that God's kingdom had arrived and was to be implemented in Jesus' way, so it screened out that kingdom inauguration which lies at the heart of the Synoptic tradition. Here is Jesus doing miracles! Well, that shows he was divine! For the Gospel writers, however, it shows that "the kingdom of God has come upon you" (Mt 10:7; Lk 11:20). The major divide, then, is not between history and canon, but between history and canon together on one side, both emphasizing Jesus' kingdom inauguration, and tradition on the other side, screening this out. This is where I should have begun my critique of *Seeking the Identity of Jesus*.

I therefore find my heart strangely chilled by Richard's quotation from Robert Jenson. I am nowhere near so interested in "the true ontology of historical being" as I am in the inauguration of the kingdom of God. But the church's dogma remains more or less silent on that topic—except to affirm it, in the creeds, in relation to the second coming. For the canon, and in history, God became king in and through Jesus, his life, death, resurrection and ascension. I believe in the creeds. But I believe in the Jesus of the Gospels a good deal more.

What difference might it make to my epistemology if I were to factor *The Resurrection of the Son of God* into my argument? Jesus' resurrection accomplishes and reveals many things. Among them, it seems to me, are the validation of the human Jesus as Messiah; with that, the validation of God's Israel project; with that, the validation of God's *human* project. Jesus is raised as a human being; changed but still the same person. Humans have a history. They think things through, they make decisions, they act. Other humans can study those actions, those decisions, those thought processes. That kind of study is vindicated, not invalidated, by the resurrection. To imply (I'm not sure that Richard quite means this) that once we can say "he is alive" we would then do all the history differently, or do something else other than history instead, seems to me unnecessary. It still makes good sense to ask, of Jesus of Nazareth during his public career, what did he think he was doing? With what mindset did he go to the cross?

So what would Karl Barth and I say to each other? If I were standing where he stood in the first half of the twentieth century, I would pray to have half his courage and his clear prophetic vision. But I'm still not sure that he meant by "history" what I mean. Yes, he meant that it all actually happened and that it matters that it actually happened. But in the world where I live it is never enough simply to reassert that. The apologetic task (so deeply suspect to Barthians) matters. I don't believe you can argue people into faith, but I do believe you can show up the weaknesses of their skepticism. In the popular media the question of God is often discussed as though Jesus didn't exist. He is presumed to be largely a figment of the church's imagination. Getting the same media to tell people that this isn't so is a hard task, but I believe that it has to be done, and that it can really help. As Ernst Käsemann saw in the 1950s, doing historical-Jesus research is difficult, but not doing it is dangerous.

3

"Outside of a Small Circle of Friends"

Jesus and the Justice of God

SYLVIA C. KEESMAAT AND BRIAN J. WALSH

SO BRIAN, HOW LONG HAS IT BEEN?

How long has what been?

How long have you and Tom been friends?

Oh, around twenty-eight years.

And why did you become friends? Was it your shared passion for the Scriptures?

Scripture certainly had a lot to do with it. But there was also music: Arlo Guthrie, Bob Dylan, Phil Ochs.

Phil Ochs?

Phil Ochs was a contemporary of the young Dylan. Tom and I were surprised to find that we both love his music. Here is the first verse of one of his most tragically ironic songs:

> *Look outside the window, there's a woman being grabbed*
> *They've dragged her to the bushes and now she's being stabbed*
> *Maybe we should call the cops and try to stop the pain*
> *But monopoly is so much fun, I'd hate to blow the game*
> *And I'm sure it wouldn't interest anybody*
> *Outside of a small circle of friends.*[1]

---

[1]Phil Ochs, "Outside of a Small Circle of Friends," *There and Now: Phil Ochs Live in Vancouver,*

I see what you mean by "tragically ironic."

Yes, and it only gets worse. The song goes on to describe the plight of the poor in the ghetto, the war on drugs, pornography, racism and even the coup in Chile under Augusto Pinochet. All heavy stuff, but the chorus always repeats, "I'm sure it wouldn't interest anybody outside of a small circle of friends."

Therein lies the question that has been at the heart of pretty much every important theological conversation that I have ever had with Tom. So what? Where does all of this exegesis go? Does this impressive and integrative Wrightian project really interest anybody outside of a small circle of friends?

This is the question that must remain at the heart of theological reflection, and I suspect that it is at the heart of many, many people who are drawn to Tom's work. The issue isn't just whether Tom's reading of the New Testament offers a more historically satisfying and integrative interpretation—as important as this might be. The question is, So what? Or as Tom himself has asked, "How do we move from the detailed historical reconstruction of this Jesus, living in the world of the first century, to our own world with all its very different contours and agendas?"[2]

Hence, the Phil Ochs song. What we are asking is whether this ambitious project actually matters to that woman subjected to violence,

or the children who are still living in the ghetto with the rats,

or to Chileans still mourning those who were murdered and tortured when the CIA orchestrated the overthrow of Salvadore Allende's elected government,

or to Oscar Romero and the countless martyrs of Latin America, gunned down by military thugs trained at Fort Benning, Georgia,

or to a ten year old girl in Sudan, raped by the soldiers who destroyed her village,

or to the Mexican peasant growing strawberries for our tables and the Indonesian garment workers producing clothing for our backs, living with violence and poverty wages.

Archives Alive Records, 1990. At the conference where this paper was first presented, Chicago musician Grant Elgersma performed the song.

[2]N. T. Wright, *The Challenge of Jesus* (Downers Grove Ill.: InterVarsity Press, 1999), p. 43.

It seems to me that we need to press again the "so what?" question. Is it fair to ask all of these kinds of questions of Tom's project?

We would be dishonoring Tom's important contribution if we didn't ask them.

But which question? Where do we focus?

There is one thing that all of these examples, and so many more, have in common. They are casualties of an economic system that is presently in crisis.

It seems to me that the issue of economics does come up more than a few times in Tom's writings.

Yes, Tom argues that Third World debt "is the number one moral issue of our day. The present system of global debt," he goes on, "is the real immoral scandal, the dirty little secret . . . of glitzy, glossy Western capitalism."[3] This is nothing less than "theft by the strong from the weak, by the rich from the poor."[4] The cross on which the developing world has been hung is unsustainable debt.

You say that this economic system is in crisis, but it looks like it is working just fine for the wealthiest nations in the world. Apart from the sheer immorality of this dirty little secret, where is the crisis?

In the fall of 2008 the world economy went into a crisis that shook it to its very core. The Christian economist Bob Goudzwaard describes this as the crisis of a "bloated financial sector."[5] Driven by an insatiable greed, our economy has no sense of enough, no sense of proper limits to affluence, no sense of justice for the poorest of the poor and the earth itself, and so it became obscenely bloated until it had to explode.

Most economists would say that things are a lot more complex than that.

Tom himself debunked the complexity argument when he spoke in the House of Lords in his response to the Queen's Speech in 2008.[6] Responding to the argument that forgiving the debts of the poorest nations isn't as simple as

---

[3]N. T. Wright, *Surprised by Hope* (New York: HarperCollins, 2008), p. 217.

[4]Ibid., p. 218.

[5]Bob Goudzwaard, Mark Vander Vennen and David Van Heemst, *Hope in Troubled Times: A New Vision for Confronting Global Crises* (Grand Rapids: Baker, 2007), p. 142.

[6]The Queen's Speech is the address to the combined Houses of Parliament wherein the government lays out its legislative plans for the next session of Parliament. As the Lord Bishop of Durham, Tom Wright had a seat in the House of Lords and offered his response to the Queen's Speech.

it seems, Tom noted that forgiving debts is precisely what the industrialized nations of the world were doing through their bailouts of financial institutions and the automotive industry. "The very rich are doing for the very rich what they have refused to do for the very poor," he insisted.[7]

So, in this crucifixion economy, nations, people and the earth itself are all offered for sacrifice before the god of unlimited economic growth.

But that god is an idol. While it may have demonic power in our lives, it is, in biblical estimation, nothing. Idols are vanity, they have no substance, and they aren't real. And the economy that collapsed in 2008 wasn't a real economy.

What do you mean it wasn't real?

The financial markets are a shady world of currency speculation, subprime mortgages and playing the stock market. In fact, 98 percent of all economic transactions every day in the world have to do only with the financial markets.[8] *This is a virtual economy, not a real economy. What got so bloated that it burst in the fall of 2008 was the financial market that essentially trades in money.*

So in this kind of economy money can grow and a small minority of people can become incredibly rich while the majority of the world's population sink deeper and deeper into poverty. I can see why you call it an idolatrous crucifixion economy. But what can we do about it?

In his response to the "Queen's Speech," Tom said that we need nothing less than a paradigm shift. "Behind the sudden squeals for help from the very rich we must listen to the long-term cries of the very poor," he proclaimed. We need, he continued, "to shape and develop a future global economic order in which all may genuinely benefit."[9]

But every paradigm tells a story. And if that great Western narrative of economic progress has proven to be hollow, then perhaps we have before us a great evangelical opportunity to tell another story.

This isn't that different from first-century Israel living within a story that was waiting for a conclusion.

---

[7]N. T. Wright, "Economy and Business: Debate on the Queen's Speech," *Empire Remixed* (blog), December 8, 2008, <http://empireremixed.com/2008/12/09/economy-and-business-debate-on-the-queen's-speech-monday-december-8-2008/>.
[8]Goudzwaard et al., *Hope in Troubled Times*, p. 93.
[9]Wright, "Economy and Business."

It seems to me that the time is ripe for hearing the story of Jesus anew. If ours is a time of endings, then we need what Walter Brueggemann has called a prophetic imagination, an imagination of both prophetic critique and prophetic hope.[10]

That brings us to the "so what" question. Do we find prophetic critique and hope in Tom's work? In the preface to *Jesus and the Victory of God* Tom wrote, "What you say about Jesus affects your entire worldview."[11] So I think that we need to look more closely at that book.

Are you kidding? Have you seen the size of that book? It's huge; it's something like seven hundred pages long!

Well, 662 to be precise. And just over half of it is a section called "The Profile of a Prophet," which provides a picture of Jesus that is deeply biblical and that answers the fundamental questions of what is wrong with the world and how God has come to put it right.

Sounds good.

It is good. But there are some gaps in the analysis. Or maybe it is better to say that there are ways that we can deepen the picture, ways that we can widen Tom's scope in his reading so that the Jesus he describes even more radically addresses the important "so what" questions that you have raised.

Even questions of economic order?

Sure. Do you think that the issues you are talking about are all brand new? They have profound parallels in the first century as well.

Recall the Gospel stories of the day laborer standing in the market all day hoping to be hired, or the poor man waiting for crumbs from the rich man's table, or the slave who owes an impossible ten year's wages,

or the rich man whose barns aren't big enough for his over-the-top harvest, or the tax collector who wants to see Jesus,

or the slave who was given a huge sum of money to make a quick and usurious profit, or the rich ruler.

In short, exactly the same kind of people that need good news today. But are the parallels really valid? I'd hate to anachronistically project our economic assumptions and problems back onto the biblical text.

---

[10]Walter Brueggemann, *The Prophetic Imagination* (Philadelphia: Fortress, 1978).
[11]N. T. Wright, *Jesus and the Victory of God* (Minneapolis: Fortress, 1996), p. xiv.

That's a valid concern. This isn't the place to go into too much detail, but the studies are everywhere showing the sharp economic divide between the very rich and the very poor in first-century Galilee and Judea.

I seem to recall that debt was also an issue. Didn't the rebels burn the debt records in the temple during the revolt? What was that about?[12]

Oddly enough, debt became an issue because of the exceptional influx of wealth into Jerusalem due to the wealth that pilgrims brought to the city.

In addition, Jews were required to take or send two tithes to Jerusalem each year: one for the Levites (who passed on 10 percent to the priests) and one that was to be spent in the city. In addition, there was a tithe for the poor in some years. Such tithes swelled the income of the city.

The priests benefited the most from the wealth entering Jerusalem, along with others associated with the temple industry.[13]

Temple industry?

Yes, the temple was an industry; it was surrounded by those who provided services so that the temple could function properly. There were services such as providing animals for sacrifice, providing and washing linens for the priests and Levites, providing wood for sacrificial fires and for building, currency exchange, providing food for both people and animals, cleaning the temple, providing rooms for rent for pilgrims—there were plenty of ways to make money if you could find a connection to the temple or its visitors.

What does all that have to do with debt?

The Jewish aristocrats had to find something to do with this excess money. They built wonderful buildings and bought what goods they could. But there was also a desire to make a profit from their money. This was accomplished in two ways: they bought land, for the income that came from rentals, thereby driving up land prices, and they made their money available by lending it out to those who needed money for seed or who needed money in order to purchase enough land to have a viable farm.[14]

---

[12]The incident is recorded in Josephus *Jewish War* 2.427.

[13]Martin Goodman, "The First Jewish Revolt: Social Conflict and the Problem of Debt," *Journal of Jewish Studies* 33 (1982): 417-27. On tithes see E. P. Sanders, *Judaism: Practice and Belief 63 BCE-66 CE* (London: SCM; Philadelphia: Trinity Press International, 1992), pp. 148-49.

[14]On the debt dynamic in Galilee see Goodman, "First Jewish Revolt," pp. 420-23; Richard A.

In Judea the excess income from the temple industry found its way into the hands of small landowners in the form of loans. And in Galilee officials—whether tax collectors, mid-level officers or priestly families—made loans available to their needy neighbors. All of this money lending yielded a considerable gain.

But weren't these loans forgiven in the seventh year?[15]

This is where the story gets interesting. You see, the rabbis instituted a ruling called "prosbul" whereby debts no longer had to be forgiven because the courts could force payment.[16] Creditors said that this was necessary in order to make it possible to get a loan in the sixth year; the effect, however, was to keep debtors on the hook with insupportable debt. The creditor could not lose, for if the debt was not repaid, a "fine" could be charged of 20 percent, and ultimately, foreclosure brought new lands and, occasionally, slaves.[17]

I am guessing that the wealthy would use all that land for cash crops.

Exactly. Grain, olive oil and grapes for wine. Throughout the history of Israel, these were the crops the wealthy grew, both for their own consumption and for lucrative export.[18]

Which brings us back to prophetic critique and prophetic hope. Did Jesus have anything to say to this situation? Tom has helpfully depicted Jesus as a prophet, so you would expect that Jesus would bring a prophetic critique to this kind of injustice.

He did indeed. But this is where we need to push Tom's exegesis

---

Horsley, *Galilee: History, People, Politics* (Valley Forge, Penn.: Trinity Press International, 1995), pp. 215-17; and Douglas E. Oakman, *Jesus and the Economic Questions of His Day* (Lewiston, N.Y.: Edwin Mellen, 1987), pp. 72-77.

[15]According to Deuteronomy 15:1-18, debts were to be forgiven and slaves set free every seven years.

[16]Goodman, "First Jewish Revolt," p. 421.

[17]Ibid., pp. 423-25. The figure of 20 percent comes from the *Discoveries in the Judean Desert* (Oxford: Clarendon, 1961), 2:100-104, no.18 line 6. The prosbul is attributed to Hillel in Sifre Deut 113. We owe this reference to E. P. Sanders, *Jewish Law from Jesus to the Mishnah: Five Studies* (London: SCM; Philadelphia: Trinity Press International, 1990), pp. 333-34. Notice the language of "fine" rather than "interest," since interest was not permitted according to biblical law.

[18]On these crops in ancient Israel and for a description of the critique of such an extractive economy by Israel's prophets, see Ellen F. Davis, *Scripture, Culture and Agriculture: An Agrarian Reading of the Bible* (New York: Cambridge University Press, 2009), p. 122. That such crops were grown for export in Galilee, see Josephus *Jewish War* 2.591; *Life of Flavius Josephus*, pp. 71-76.

somewhat. While on the one hand Tom makes it very clear that Jesus has come with a word of judgment and that Jesus echoes the prophetic call to repentance, he also interprets that call to repentance almost entirely in terms of nationalistic zeal.[19]

But what about other issues that Jesus addresses? What about the critique of riches, of mammon, of possessions?

Again, Tom's preferred interpretation is to see all of this in terms of a critique of nationalistic zeal. Possessions refer primarily to land in ancient Israel, and land evoked the nationalist feelings that first-century Jews were willing to stake their lives and future on.[20]

To be fair, this is a central part of Jesus' prophetic critique. And it is an incredibly important part of what he was saying. The call to turn the other cheek, to pray for one's enemies, to walk the second mile, to be peacemakers (Mt 5:38-48; Lk 6:27-36)—all of this becomes pretty central in early Christian practice and belief.

I'm not denying the importance of the prophetic critique of Jewish nationalism—it was at the heart of Jesus' teaching and is a message we desperately need to hear today as well. But notice that the passages that list these commands in Matthew and Luke also include this command: "Give to everyone who begs from you" and Matthew adds: "Do not refuse anyone who wants to borrow from you" (Mt 5:42). In Luke the passage ends with this: "Lend, expecting nothing in return!" (Lk 6:35).

The point is that while the abandonment of nationalist zeal is clearly one of the things Jesus is calling for in his ministry, loving your enemy is linked in these verses with a certain kind of *economic* practice.

There are plenty of calls to repentance in the Gospels that are not speaking of nationalist zeal, like the rich ruler or Zacchaeus or the rich man who feasted while Lazarus waited for a crumb from his table or the man who built the bigger barns or even the tax collectors and sinners.

And we also need to remember the prophetic tradition. Tom argues convincingly that Jesus saw himself as one of a long line of prophets

---

[19]The following references are all from *Jesus and the Victory of God*. That Jesus has come with a message of judgment and repentance: pp. 183, 249, 323, 339, 446. That Jesus' audience needs to repent of nationalistic zeal: pp. 241, 249, 290, 325, 384, 390, 404, 407, 417-19, 449-50, 569.
[20]Ibid., pp. 403-5.

come to call Israel back to its true calling to be a light to the nations, to demonstrate to the world what it is to be the image of the one true God. Like the prophets, Jesus has come to call Israel back to covenant faithfulness—but he does so in a way that Israel did not expect, providing an ending to the story that is completely different from any other telling in the first century. So far so good.

But here's the problem. When Tom quotes the prophetic texts, either of judgment or of expectation, he tends to pull back. He tends to not discuss the places where justice and righteousness are talked about or where there is a critique of economic injustice.

Because he does not emphasize the socioeconomic sins that the prophets focus on,[21] he downplays these themes in the Gospels as well. For instance, in commenting about the rich young man he says: "The command to forsake riches and to follow Jesus appears to have been very specific to this young man. We are not told that Jesus said this sort of thing regularly, even often (though the warnings against riches, and trust in them, is of course frequent)."[22] According to Tom's comments here, Jesus' command to the rich young man is a one-off thing.[23]

What about the story of Zacchaeus? Surely this is a story about economic justice and the kingdom of God.

Actually, Tom downplays the economic aspect of the Zacchaeus story. He writes, "The crucial issue in the Zacchaeus episode . . . is that, whatever Zacchaeus did or did not do with his money, Jesus declared on his own authority that Zacchaeus is a true son of Abraham and that salvation had 'today' come to his house."[24]

Are you sure that you are being fair here? In his popular commentary on Luke, Tom describes Zacchaeus as a symbol of the renewed Israel because he

---

[21]On not caring for the aliens, orphans and widow see Is 1:23; 10:2; Jer 5:27-29; 7:5; 22:3-6; Ezek 22:7; Zech 7:8-14; Mal 3:5; on failing to practice mercy and justice: Is 5:7; Jer 22:13-17; Hos 12:7-8; Amos 5:7; 6:12; Mic 6:1-12; on grinding down the poor and needy see Is 3:14-15; 10:2; 32:7; 58:3; Jer 2:34; Ezek 22:29; Amos 2:6-7; 4:1; 5:11; 8:4-8; cf. Job 24:9-14; Ps 37:14; 109:16.

[22]Wright, *Jesus and the Victory of God*, p. 302.

[23]In a later book, Tom changes his interpretation, referring to the kind of economic redistribution that we meet in Acts 2 as a fulfillment of what was said to the rich young man of Mark 10. See N. T. Wright, *After You Believe: Why Christian Character Matters* (New York: Harper-Collins, 2010), p. 227.

[24]Wright, *Jesus and the Victory of God*, p. 257.

has repented of his greedy ways and made amends.[25]

That's true, we do find in *Luke for Everyone* more attention to this issue than we find in *Jesus and the Victory of God*. But my point is that when we look at the larger pattern there is a significant lacuna in Tom's exegesis of these stories and in his description of Jesus as a prophet.

Perhaps the best way into the topic is by way of a prophetic image that comes up again and again in both the Gospels and in Tom's description of Jesus' prophetic task. The image is that of fruit.

Fruit? As in the parables of the sower and also the tenants?[26]

Those are the parables. And Tom's brilliant reading of both of them in terms of the story of the people of Israel breathes new life into the text, while his rooting of these stories in Isaiah 5–6 provides the important prophetic background.[27] But his exegesis of both parables begs the question: What is the fruit that God is calling Israel to bear? What is the fruit that the prophets consistently asked for from the people? What is the fruit that the son has come to collect? What is the fruit that results from God's word being sown?

Isaiah's parable of the vineyard answers these questions with considerable clarity:

> *For the vineyard of the* LORD *of hosts*
> *is the house of Israel,*
> *and the people of Judah*
> *are his pleasant planting;*
> *he expected justice [mishpat],*
> *but saw bloodshed [mispakh];*
> *righteousness [tsedaqah],*
> *but heard a cry [tse'aqah]! (Is 5:7)*

Justice and righteousness, not bloodshed and cries. And the rest of Isaiah 5 goes on to describe what has given rise to bloodshed and cries: they add house to house and field to field, thereby depriving their neighbors of land rights; the nobles glut themselves on wine and feasts;

---

[25]N. T. Wright, *Luke for Everyone* (London: SPCK, 2001), p. 217.

[26]These are not, of course, the only references to fruit in the Gospels, but have been chosen as representative.

[27]On both of these parables see Wright, *Jesus and the Victory of God*, pp. 232-39.

the courts acquit the guilty for a bribe and deprive the innocent of their rights (Is 5:8, 11, 23).

But we don't have to rely only on this text to show the prophetic background to this imagery. Other prophetic texts whisper through the passages about the fig tree in Mark 11 and Matthew 21.

Doesn't Tom root the fig tree image in the context of Jeremiah?

Yes. In Mark the temple action is framed by the incident of the fig tree, which evokes Jeremiah 8. Tom quotes these verses from Jeremiah 8:11-13 to show the connection:[28]

> They have treated the wound of my people carelessly,
>> saying "Peace, peace"
>> when there is no peace.
> They acted shamefully, they committed abominations;
>> yet they were not all ashamed,
>> they did not know how to blush.
> Therefore they shall fall among those who fall;
>> at the time when I punish them, they shall be overthrown,
>>> says YHWH.
> When I wanted to gather them, says YHWH,
>> there were no grapes on the vine,
>> nor figs on the fig tree;
> even the leaves are withered, and what I gave them has passed away
>> from them. (Jer 8:11-13)[29]

What is significant here is that Tom has begun the quotation in the midst of a longer paragraph. The previous verse gives this reason for the judgment:

> From the least to the greatest,
>> everyone is greedy for unjust gain;
> from prophet to priest,
>> everyone deals falsely. (Jer 8:10)

So it isn't just that the priest and prophets have declared peace when there is none, but that they have done so in a context of deep economic injustice.

---

[28]Wright, *Jesus and the Victory of God*, pp. 421-22.
[29]Ibid., p. 421.

Isn't this also the context of the temple sermon in Jeremiah 7, which Jesus cites in his own judgment on the temple?

That's right. The problem in Jeremiah 7 is that the people are oppressing the alien, the orphan and the widow, they are shedding innocent blood, they are going after other gods, stealing, murdering, committing adultery, swearing falsely (Jer 7:6-8; Jesus quotes from v. 11).[30] The temple was the place both where injustice was perpetrated and where the oppressors came to practice their piety in spite of their unrighteous actions (cf. Is 58).[31]

But did the temple have these associations in Jesus' time as well?

Of course it did! Remember the burning of the records of debt? They were kept in the temple because it was the center of judicial and economic power for first-century Jews. The temple was the place where judgments were carried out that forced people to pay debts even after a Sabbath year. The temple officials were wealthy aristocrats who held those debts, who collected the rents, who exported the luxury crops.[32] Where did the taxes end up that people like Zacchaeus collected? Some of them ended up in Roman pockets. The rest ended up at the temple.[33]

So if we hear Jesus' references to fruit in light of the prophets, it is clear that when Jesus says that the word that is sown in good soil bore fruit thirty, sixty and a hundredfold, he means the fruit of justice and righteousness. And when the owner of the vineyard came to collect the fruit, he was expecting to see justice and righteousness but instead saw bloodshed and heard cries.

---

[30]The same overtones are present in Mic 7:1-3, also evoked by the fig tree action.

[31]Ellen Davis outlines the clear connection between Israel's oppressive food economy and the priesthood (*Scripture, Culture and Agriculture*, p. 133). The priests issued loans for animals and seed, they calculated and collected taxes, and the sanctuaries were the centers of food processing, along with storage and redistribution.

[32]See Goodman, "First Jewish Revolt," pp. 420, 422; Horsley, *Galilee*, pp. 215-19; and Sanders, *Judaism: Practice and Belief*, pp. 147-55. Josephus describes priests who had come with him to Galilee, collecting "a large sum of money from the tithes they accepted as their priestly due" (*Life*, p. 63). The abuse of this privilege by the high priest is recorded in *Antiquities* 20.181, 205ff. Jonathan A. Draper describes the Pharisees as retainers of the temple system ("Jesus and the Renewal of Local Community in Galilee," *Journal of Theology for South Africa* 87 [1994]: 33).

[33]While Tom does note the economic abuses associated with the temple in *Jesus and the Victory of God* (pp. 412, 417), this does not seem to have much impact on his larger argument. In fact, he argues later that rather than having an economic focus, the temple had become the talisman for nationalist violence (ibid., pp. 419-20).

Exactly. Giving voice to the pain that is suppressed by injustice is at the heart of prophetic critique. The prophets name the pain that the empire denies. Tom describes very well the pain that violent nationalism will bring to the first-century inhabitants of Galilee and Judea, but he also needs to describe the pain that results from economic injustice.

Jesus gives evocative expression to that pain in the story of the rich man and Lazarus—there it is double edged: the pain of Lazarus in this life and that of the rich man in the life to come. He gives voice to this pain in the parable of the persistent widow in Luke 18. He names a world of astonishing debt and torture in Matthew 18 and Luke 16, and of unscrupulous profits in Luke 19 and Matthew 25.

What do you mean a world of unscrupulous profits? What are you talking about?

I am talking about the parable of the nobleman and his slaves in Luke 19 (also known as the parable of the pounds). It is really a part of the story of Zacchaeus. Just after pronouncing that Zacchaeus is a true son of Abraham, Jesus tells this parable to the guests in Zacchaeus's house.

I've always wondered why Zacchaeus gave away half of his possessions and paid back four times everyone that he had defrauded.

Think about it. We meet Zacchaeus in Luke where Jesus' journey to Jerusalem has been characterized by stories about food and drink and money. Luke 12 tells the story of the rich man who builds bigger barns to store his excess grain—only to discover he has built up treasure in the wrong place. This story is followed by a teaching about trust and anxiety that ends with the command by Jesus to the disciples to sell their possessions and give alms (Lk 12:33). Jesus then moves to a comparison between the faithful servant, who gives the other servants their food and drink at the proper time, and the unfaithful servant who eats and drinks the food himself (Lk 12:42-46; cf. Ezek 34:2-5). In Luke 14 Jesus tells those who would follow him to invite to their banquets the poor, the crippled, the lame and the blind—in short those who cannot repay their hospitality (Lk 14:12-14). Luke 14 ends with this saying: "none of you can become my disciple if you do not give up all your possessions" (v. 33).

He puts it that bluntly?

You can look it up. And it goes on.

In Luke 16 we meet the parable of the rich man and Lazarus—which ends with the assertion that if the brothers cannot hear the call to economic justice in the law and prophets, they won't hear it from someone who rises from the dead (v. 31). And, of course, in Luke 18, we have the story of the rich ruler who is told by Jesus to sell all that he has and to distribute the money to the poor. This is no one-off saying. This is the third time this command occurs in the journey to Jerusalem in Luke.

Zacchaeus wanted to see Jesus. Surely he had heard about him, heard the stories he had been telling, heard about what he had said again and again.

So that is why his first reaction is to give his money away. He understood the economic meaning of following Jesus. In fact, it is as if Zacchaeus is fulfilling the prophetic hope, realizing the jubilee hope that Jesus promised in Luke 4:18!

And that is why Jesus told the next parable, the parable of the pounds in Luke 19:11-27. We are told that Jesus tells this parable because he was near Jerusalem and the people supposed the kingdom of God was to appear immediately (v. 11). Why might the people expect that the kingdom of God would appear immediately?

There could be few possible reasons. First, Jesus had just declared that salvation had come to the house of Zacchaeus. That would be seen as kingdom language. Second, Jesus was on his way to Jerusalem. Everyone knew that Jerusalem was the place where Jesus would need to be if he was going to bring in the kingdom and overthrow the Romans. Expectation would rise the closer he got to Jerusalem. And, third, when the prophet who is on his way to Jerusalem declares salvation and rich tax collectors start giving away their money, this sure sounds like good news for the poor. It sounds like the kingdom of God has arrived. All of these things would reinforce the others, wouldn't they?

So Jesus tells this parable in order to sober them up, in order to show them that the coming of the kingdom isn't going to mean that the rich give their money away and all will be fine. This parable demonstrates that the economics of Jesus, the radical economics just demonstrated by Zacchaeus, must live in the real world of crucifixion economics. The parable functions as a reality check in the context of an understandable kingdom enthusiasm.

I'm sorry, I have no clue what you are talking about. Isn't this parable about the kingdom of God coming in Jesus?

Nope. This one doesn't begin "The kingdom of God is like . . ." In fact, as almost everyone points out, this parable begins with distinct parallels to Archelaus heading off to Rome to get royal power for himself. He is followed by a contingent of the citizens of his country, who oppose his rule. That story is recorded in Josephus, and everyone listening to Jesus would have heard the parallel. This is not a nobleman they would have equated with God.[34]

But the bit about the money, surely that is about God. About how Israel has been given gifts, or responsibilities over creation, and how Israel—and we too—need to be good stewards and develop them.

Remember how you said that you would hate to project your own economic assumptions on the biblical text? Well that is what we do when we read this parable in terms of stewardship. We read it as if making a 1,000 percent profit was a good thing! But that is a late capitalist assumption! In the first century, Jesus' audience would have been appalled at this rate of return: what a crook! He started with one mina and now he has ten? Or, to put it in contemporary terms, he started with $6,000 and now he has $60,000? What kind of a greedy grasping moneylender is this who wrings this kind of interest out of people?[35]

I guess our response betrays our socioeconomic context, doesn't it? We are the ones who like to make money. If we were at the mercy of loans to sow our seed or keep our land, we would also be properly appalled.

---

[34]Josephus *Jewish War* 2.1-38, 80-100; *Antiquities* 17.219-49, 299-320; Wright, *Jesus and the Victory of God*, p. 633.
[35]Similarly, Bruce J. Malina and Richard L. Rohrbaugh, *Social Scientific Commentary on the Synoptic Gospels* (Minneapolis: Fortress, 1992), p. 390; Ernesto Cardenal, *The Gospel in Solentiname*, trans. Donald D. Walsh (Maryknoll, N.Y.: Orbis, 1982), 4:38-48, 76-81; and Deborah Storie, review of *Jesus Through Middle Eastern Eyes: Cultural Studies in the Gospels*, by Kenneth E. Bailey, in *Pacifica* 96, no. 22 (2009): 103.

Actually, most people in the world are at the mercy of loans to sow their seed and keep their land. It is just the urban West that is out of touch with this kind of economic dependence. Our economic assumptions have dictated the hero of this story for us. But what if we look at the text through the lens of the prophets, through the lens of Zacchaeus, through the lens of what Jesus has to say about money?

Well, then we would notice, I guess, that the person who praises the first two slaves is the master who is later described as harsh, taking what he did not deposit and reaping what he did not sow. He seems to be described in the terms of a wealthy man who takes the crops that others have done the hard work of sowing and who forecloses on other's savings.

Exactly. How would these slaves have made their money grow? By lending to those in need and then by foreclosing when they couldn't repay. That's a quick way to make money beget money without actually benefiting anyone other than the creditor.

That sounds familiar. You don't need to project our economic crisis onto the first century to see the striking parallels.

Yes, and the reward of land for the rapacious slaves is appropriate—it is by taking land that they have done their dirty work.

Seems a far cry from any sense of covenant economics.

The distance between the work of the first two slaves and covenant economics is also underlined in verse 23, where the nobleman says to the third slave that at the very least he should have been able to collect his money with interest (*tokē*). This Greek word literally means "offspring" and hence the word that we translate as "interest" has the overtones of money breeding money. This is the same word used throughout the Septuagint to indicate that charging interest is prohibited by those who are righteous and who follow Torah.[36] And, incidentally, charging interest was still forbidden to Jews in Jesus' day.

---

[36]Ex 22:24; Lev 25:36-37; Deut 23:20; Ps 15:5 (14:5 LXX); Ezek 18:5-18. Note that in this last passage the NIV has softened the meaning by inserting the word *excessive* into the translation. There were also no banks in the first century and no savings accounts to accrue interest. The word translated as "bank" is actually a table (*trapeza*)—something like the table the moneychangers kept their money on, the ones that Jesus turned over in the temple (Mt 21:12/Mk 11:15). We owe these points about the table and interest to Ched Myers in private correspondence.

But if this behavior is prohibited in Torah, then there is no way that this nobleman can be God! His economic behavior is not only inconsistent with the rest of Luke, it is inconsistent with the rest of the Scriptures!

That's right, and the third slave recognizes it for the dirty work that it is. That is why he wraps the money in a cloth (*soudari¢n*) used to wipe sweat or snot or to clean corpses. This is dirty money, and it deserves nothing more than an unclean burial.[37]

So that is why the story ends so brutally, both for the slave, who loses everything, and for those who opposed the rule of this king and are slaughtered.

The ending is harsh because this isn't really about the kingdom. This story is told in Zacchaeus's house for Zacchaeus's sake. You see, sometime in the near future Zacchaeus is going to have some appointments with the bureaucrats above him. He is supposed to have collected the tax amount and some extra to line the pockets of the men above him. He was probably chosen for his job because he was the best at squeezing money out of the people in the village. As a result of meeting Jesus, he won't have extra for kickbacks. He is going to be like that third slave—unable to deliver the economic goods to the harsh ruler.

And like the third slave he is probably going to have everything taken away—his authority over his city will be taken and given to someone who doesn't mind violence for profits.

So Jesus is saying, "I know it looks good, but the kingdom isn't going to come with good news for the poor without a price. When people start opting out of this abusive economic system, there is going to be more abuse. There is going to be suffering. Because the powers that be aren't going to like it at all." That's the point of this parable.[38]

---

[37]We also owe this point about the cloth to Ched Myers in private correspondence.

[38]This reading of the parable of the pounds is not without precedent. See also Elizabeth Dowling, *Taking Away the Pound: Women, Theology and the Parable of the Pounds in the Gospel of Luke* (London: T & T Clark, 2007), esp. chap. 2; Merrill Kitchen, "Rereading the Parable of the Pounds: A Social and Narrative Analysis of Luke 19.11-28," in *Prophecy and Passion: Essays in Honor of Athol Gill*, ed. David Neville (Adelaide: Adelaide Theological Forum, 2002), pp. 227-46; William R. Herzog, *Parables as Subversive Speech: Jesus as Pedagogue of the Oppressed* (Louisville: Westminster/John Knox Press, 1994), pp. 156-168; Oakman, *Jesus and the Economic Questions of His Day*, p. 171, n. 22; and Deborah R. Storie's forthcoming Ph.D. dissertation, *Contesting Public Transcripts in Biblical Studies: An Adventure with Zacchaeus* (Melbourne: Melbourne College of Divinity, 2011). Storie offers a taste of her interpretation in a critical engagement with Kenneth Bailey's reading of the parable in her review of *Jesus Through Middle*

A crucifixion economics indeed. And this third slave is saying that he won't play by the rules of this economic game. He names the ruler for the unscrupulous and violent man that he is, he refuses to invest his money in a way that is only concerned about generating more money and he suffers the consequences.

Recognizing that this parable has clear allusions to Archelaus, Tom offers this interpretation: "But now, Jesus is implying, the unwanted King is coming back in power: not another wicked Herod, but the true King, the King who comes with a message of grace and peace, the King who was rejected because his people wanted to keep the kingdom for themselves."[39]

The problem is that no such king can be found in this parable. This king is, by his own admission, a harsh man who takes what he did not deposit and reaps what he did not sow. There is no suggestion that he reaps the fruit of justice and righteousness. Quite the opposite! Even the bystanders recognize the unfairness of this king's actions. There is no grace and peace to be found in this story.

In fact, just after this Jesus weeps over Jerusalem saying that they "did not know the things that make for peace" (Lk 19:41-42). While the king of the parable wreaks vengeance on those who oppose him and imposes an economics that certainly cannot make for peace, all Jesus can do is weep.[40]

This is all sounding familiar. Doesn't Ched Myers do a similar reading of the parable of the talents in Matthew 25?[41]

Yes, and there the parable is paired with the parable of the sheep and

---

Eastern Eyes, esp. 102-4; and in Deborah Storie and Mark Brett, "The Church in the Economy of God," *Zadok Perspectives* 102 (2009): 5-10.

[39]Wright, *Luke for Everyone,* p. 227.

[40]Cf. Malina and Rohrbaugh, *Social Scientific Commentary,* p. 392.

[41]Ched Myers and Eric DeBode "Towering Trees and Talented Slaves: Jesus' Parables," *The Other Side* 35, no. 3 (1999). Even though the story in Matthew is framed differently, the parables have very strong similarities, especially at the climax. In both stories the first two slaves make an exorbitant profit on their money. In both the master is described as a harsh man who reaps what he did not sow (Mt 25:24-26//Luke 19:21-22), and, significantly, in both stories the master makes it clear that he expected his money to be returned with "interest," which was not only expressly forbidden in Torah but was also forbidden in first-century Judaism. The behavior of the master in Mt 25 also stands in stark contrast to the behavior of those who inherit the kingdom in the following description of the sheep and the goats.

the goats. Who are the ones who inherit the kingdom in that parable? Those who use their resources in ways that subvert the economic order by feeding the hungry, giving drink to the thirsty, welcoming the stranger, clothing the naked and caring for the sick and imprisoned. They are those who see Jesus precisely in the places of outer darkness, which is where the slave has been cast (Mt 25:14-46).

So what we are seeing here is that Jesus offers a radically alternative vision of economic life; an economics that bears the good fruit of justice, that refuses to place the acquisition of money over the care for the least of these.

We also see that Jesus' prophetic critique is wider than Tom allows. Jesus not only names the death dealing and pain that comes from violent nationalism—and he does do that at length—but he also names the death dealing and pain that comes from economic injustice. What is more, his language of prophetic hope points to a future that judges these things as well.

Prophetic hope. Isn't that where Brueggemann talks about prophetic imagination? About envisioning new symbols, about describing a new reality that stands in stark contrast to what the empire would have us believe to be true?

That's right, although Jesus' symbols are not entirely new. They are deeply embedded in visions of prophetic hope found in Israel's Scriptures.

Jesus' critique draws on texts like Isaiah 65, which stand in judgment on the harsh ruler of the parable of the pounds:

> They shall build houses and inhabit them;
>> they shall plant vineyards and eat their fruit.
> They shall not build and another inhabit;
>> they shall not plant and another eat. (Is 65:21-22)

Or consider these verses from Isaiah 61 that Jesus quotes in Luke 4:18-19:

> The Spirit of the Lord is upon me,
>> because he has anointed me
>>> to bring good news to the poor.
> He has sent me to proclaim release to the captives
> and recovery of sight to the blind,

to let the oppressed go free,
to proclaim the year of the Lord's favor.[42]

I guess what is so striking about this is how it was carried forward into the *early church. Why else would there be so much emphasis in Acts on selling one's* *possessions and bringing the money to share it with the poor if it hadn't been* *central in Jesus' ministry (Acts 2:42-47; 4:32-37)?*

And why else would Paul criticize the fact that some go hungry and some get drunk at the Lord's Supper in Corinth unless that meal was supposed to symbolize a different kind of body than the imperial body politic—a meal where no one goes hungry and no one overconsumes (1 Cor 11:17-34)?

It is no wonder that this early movement of Jesus followers experienced *an ever-expanding circle of friends. Which brings us full circle, right back* *to where we started. Does this gospel matter outside of a small circle of* *friends?*

Or maybe we could ask, does this telling of the story of Jesus, which offered a radically new ending to the unfinished story of Israel, offer a radically new beginning for us facing an economy in crisis?

That's exactly the question. When the governments of the West were bail- *ing out the failing financial markets and their institutions in 2008, the com-* *mon refrain was that there was "no option." There was nothing to do but to* *pour the resources of the public treasury into these failing private corporations.* *No other story was available.*

Well, both Zacchaeus and the third slave could have pled that they had "no choice" but to play the economic game according to the oppressive rules of the empire. But they didn't. They embraced the story of Jesus.

Maybe that's our problem. We still play by the rules. We still live out of a story that is bankrupt.

That's right. Every one of us in the Christian community in the West *benefits from the virtual economy that we have seen collapsing. That's*

---

[42]Note that Jesus stops his citation of Isaiah short. After the phrase "to proclaim the year of the Lord's favor," the prophet continues, "and the day of vengeance of our God." While Jesus refuses to frame his jubilee kingdom in terms of vengeance, we have seen that the king in the parable of the pounds is known to be a vengeful man and demonstrates that his is a kingdom of vengeance. The contrast couldn't be clearer.

why all the Christian colleges in North America took a hit with the stock market crisis. So much Christian money has been invested in the financial market; whether we are talking about endowment funds, denominational resources, pension plans or personal portfolios. We have fallen for the economic idolatry of money giving birth to money. But that's not what money is for.

So what do we need to do?

Well, for starters, we need to get out of the markets. Christians need to abandon the financial markets and begin to develop more just ways to invest the resources entrusted to us. A good example is the United Methodist Church, which has invested its money in affordable housing rather than the financial market.[43]

I guess my question is this: what does this look like for your average Christian like you and me. Lots of people don't have investments in the market, nor do they have money to invest in affordable housing. What is the economic word of hope for those of us who are enmeshed in the system, not because of our investments but because we are a cog in the wheel?

I don't think that we can answer that question with specific directives, like a voice from on high. Not because there are no answers but because it is too cheap to say "Here is your answer to the dilemma of what a Christian should do with her money. Do this with your money and you will be okay." Rather, when we have struggled with the way that the biblical text challenges our own cultural assumptions about money, then the hard work begins of on-the-ground Christian discernment.

You are saying that what we do with our money is something that we need to struggle with in prayer, in the context of a community of other believers, and in the context of the local needs and challenges in which our lives are situated?[44]

---

[43]The affordable housing portfolio of the United Methodist Church is worth over a billion dollars. See "Sharing the Dreams: A Place Called Home," *General Board of Pensions and Health Benefits of the United Methodist Church* <www.gbophb.org/sri_funds/articles/housing.asp>. For further reflection on a Christian economic perspective in relation to homelessness, see Steven Bouma-Prediger and Brian J. Walsh, *Beyond Homelessness: Christian Faith in a Culture of Displacement* (Grand Rapids: Eerdmans, 2008), chaps. 3-4.

[44]See Michael Schut, ed., *Money and Faith: The Search for Enough* (Denver: Morehouse Education Resources, 2008), which includes essays on various aspects of money and Christian dis-

Precisely. How we use our money in ways that are faithful will differ from other Christians in other places. Consider Alan, who left a life in real estate development to pour his money and time into the creation of Mobile Loaves and Fishes in Austin, Texas, providing food and housing for the poorest of the poor. Or Sharon, who makes her money available for a story-telling program for inner-city kids in Hamilton, Ontario. Or the Quaker community in Oxford, which pools their money so that those without income can pay the poll tax. Or Jasmine, who left her position at a large bank in order to help start a credit union in an underserviced part of town. Or the countless folks in cities who are supporting local agriculture through Community Shared Agriculture relationships with organic farmers. Or those who have begun microfinancing programs in various parts of the world. Or all of those people who refuse to give their money to companies that abuse their workers.

Part of our task, then, is to share these stories of how people are living out of a biblical vision in relation to their money.

And these people are often living this biblical vision because they are asking different questions about their place in the economic system; questions shaped not by concerns about profit or security, but questions shaped by the kingdom of God.

The questions must be pretty wide in these contexts. They would have to do with where money comes from, the effect that it has in the present and where it goes.

I'm not sure what you mean by that.

Well, for example, when we ask "Where does our money comes from?" we are asking whether creation was harmed in order for me to have this money and whether community was created or destroyed in order for me to have this money.

That's a pretty tough question—someone's job could be on the line as a result of answering that question.

Does that matter for the sake of the kingdom? Is your job the non-negotiable? Do we try to live faithfully, unless it harms our jobs?

Okay, I guess not.

cipleship, along with a study guide for groups who are struggling with these issues, and a detailed bibliography for further reading.

But if that is too hard a path of discipleship, ask the other questions. When we invest or spend this money, what is the result, where do our economic resources go? Am I giving this money to benefit a company that despoils God's creation or harms the community God has created us to live in? Might this investment end up destroying relationships and livelihoods? Or am I investing or spending this money in organizations and business enterprises that contribute to a vision of healing, redemption and shalom for life on this earth? That is a very simple question. Or there is the question that Deborah Storie and Mark Brett encourage us to ask when our communities, or we ourselves, see our investor statements: "What human realities do such statements camouflage? Are we reaping what we did not sow?"[45]

These are questions of justice, in the end, aren't they?

Precisely. They are the questions that arise when Jesus and the "victory" of God meets Jesus and the "justice" of God.

And this victory and this justice meet, Tom has powerfully taught us, on a cross. So maybe we need to reimagine crucifixion economics. One of the most powerful lines in all of Tom's writings is this: "The cross was not the defeat of Christ at the hands of the powers. It was the defeat of the powers at the hands—yes the bleeding hands—of Christ."[46] The powers of exclusion are defeated by the power of love. Yes, a crucifixion economics, but not the crucifixion of the poor for the sake of the rich. No, a crucifixion of our greed, of our gluttony, of our insecurity, of our consumptive way of life—a dying with Christ—so that we might be raised with him.

From a crucifixion economics to a resurrection economics.

Yes, an embrace of economic suffering, of economic restraint in the hope of a rebirth to an economics of radical generosity, an economics that bears the good fruit of justice and righteousness,

an economics that feeds the hungry by allowing them to feed themselves and not grow cash crops for us,

an economy of care that will place justice, compassion, stewardship and

---

[45]Storie and Brett, "Church in the Economy of God," p. 9.
[46]N. T. Wright, *Following Jesus: Biblical Reflections on Discipleship* (Grand Rapids: Eerdmans, 1994), p. 19.

love over any narrowly conceived notion of economic efficiency.[47]

Now that just might be of some interest . . . outside of a small circle of friends.[48]

Response to Sylvia Keesmaat and Brian Walsh
N. T. WRIGHT

I did think of writing my Walsh-Keesmaat response as a dialogue between myself in 2010 and myself in 1982, when Brian and I first met. Another time, perhaps. It is great fun to have a paper in this discursive style, as it is to find Martin Goodman and Bruce Cockburn bumping into each other in the footnotes. Let me focus on two central points.

First, if I were writing *JVG* today I would certainly want to highlight economic issues more than I did then. The critique of violent nationalism is important and central, but economic issues are vital too. I loved the way Sylvia drew out these dimensions of the text. I am slightly concerned that several of her secondary sources have such a clear agenda, but then so, of course, do all those earlier scholars who were happy with the economic status quo.

Second, Sylvia's proposed reading of the parable of the pounds/talents causes me problems. Yes, the urban West is out of touch with living at the mercy of loans for seed and land—though the urban West I know knows all about living at the mercy of loans for other necessi-

---

[47]Such an economic vision and theory is further developed in Bob Goudzwaard and Harry de Lange, *Beyond Poverty and Affluence: Toward an Economy of Care* (Grand Rapids: Eerdmans, 1995); and Herman Daly and John Cobb Jr., *For the Common Good: Redirecting the Economy Toward Community, the Environment and a Sustainable Future* (Boston: Beacon, 1989). For a deepening of an alternative economics from a richly agrarian perspective see Wendell Berry, *Home Economics* (New York: North Point, 1987); and his *Sex, Economy, Freedom and Community* (New York: Pantheon, 1993). See also the bibliography in Schut, ed., *Money and Faith*, which has sections on "Fair-trade and Micro-lending," "The Corporation," and "Investments, Consumption and the Individual." See also Byron Borger, "Reading for a Global Perspective" in *Do Justice: A Social Justice Road Map* (Three Rivers, Mich.: *culture is not optional, 2008), pp. 69-79. This annotated bibliography, by one of the most well-read Christian booksellers in the United States, is a wealth of information and helpful sources. *Do Justice* is available from <www.cultureisnotoptional.com>.

[48]Our thanks to Justin Van Zee and Ben Stevenson, who talked through this paper with us and provided helpful questions and fruitful insights.

ties. But I don't think we can read the parable with the master playing the villain and the third servant the hero.

For a start, this makes the parable metonymy rather than metaphor. Some parables may work like that, but I need convincing. The parable of the sower is not a comment on farming practice. The "great supper," especially in Matthew, is not about social behavior (or is the real hero the underdressed guest?). The "unjust steward" is not supposed to legitimate sharp financial practice. Yes, it is possible that Jesus might suddenly tell a story which was a moral tale rather than a parable. I doubt it here, for literary reasons.

Yes, the hearers might have quickly taken a point of view, but parables often subvert that. Jesus' audience would have supported the Pharisee over the tax collector all the way. He's holy, righteous, not like that swindler (Lk 18:9-14). But the final verse takes their breath away: it was the tax collector who was justified. So, just because many in Jesus' audience might have heard the story about the pounds as a tale about an arrogant fat cat and two of his servants colluding with him, that doesn't at all mean that the punch line—the condemnation of the third servant—wasn't actually the sting in the tail, or perhaps the tale, that made them suddenly realize it worked quite differently. As with another Lukan parable, the "unjust judge" (Lk 18:1-8), the audience would be angry with the unjust judge, yet the story still works. Just as Jesus was solidly opposed to Roman brutality, yet didn't support the zealot cause, so he may have been appalled at economic exploitation without endorsing the normal populist reaction.

This doesn't at all detract from the economic impact of Jesus' teaching, any more than God's strange calling of Hosea meant that God approved of his wife's prostitution. Rather the reverse. Jesus could have been using the apparent weight of the economic assumptions of his hearers to push home a quite different point: that Israel, as God's servant, has been given gifts with which to work for the master, but has buried them in the ground. The Lukan context, I believe, supports this reading. The story isn't about Jesus going away and returning at the parousia, but about God going away and now coming back in the person of Jesus to call in accounts. Certainly Luke 19:44 takes it this way:

Jerusalem "did not know the time of its visitation."

That Lukan context, both of how parables work and of what Luke seems to think this one means, thus strongly inclines me to reject Sylvia's interpretation. In discussion after the paper I pointed out that this parable was central to my reading of Jesus' self-understanding, and Sylvia said she thought this could be established by other passages. I want to respond in kind: I agree with most of what she and Brian say about economics, but I think that this can be established in the Gospels (not least the Jubilee passages) without reading this parable this way.

I also have a problem about the realism—or lack of it—of the exciting concluding suggestions. Far be it from me to dampen reforming enthusiasm. I have long been aware of the warnings of T. S. Eliot and C. S. Lewis, to look no further, on the danger of the Western world living by the principle of compound interest, which was clearly forbidden in the Bible (and in the Qur'an). (British society has made legal provision for Muslims to run their economic lives differently; wouldn't it have been good if it had been Christians agitating for that?) But just as you can't turn a polygamous society into a monogamous one overnight by telling the men to dismiss all but one wife at once, so it may not be possible to turn around our entire Western economy in one fell swoop. As well as the prophetic witness of those who have found ways to live differently, it would be good to see realistic proposals, worked out perhaps with bankers and financial experts, on how to take the several steps from where we now are to where it would be good to be. I say this not to blunt the challenge or slow down the process, but precisely to sharpen it and speed it on its way. Jesus' kingdom command—repent and believe the good news—has to be translated into proposals that will commend themselves, not just to keen individuals but to numbers large enough to effect real change.

4

Jesus' Eschatology and Kingdom Ethics

Ever the Twain Shall Meet

NICHOLAS PERRIN

IN THE CLOSING PAGES OF HIS 1974 classic monograph *The Gospel and the Land*, W. D. Davies examines the relationship between Israel's land and the kingdom with reference to two contemporary but diametrically opposed thinkers: the Heidelberger Günther Bornkamm, a student of Bultmann, and the Oxoniensis George B. Caird, a student of C. H. Dodd. For the former, as Davies points out, the kingdom of God is neither politically laden nor apocalyptically oriented. As Bornkamm saw it, Jesus never drew attention to an impending apocalyptic crisis and remained decidedly disinterested in Israel's national aspirations. After all, because the kingdom of God had already arrived in the present with Jesus himself, political realities stood decisively relativized.[1] Thus, according to Bornkamm, Jesus expected his ethics to be worked out within a framework of a realized eschatology, one that saw the kingdom as an ever-present and timelessly transcendent reality. In short, Jesus' ethical call was a strictly personal affair.

Caird's Jesus, by contrast, confronted not the individual hearer in his or her subjective experience, but Israel as a whole in light of an impend-

---

[1] W. D. Davies, *The Gospel and the Land: Early Christianity and Jewish Territorial Doctrine* (Berkeley: University of California Press, 1968), pp. 344-47; cf. Günther Bornkamm, *Jesus of Nazareth* (New York: Harper, 1960), pp. 61-67, 121-23.

ing national crisis.[2] As the Oxford scholar saw it, Jesus' ethical summons focused on a future but imminent eschatological moment at which—short of repentance—the temple would be destroyed. Such a catastrophic event would both vindicate Jesus' own cause and actualize grim judgment against a disobedient Israel who resisted it. Thus, Jesus' ethical program was directed toward one overwhelming conviction, namely, that "Israel was at the cross-roads, that she must choose between two conceptions of her national destiny, and that the time for choice was horrifyingly short."[3]

While the positions of Bornkamm and Caird are internally consistent, between the two historians we are left with two rather divergent portraits. To be sure, both agree that the historical Jesus issued an ethical appeal to his contemporaries and grounded that appeal within an eschatological framework. But both dramatically disagree as to the nature of Jesus' eschatological expectation and the substance of his message, that is, whether he meant to enjoin a personal or sociopolitical ethic.

Davies's briefly juxtaposing Caird and Bornkamm in 1974 was in its own way prescient. Like the Roman poet Virgil, whose account of the hapless relationship between Aeneas and Dido was meant—*vaticinium ex eventu*—to presage later conflicts between the two great nations of Rome and Carthage, Davies's pitting of Caird against Bornkamm seems in retrospect to have prefigured a seismic scholarly conflict that has endured to this day. It is the conflict between the post-Bultmannian New Quest of the Historical Jesus, on the one side, and the so-called Third Quest, on the other. Whereas the Bultmann-Bornkamm line has tended to see Jesus as a politically innocent sage declaring timeless and universal truths that transcend Jewish particularity, the so-called Third Quest has above all been characterized by taking Jesus very seriously as a sociopolitically minded Jew, one who spoke forthrightly into the political arena of his day. In contemplating these two very different approaches to Jesus, moving more or less in opposite directions, I am reminded of the well-known line from Rudyard Kipling,

---

[2]Davies, *Gospel and the Land*, pp. 347-53; cf. George B. Caird, *Jesus and the Jewish Nation* (London: Athlone Press, 1965), pp. 8-10.

[3]Caird, *Jesus and the Jewish Nation*, p. 8, quoted in Davies, *Gospel and the Land*, p. 347.

which declares with resigned satisfaction: "East is East, and West is West, and never the twain shall meet."

In properly appreciating the Jesus scholarship of my mentor and friend, N. T. Wright, we will want to locate his work within this opposition, more specifically, within this Cairdian trajectory. Surely, if G. B. Caird was the Aeneas-like progenitor of the Third Quest, who endured a kind of scholarly isolation and exile while carrying on his back the influence of his *Doktorvater*, C. H. Dodd; and if Dodd in turn in his own day defended with Anchises-like valor the historicity of Jesus' life against the slings and arrows of outrageous skepticism; then Bishop Tom Wright must be assigned the role of Aeneas's son, Ascanus. Just as the youthful Ascanus was escorted out of burning Troy by the hand of his father only in his later years to found an empire, Tom's career has spanned a felicitous shift of scholarly opinion. Caird's distinctive conjoining of a this-worldly eschatology and first-century political critique had humble beginnings, for in 1965 the much-beleaguered Dean Ireland's Professor of Exegesis, with his lecture "Jesus and the Jewish Nation," was among the few to brandish a sword in Bultmann's direction. Eventually, however, the same basic line would—particularly through Tom's works like *Jesus and the Victory of God* (1996) and *The Challenge of Jesus* (1999)—undergo further development, attaining a considerable degree of refinement, plausibility and even ascendancy. Today, whether or not one agrees with the particulars of Tom's portrait of the first-century Galilean, nearly all would agree that his account remains one of the most influential—not to mention one of the most brilliant—reconstructions within contemporary historical Jesus studies.

Fourteen years after the publication of *Jesus and the Victory of God*, after the reviews and rejoinders, after the responses of rejoicing and retort, it is time not only to celebrate the achievement of this fine book but also to ask, How might Tom Wright have represented Jesus differently—for the better? I believe that the true value of a scholarly contribution may be assessed by whether it raises the kind of questions that demand to be taken seriously. Or, as Christopher Morse puts it, the historical value of a given piece of scholarship should be judged above all by "the quality of its provocation." If Tom Wright has admirably provoked us all to think about the historical Jesus in different ways, I count this paper as my humble attempt to express gratitude for such provocation but also to return the favor in a small way. There is much to be said for the promise of Wright and his Jesus; there is also room to explore the limitations of the Cairdian model, as it embodied the same Jesus.

THE PROMISE OF WRIGHT AND WRIGHT'S JESUS

It is a rarity when a room full of scholars comes to agree on any given point. I suspect that future assessments as to Bishop Wright's long-term significance for New Testament theology will prove no exception, even as assessments up to this point have sometimes proven controversial. Without taking the time to explain why I settle on these and not others, I wish to advance three points.

My first point bears on what I see as Tom's groundbreaking methodology. Although one does not hear very much these days about the Jesus Seminar, in the late 1980s and early 1990s this was not the case.[4] Thanks to the marketing savvy of the late Bob Funk, the Jesus Seminar had virtually become a household term, referring in the popular mind to a collection of scholars who knew what Jesus *really* said, and knew too how he had been egregiously misquoted by the early church. Through the radical application of source-critical tools, including the various criteria of authenticity, Jesus Seminar fellows took it upon themselves collectively to peel away countless layers of supposedly extraneous traditional material that had accumulated around the isolated sayings of Jesus so as to identify what Jesus really did (and did not) say. The net yield of authentic Jesus sayings, the Jesus Seminar promised, could then provide a new and properly scientific basis for painting a fresh portrait of the historical Jesus, all in keeping with "the assured results of critical scholarship."[5] Unfortunately, because this yield was so small, the portrait rendered but a shadow of the Galilean, or to use

---

[4]The Seminar's most important publication remains *The Five Gospels: The Search for the Authentic Words of Jesus: New Translation and Commentary*, ed. Robert W. Funk. et al. (New York: Macmillan, 1993).

[5]Ibid., p. 34.

Tom's metaphor, "a silhouette," one which told us actually almost nothing about the historical Jesus except perhaps that he surely would have
been environmentally minded and voted against Ronald Reagan.[6] Nature abhors a vacuum, and silhouette portraits of Jesus have a way of
inducing us to make him after our own image, even in the name of
objective history.[7]

Whereas Ben Meyer (*The Aims of Jesus* [1972]) and E. P. Sanders
(*Jesus and Judaism* [1985]) had each in their own way sought to circum-
vent the more stultifying constraints of the standard criteria of authenticity, even as they were forced to work within them, Tom's project served
to make a clean break altogether. By applying his quadrilateral of worldview questions to data that could be provisionally vouched for by his
novel criterion of double similarity (whereby Jesus material explicable as
bridging the concept world of Judaism and the early church may be
deemed authentic), his critical-realist model provided—in the eyes of
many readers—a more supple and satisfying model of historiography.[8]
This method commended itself not because it gives us a Jesus who pretty
much said and did what the Gospels say he said and did, but because it
reflected due suspicion of an affectedly scientific procedure that excludes
a bulk of the Synoptic tradition ahead of time, and did so—quite unself-
consciously—on the basis of narrowly conceived and theologically vested
grounds. In the game room of Jesus scholarship where we have been trying to assemble a jigsaw puzzle of the historical Jesus without a box top,

---

[6]N. T. Wright, *Jesus and the Victory of God* (Minneapolis: Fortress, 1996), pp. 3-124, esp. pp.
3-11.

[7]Criticism against the Jesus Seminar has come from other quarters as well: Richard B. Hays,
"The Corrected Jesus," *First Things* 43 (1994): 43-48; Birger A. Pearson, "The Gospel Accord-
ing to the Jesus Seminar," *Religion* 25 (1995): 317-38; Ben Witherington III, *The Jesus Quest:
The Third Search for the Jew of Nazareth* (Downers Grove, Ill.: InterVarsity Press, 1995); Luke
Timothy Johnson, *The Real Jesus: The Misguided Quest for the Historical Jesus and the Truth of the
Traditional Gospels* (San Francisco: HarperSanFrancisco, 1996); Craig A. Evans, *Fabricating
Jesus* (Downers Grove, Ill.: InterVarsity Press, 2006).

[8]This worldview quadrilateral is developed at length in *The New Testament and the People of God*
(1992). Wright (*Jesus and the Victory of God*, p. 132) provides a succinct argument for the criterion of double similarity: "Along with the much-discussed 'criterion of dissimilarity' must go a
criterion of double similarity: when something can be seen to be credible (thought perhaps
deeply subversive) within first-century Judaism, *and* credible as the implied starting-point
(though not the exact replica) of something in later Christianity, there is a strong possibility of
our being in touch with the genuine history of Jesus."

our author is more or less saying, "Instead of examining one piece at a time without reference to their potential interconnectedness, why not get all the pieces on the table, see what fits, and then decide what the box top must have looked like?" Some call this overly credulous; in my judgment and in the judgment of many, this strategy makes far more sense than the reductionisms that were once touted as "assured critical results." Against the sterile, atomizing tendencies of the Jesus Seminar, which regularly preempted data on dubious a priori grounds, our author has provided an alternative approach that remains by comparison open-minded and heuristically rich.

In retrospect, the critical methodology employed in *Jesus and the Victory of God* seems to be almost as important as—if not more important than—its critical results. Not that this volume gives us the final word on how to do Jesus (Tom himself, I believe, would shudder at the thought), but it came at just the right time, when historical Jesus studies would either have to move outside the confines of its self-constructed cardboard box—or suffocate. Because historical Jesus studies had up to this point been largely dominated by the shadow of Bultmann, and because, too, the Marburger's theology necessarily assumed that our Jesus puzzle box was something of a garage sale giveaway, containing pieces of not one but several puzzles jumbled together, leaving precious little hope of connecting the pieces of *Sitz im Leben Jesu* (Jesus' setting in life), Tom's proposed method constituted a clear break from business as usual. To be sure, the Jesus Seminar was certainly not the only show in town when Tom Wright wrote *Jesus and the Victory of God*, but his focus on certain interlocutors (John Dominic Crossan, Burton Mack and Marcus Borg—all members of the Jesus Seminar) and his relative neglect of others (one would otherwise perhaps expect more interaction with J. P. Meier) signaled his own interest in taking on the New Quest head on.[9] Although Ben Meyer also should be noted as having set forth

---

[9]John Dominic Crossan, *The Historical Jesus: The Life of a Mediterranean Jewish Peasant* (San Francisco: HarperSanFrancisco, 1991); Burton Mack, *The Lost Gospel: The Book of Q and Christian Origins* (San Francisco: HarperCollins; Shaftesbury, U.K.: Element, 1993); Marcus Borg, *Meeting Jesus Again for the First Time: The Historical Jesus and the Heart of Contemporary Faith* (San Francisco: HarperSanFrancisco, 1995); J. P. Meier, *A Marginal Jew: Rethinking the Historical Jesus*, vol. 1, *Origins of the Problem and the Person* (New York: Doubleday, 1991); and, *A*

a fresh approach to what had become a stale problem, it was Tom's work which broke the methodological hegemony of the New Quest.

Jesus and the Victory of God's second great contribution, which I will treat briefly, lies in its recovery of Jesus as a reader of Israel's Scriptures. Because redaction criticism had typically claimed the scriptural quotations and allusions within the Gospel tradition as its own territory, that is, as the byproduct of the evangelists' theological agenda, Jesus scholars in general had long been hesitant to ascribe scriptural quotations to Jesus himself. This of course also works hand-in-glove with a separate but related agenda that seeks to distance Jesus from his own Hebrew Scriptures. The vision of Jesus as operational proto-Marcionite, as Francis Watson has well argued, lies very close to the heart of the Bultmannian program.[10] Since Bultmann had conceived of Jesus as the one who dared to transcend the legal trammels of his Judaism, which inevitably entailed transcending its Scriptures, the greater part of twentieth-century Jesus scholarship took little notice of Jesus as scriptural theologian. Third Questers, on the other hand, proved much more sanguine about Jesus as a reader of Scripture. But I believe that it was above all Tom who granted this component of the Jesus tradition fresh historical explanatory power by seeing Jesus' reading of Scripture as a function of his prophetic role. If the present day of Jesus scholars are forced to think twice before casting Jesus as a romantically inclined Marcionite born before his time (Caird's other famous student, Marcus Borg, may have thought twice but decided to go for the Marcionite Jesus regardless), we have Tom Wright to thank for it.

Third, and on a related point, I maintain that few proposals in the history of Jesus scholarship have promised greater theological dividends than Tom's recurring suggestion that Jesus identified himself with Israel precisely as he identified himself as its royal Messiah. By "Israel," here, I mean (just as Tom means) not simply Israel in a static sense, a body politic in the Palestine of Jesus' day, but rather the entire historical

Marginal Jew: Rethinking the Historical Jesus, vol. 3, *Mentor, Message, and Miracles* (New York: Doubleday, 1994).
[10]Francis Watson, *Text and Truth: Redefining Biblical Theology* (Grand Rapids: Eerdmans, 1997), pp. 153-69.

trajectory leading up to, including and climaxing in his ministry. As messianic herald of the kingdom, Jesus was claiming to be both the embodiment and fulfillment of storied Israel. As such, he not only had a pivotal role within the unfolding drama of redemption, he was also the billboard and the stage of the drama itself.

In order to understand the drama properly, Tom insists, it is first necessary to get the setting right: according to his program Jesus' Israel finds itself in the gloomy shadows of ongoing exile. True, a remnant had returned to the land under Cyrus, but this geographical fact was of secondary importance. So long as Israel's enemies retained political control and YHWH had not returned to Zion, Israel was indeed in exile. For a proper understanding of Tom's larger argument, this point can hardly be overstated. For him, exile is not simply yet another unhappy circumstance attending Israel's woeful existence: exile is *the* narrative conflict, which, so far as Jesus is concerned, finds climactic resolution in Jesus himself.

In advancing this claim, repeatedly and on a largely implicit level, Jesus was by no means presenting his hearers with a *novum*. Steeped in the Scriptures, God's people had for centuries expectantly looked forward to a time when Israel would one day return from exile, evil would be dealt with decisively and YHWH himself would return to take the throne.[11] On observing intimations that the threefold complex of events was underway, Jesus' contemporaries could only infer that if he was right, then the kingdom of God was truly at hand and Israel was on its way to being restored, an event palpable in the current time-space continuum. Since exile by definition denoted a situation in which the wrong people were in power (namely, the Gentiles or Jews who acted like Gentiles), the reverse of the curse of exile would have to include a similar reversal in the political power structures of the day.

While I take slight issue with how this notion of exile gets worked out in *Jesus and the Victory of God*, a point to which I will return momentarily, I find Tom's reconstruction and deployment of a first-century Jewish metanarrative of exile and restoration to be persuasive. I am

---

[11]Wright, *Jesus and the Victory of God*, pp. 206, 227.

convinced with him that there was an essential ancient Jewish metanarrative, variations notwithstanding, even as most reading this book have a rough idea of what is meant by the narrative of "the American dream," variations notwithstanding. Indeed, I might be so bold to say that in bringing exile to the forefront, Tom has supplied the great missing link of modern Jesus studies, even, perhaps the missing link of New Testament theology.

I can still remember picking up *Climax of the Covenant* almost twenty years ago and inwardly resisting at every turn Wright's interpretation of Galatians 3:10-14, only in the end to find myself declaring, "But of course, unless Paul arbitrarily employs certain Scriptures to trump other Scriptures, how could it be any other way?" (Time forbids us lingering on other passages, the Magnificat or Romans 8, for example, which, apart from a backdrop of exile, present insurmountable exegetical problems.) In the end, my resistance stemmed not from any superior counterexplanation, nor even from the fact that Wright's interpretation struck me as novel, but rather because I had been hermeneutically conditioned to read Scripture as God's saving Word to me as an individual rather than—what I believe it is today—God's saving Word to the Israel of God, even the church. So today I hope I am forgiven for wondering aloud as to whether the mother lode of controversy swirling around Tom's understanding of salvation arises not so much from any exegetical conclusions or confessional commitments (although there may be quibbles to be had in both these areas), but from an unexamined commitment to a post-Enlightenment interpretive framework that refuses to accede to the fact that YHWH's revealed salvation has always been essentially corporate—dare one say covenantal—rather than individualized in orientation.

Tom's portrayal of Jesus as the recapitulation of Israel-returned-from-exile also has ramifications for combating reiterations of docetism within the church. By eschewing, on the one side, ahistorical pietism ("You ask me how I know he lives? He lives within my heart"—A. H. Ackley) and, on the other side, antihistorical skepticism ("No one is any longer in the position to write a life of Jesus"—Bornkamm), Tom has made a strong bid to reinstate Jesus as a historical figure with the church's ongoing theological calculus.[12] This is important, not least because modern Protestantism has long struggled with the life of Jesus. When the church has not found itself forcing its master awkwardly into the mold of moral exemplar (resulting in something like, "Jesus shared his bread with five thousand people and you can't even bring a dessert to the church potluck dinner!"), it often makes the opposite error of reducing his task to simply dying for our sins, a notion which undoubtedly prompted Martin Dibelius and countless others to see Mark 1–14 as a protracted clearing of the throat before the real meaning of Jesus is finally articulated in chapters 15-16. By extending Jesus' mission to a historical-political dimension, while reaffirming Jesus' self-consciousness as the divinely sent substitutionary atonement, Tom has not only provided an antidote to rampant docetic tendencies in theologically conservative and liberal circles, but has also redeemed the homiletical value of the Gospels. So long as the meaning of Jesus' life retains only a vague connection to the meaning of his death, the Gospels will continue to be regarded either as a catalog of assorted interesting things Jesus did or as the optional chips and dip leading up to the meat-and-potatoes main course of Pauline theology.

Along similar lines, "Jesus' story as Israel's story" also lays the groundwork for an integrative biblical theology. Against Bultmann, who saw Jesus' message as the "presupposition" of New Testament theology,[13] thereby implying successive radical breaks between Judaism, Jesus and early Christianity, Tom offers Jesus as a true bridge figure. To put it otherwise, so long as the discipline of biblical theology is on the lookout for a unifying thread that binds the canons together, in *Jesus and the Victory of God* we find at least one such thread available: Israel itself. For those inclined to undertake biblical theology through the lens of a narrative theology, Tom's paradigm grounds such a reading strategy in the historical Jesus himself and thereby provides

---

[12]By "antihistorical" I refer not to the historical-critical process, which of course constitutes the very act of doing history, but the low expectation of there being any measurable historical results at the end of the process. The Bornkamm quote is found in his *Jesus of Nazareth*, p. 13, cited in Wright, *Jesus and the Victory of God*, p. 3.

[13]Rudolf Karl Bultmann, *Theology of the New Testament*, trans. Kendrick Grobel (New York: Charles Scribner's, 1951), 1:3.

hard backing, the gold standard of history.

Finally, given the co-identification between Tom's Jesus and Israel, we are afforded new opportunities for integrating soteriology and ecclesiology. At its worst, Western Protestantism has functionally defaulted to a notion that views the church as little more than a loose association of the equivalents of Jesus' Facebook friends. There are, I suspect, various reasons for this, any serious consideration of which would take us off track. But by casting Jesus as a prophet to Israel for Israel, Tom has very clearly framed his saving intentions within the context of community. By following him on this score, we are much better poised to advance ecclesiology not as an extraneous afterthought to the dogmatic enterprise, but as integral to it.

Unfortunately, this point is almost entirely lost on the current, popular reception of Bishop Wright, not least, ironically enough, among conservative Reformed theologians like myself. However, if I were to believe in ghosts, then I would also have to believe that every time that Tom preached as the Canon Theologian of the Westminster Abbey, the spirits of the seventeenth-century Westminster Divines who haunt the Jerusalem Chamber would rise up and applaud him for his robust doctrine of the church. I believe that if contemporary Reformed theologians would take as seriously as Bishop Wright the thrust of the Westminster creedal statement that "the visible church . . . is the kingdom of the Lord Jesus Christ . . . out of which there is no ordinary possibility of salvation" (25.2), contemporary Reformed theology and Protestant theology as a whole would be in a much better place. We ought to ask whether and to what extent the historical Jesus' putative self-identification with Israel could serve as a resource for Protestantism in the midst of its present-day ecclesiological identity crisis, a crisis precipitated by postmodern culture's attaching new probative force to tradition, not least the ecclesiological traditions of Rome and Orthodoxy. While it is certainly fair to raise the question as to whether Tom's thought is consistent with classical seventeenth-century formulations of imputation, it would be rather unfortunate if this particular discussion entirely eclipsed other pressing issues such as this one.

Another implication that the contemporary church is just beginning to draw bears on social ethics. Because Tom's Jesus was convinced that sociopolitical flourishing—righteousness—was an integral component of salvation, and that these are primarily matters of not personal but corporate concern, the church may stand to be redeemed from its "Everyone did what was right in his own eyes" approach to social ethics. Again, the kind of thinking we have in *Jesus and the Victory of God* provides an opportunity to move forward in the church's mission. In my judgment the most looming obstacle to the Western Protestant church's framing a univocal and coherent social ethic within the contemporary marketplace of ideas is the absence of any clear ecclesial self-identity. It would be tragic if we became so preoccupied by explicating and controverting Tom's implicit *ordo salutis* that we failed to take a step back and avail ourselves in very practical terms of his unique synthesis of Christology, praxis and community.

Fourteen years after the release of *Jesus and the Victory of God*, we still have much to reflect on and ponder. New methods have brought us new and refreshing results. A greater appreciation of the role of Torah in Jesus' eyes shapes both our doctrine of the Word and our Christology. Most of all, the believing church stands provoked by his insistence that Jesus *qua* Israel is no post-Easter construct, but deeply embedded within his self-consciousness as prophetic Messiah. Jesus' self-consciously taking on the role of Israel requires our rethinking New Testament theology, and by extension, other branches of theology as well.

QUESTIONS

All this, however, is not to say that there is no room for improvement or even that Tom himself would consider his writings from the 1990s to be the definitive study of the historical Jesus. If a mind as expansive as Calvin's made successive changes to his *Institutes* over the years, we should not begrudge Bishop Wright at least a theoretical opportunity to do the same. So, looking back, what might have Tom done differently?

Toward my answering this question, I return to Davies's discussion in which he provides his own critique of both sides of the Caird-Bornkamm debate. Bornkamm he criticizes for ignoring the communal aspect of Jesus' ethical teaching; Caird, for his understanding of eschatology. Eschatology in Caird's own words, quoted disapprovingly by Davies, "refers to . . . a new, entirely different, state of things, without in so doing, necessarily leaving the framework of history."[14] In short, according to Davies, "Bornkamm has sacrificed the communal dimension of the Kingdom of God to an exaggerated individualism; Caird has sacrificed the personal and transcendent dimensions of the Kingdom to an exaggerated politico-national concern."[15] By this Davies presumably means that just as Bornkamm is insensitive to Jesus' interest in forming a community around himself, an interest that few if any present-day Jesus interpreters dare to deny, Caird, for his part, has failed to detect any sense that Jesus intended his call to force an existential crisis to which the individual must respond, for personal weal or woe.

Criticisms of this nature have also been leveled against Tom, but here we must be careful. In the first place, it is important to show awareness of the context in which our author speaks. I believe that in future years, when scholars survey his corpus, as they undoubtedly will, they will likely agree that one of the most important theological threads in his writings, not least in his writings on Jesus, is in fact a two-ply cord. This cord involves a commitment not only to challenging what Davies calls the "exaggerated individualisms" (among other Gnostic tendencies) that today crowd various accounts of Paul and Jesus, but also to offer a compelling apologia—on both a historical and theological level—for a historically rooted and politically relevant Christian faith.

Unless I am mistaken, I believe that our interpretation of Tom must take into account two implicit conversation partners, one on either shoulder, to which he turns again and again. One the one side is that sizeable swathe of old liberalism that emphasizes Christian faith as an essentially subjective experience bearing strictly on interior realities; on the other side is a world-denying fundamentalism, which for all its stated commitment to an objectivized Christian faith, nonetheless comes full circle back to Bultmann in its refusal either to think historically or to entertain the possibility that such things as history and poli-

---

[14]Caird, *Jesus and the Jewish Nation*, p. 20, cited by Davies, *Gospel and the Land*, p. 348.
[15]Davies, *Gospel and the Land*, p. 348.

tics bear their own theological significance. For Tom, both the Bultmannian New Quester and fundamentalists are like Priam's Greeks
who are not to be trusted. Their exegetical gifts are like a large, wooden
horse, by which anticreational gnosticisms of various sorts are smuggled
in—all yielding dire results. In this respect, inasmuch as Bishop Wright
has made a career of playing the priest Laocoön, who cried out, "Do not
trust the wooden horse!" it comes as no surprise that he has also been
criticized, like Caird, for "sacrificing the personal and transcendent dimensions of the kingdom to an exaggerated politico-national concern."
So long as these criticisms betray their own obliviousness to the author's intentions and, in particular, the conversation I have just described, they ask to be taken with a grain of salt.

Tom himself is aware of the possibility of extremes and so seeks to
establish a balance on the matter that Caird perhaps lacked. In chapter
seven of *Jesus and the Victory of God*, a chapter in which our author begins to discuss the correlation between Jesus' eschatology and ethics,
he writes:

> Scholarship has moved on somewhat from the idea that Jesus' message
> was for the "individual" as an isolated entity. . . . We have, in the last
> forty years, "discovered" that Matthew, Mark, Luke, and John—and
> even, according to some, Q and *Thomas*—had a great interest in "com-
> munity." It ought to be just as clear, if not clearer, that Jesus himself was
> deeply concerned about the social and corporate effects of his kingdom-
> announcement. (In case this paragraph should itself be misunderstood,
> let me say as clearly as possible that the *corporate* meaning of the stories
> does not undermine, but actually enhances, the personal meaning for
> every single one of Jesus' hearers. It is *individualism* and *collectivism* that
> cancel each other out; properly understood, the *corporate* and the *per-
> sonal* reinforce one another.)[16]

Tom's distinction between individualistic and personal, collectivistic
and corporate, is a salutary one. It is hard to disagree with the proposition that the categories of "personal" and "corporate" need not be mutually exclusive but in fact carry most weight when understood as mutu-

---

[16]Wright, *Jesus and the Victory of God*, p. 246.

ally defining terms. With such a caveat in place Tom is clearly signaling his intention to offer a nuanced position, which seeks to spell out an appropriate response to Jesus' kingdom preaching on both a corporate and personal level.

However, whether this intention manages to work out in practice is another question. As Tom describes it, when Jesus proclaimed the kingdom, he issued a proclamation that entailed four aspects: welcome, challenge, summons and, most importantly for our purposes, invitation. By invitation he simply means repentance. But repentance does not pertain to the "world of individual conduct" but refers to "*what Israel must do if her exile is to come an end*," evident in the restoration of national fortunes.[17] At this point Tom makes a further, critical move by saying that repentance "can also have a much more down-to-earth ring: *to abandon revolutionary zeal*."[18] Then, drawing on a passage from Josephus, Tom argues that for Jesus, as for Josephus, repentance not only *could* mean abandoning revolutionary inclinations but in fact *did* mean just that without remainder. Thus, the call to repent

> was an *eschatological* call, not the summons of a moralistic reformer. And it was a *political* call, summoning Israel as a nation to abandon one set of agendas and embrace another. "Repentance" in Jesus' first-century context is not to be conceived simply as one feature within the timeless landscape of a non-historical religion. . . . Rather, precisely as a would-be prophet, and a prophet of the eschaton at that, he summoned Israel to a once-for-all national repentance, such as would be necessary for the exile to end at last. This was not simply the "repentance" that any human being, any Jew, might use if, aware of sin, they decided to say sorry and make amends. It is the single great repentance which would characterize the true people of YHWH at the moment when their god became king.[19]

Like the scriptural prophets, Jesus' call was both eschatological and political in nature. But unlike the scriptural prophets, who as far as I can tell used the term *repentance* to indicate Israel's duty to forsake a

---

[17]Ibid., p. 247, 249-50.
[18]Ibid., p. 250.
[19]Ibid., p. 251; cf. Josephus *Life of Flavius Josephus* §110.

broad range of sins, including such things as idolatry, oppression of widows and orphans, bribery, and deceit (Is 1:27; Jer 9:5; Ezek 14:6), Tom's Jesus employs *repentance* in a specialized sense, by which he focuses his call very specifically on the issue of Israel's violent militancy. It was in this disposition "that Jesus saw the true depth of Israel's present exile."[20] For Tom's Jesus there presumably would have been other charges that may have been laid at Israel's collective feet, but violent militancy acquires a metonymic status; it functions as a kind of national meta-sin, the repudiation of which would avert judgment and indicate the end of exile.

Seeing the temple as the quintessential "talisman of nationalist violence," Tom's Jesus prophesies against it—through actions and words—so as to serve public notice. His point was clear: should Israel fail to heed his call to repent and remain in a state of exile, the result would be national catastrophe.[21] It was to be through the destruction of the temple that disobedient Israel would be judged for its violent ways; it was also through the same that the remnant would—after passing through the dark tunnel of tribulation—emerge from exile as the newly reconstituted Israel.[22] Finally, it was through the fall of the temple that Jesus' proffered path of peace would be vindicated.[23] As his agenda would be vindicated, so too would his status as prophet and Messiah.[24] In sum, the predicted destruction of the temple would retrospectively point back to the disobedience of Israel and the righteousness of Jesus' ways, and point forward to an exile-free existence for those who proved faithful to those ways.

In my view Tom's decision first to identify the impending destruction of the temple with the climactic end of exile, and then to make this imminent disaster the fundamental basis for Jesus' kingdom ethics provides a plausible explanation for Jesus' social ethics. However, the same framework does not serve very well for providing a coherent personal ethic. If Tom's Jesus' directed his message to Israel as a whole as it stood

---

[20]Wright, *Jesus and the Victory of God*, p. 253.

[21]Ibid., p. 420. Similarly, Marcus Borg, *Conflict, Holiness and Politics in the Teachings of Jesus* (New York: Mellen Press, 1984), pp. 163-70.

[22]Wright, *Jesus and the Victory of God*, pp. 336-68.

[23]Ibid.

[24]Ibid., pp. 343, 362, 511.

at its own national crossroads, calling the question as to whether the nation should persist in or desist from its violent militancy, and if, too, the nation's failure to comply with Jesus' invitation would result in negative consequences (so far as we know) strictly on a corporate level, then there is no sense in which Jesus' eschatology has any direct bearing on the individual's response to Jesus. Although a critical mass of personal decisions to heed Jesus would have presumably averted YHWH's judgment, the virtual disconnect between one's immediate response to Jesus and the national response with its corresponding just deserts means, in short, that Jesus never—as far as we know—preached any connection between the individual's response to the kingdom invitation and the eschatological future.

There are, I think, sufficient indications that Jesus did in fact frame his invitation both as a corporate call on Israel as a whole and as a personal call, with eschatological implications hanging equally in the balance in both spheres. For example, we might think of the Gospel account of the young man who falls at Jesus' feet in quest of eternal life (Mk 10:17-22 par.). The passage ranks high for authenticity. Jesus' denial of being good ("No one is good but God alone") would not be the kind of thing we would expect from the early church, which was normally disposed to speak of Jesus in much more exalted terms. Furthermore, both the young man's question and the ensuing catalog of core commandments were typically known to be the stuff of rabbinic dialogues. With Tom and Bornkamm, we accept the episode as reflective of Jesus' own setting.[25]

First, it is to be noted that the man's inquiring after eternal life was simply a way of asking, "How do I know that I will attain to the resurrected state?" After all, in Second Temple Judaism "eternal life" was nothing more and nothing less than the resurrected existence.[26] Strikingly, Jesus' command ("Sell what you own, and give the money to the

---

[25]Bornkamm, *Jesus of Nazareth*, pp. 147-48.; Wright, *Jesus and the Victory of God*, pp. 301-3. For further discussion of the historicity of this pericope and its place within Jesus' agenda, see my *Jesus the Temple* (London: SPCK; Grand Rapids: Baker Academic, 2010), pp. 121-30.

[26]For "eternal life" as the resurrected state, see *Psalms of Solomon* 3.16; *1 Enoch* 37.4, 40.9, 58.3; *Testament of Asher* 5.2. See also N. T. Wright, *The Resurrection of the Son of God* (London: SPCK, 2003), pp. 441, 463.

poor, and you will have treasure in heaven; then come, follow me") coordinates the man's final destiny with the double condition of self-divesture and attaching to Jesus' movement. With the phrase "and you will have treasure in heaven," Jesus is apparently connecting the offer of self-divested discipleship and resurrection hope with investiture in the heavenly treasury, which, in short was the heavenly temple. To follow Jesus personally on his terms was to share in the hope of physical resurrection, which was also to participate in the corporate eschatological temple, even as it was being provisionally unleashed in the present through the ministry of Jesus.[27]

This episode provides a brief but I think convincing example in which Jesus confronts an individual with an existential choice that must either be refused or accepted in the immediate moment. The framing of the decision is entirely in eschatological terms, even as is the initial question. To follow Jesus, the man would have to cash out his properties, transfer the proceeds to the poor and, in short, abandon the social standing and way of life he had come to depend on. Jesus asked the man to cash out not because ownership of wealth was inherently wrong, but because in the case of this particular individual to do so would be the necessary entailment of repentance. In this vignette personal repentance, together with following Jesus, provided its own assurance for securing one's lot in the resurrection.

Resurrection in turn was not simply a personal event but a corporate reality, the culmination of God's temple purposes, which were already being realized in the present through Jesus' kingdom preaching. These same temple or kingdom purposes were proving to be at odds with the religiopolitical interests of the regnant priesthood. I believe it is in light of this fundamental conflict, symptomatic of a broad-spanning covenant fracture on a national level, which explains Jesus' prophecies against the temple. Israel and its temple stood to be judged not simply by virtue of its violent militancy, though that was no doubt part of the equation, but on account of its refusal to disown its idolatries, which stood in the way of its basic remit to worship the one true God. As is clear from the

---

[27]This comes more to the fore in Wright's discussion of the same passage in *After You Believe: Why Christian Character Matters* (New York: HarperCollins, 2010), p. 227.

apocalyptic literature of the period, eschatological judgment against idolatry was meted on both a personal and corporate level.[28]

In my judgment, from Jesus' point of view, the destruction of the temple was not the eschatological terminus but a milestone marker which demonstrated that the eschaton was underway. It betokened, as Tom correctly points out, the disobedience of Israel and Israel's temple; it indicated too the justice of Jesus' cause, that he was, despite the objections of his gainsayers, the true temple builder, and in some sense, the true temple as well. But it does not seem to be the case that the destruction of the temple marked the end of exile—only that the return from exile was underway, even as a resurrected creation was slowly taking shape through the expanding impress of the preached kingdom. While Tom's Jesus confines the eschaton to the events of A.D. 70, I believe that these same realities were for Jesus a kind of down payment of the eschaton; they were the dawning beams of light that the exile stood to be reversed and that the kingdom was both here and on its way.

I would similarly suggest that as ingenious as Tom's metanarrative may be, it stands in need of adjustment. Certainly his conjoining end of exile, vanquishing of evil and the enthronement of YHWH draws on the major elements of the ancient Jewish story as a useful backdrop to Jesus' implied script. But the difficulty for us two thousand years later consists in distinguishing ancillary features of the Second Temple Jewish narrative from its most fundamental components, that is, its narratival telos and driving logic.

What is *The Aeneid* about? Is it about arms and men, broken love affairs, wind-swept ships, trips to the underworld, and Aeneas's return from exile? Well, yes, in a sense. But it is more fundamentally about Aeneas's fulfillment of destiny to father the future rulers of Rome. Similarly, what is the metanarrative of Second Temple Judaism about? Is it about arms and men, the vanquishing of evil, YHWH's return to Zion, and return from exile? Well, yes, in a sense. But I suggest—and

---

[28]The *Apocalypse of Abraham*, for example, echoes countless Second Temple texts, when it "defines the religion of Abraham as the rejection of idolatry, and it suggests that idolaters are ultimately doomed to destruction" (J. J. Collins, *The Apocalyptic Imagination: An Introduction to Jewish Apocalyptic Literature*, Biblical Resource Series, 2nd ed. [Grand Rapids: Eerdmans, 1998], p. 226).

indeed Tom himself more recently suggests—that is more essentially about Israel's fulfilling its destiny to be YHWH's kingdom of priests.

The issue with defining Israel's basic problem as the problem of exile, as accurate as this may be in some sense, is that it cannot offer a positive account of what it means for Israel to finally be true to its own self. The condition of exile is essentially a negative condition. The reverse of exile, I would submit, for Jesus as much as for the Maccabean mother of 2 Maccabees 7, is a resurrected temple existence.

As it so happens, this is more or less what Tom also argues in his trilogy: *Simply Christian* (2006), *Surprised by Hope* (2008) and *After You Believe* (2010). In each of these three recently published books, we find an unswerving commitment to a line of ethical reasoning undertaken with pointed reference to the future resurrected state. In the most recent of the three, Tom states: "The basic point is this: Christian life in the present, with its responsibilities and particular callings, is to be understood and shaped in relation to the final goal for which we have been made and redeemed."[29] That "final goal," characteristically for Tom, is the establishment of the new heaven and new earth, into which redeemed humanity will be bodily raised. Clearly in Tom's later writings, ethical reflection depends for its starting point on resurrection and the creational realities which resurrection reaffirms.

To this I can only add a hearty "Amen!" But what about the hero of *Jesus and the Victory of God?* Did he see things *roughly* along these lines? According to Tom, it seems that we have little evidence to this effect. But if the historical Jesus did not situate his call to repentance within a broader resurrection hope, demanding an existential decision of personal repentance, then Bultmann would be right after all: the message of Jesus would be the presupposition of New Testament theology, not part of that theology itself. Likewise, if Jesus called Israel to himself strictly with reference to his political agenda and without more fundamental and transcendent framework, then we can only surmise that Jesus claimed no distinctive role in the "age to come." And if Jesus claimed no role in the "age to come," then it is hardly likely for him to

---

[29]Wright, *After You Believe*, p. ix.

have spoken with authority about the kingdom as an objective, transcendent reality. And if the kingdom is not in fact an objective, transcendent reality, then we are again back to Bultmann, whose greatest contribution, according to Norman Perrin, "lies in the way in which he has fearlessly accepted the challenge of the modern view of the world."[30] In my judgment, if we follow Caird too closely, so that eschatology does in fact refer to "a new, entirely different, state of things, without . . . leaving the framework of history," we end up falling into the same closed continuum that Bultmann so fearlessly and unquestioningly accepted, albeit by a different door.

It seems to me that ethics without reference to a history-transcending eschaton will always ultimately force us to choose between Bornkamm's individualism or Caird's collectivism, that is, to privilege the individual over the corporate or vice versa. It is only in correlating the individual and the corporate, the true Israelite and true Israel, with reference to the resurrected future, that both of these attain their proper creationally ordered place and the extremes are finally transcended. But perhaps the Caird-Bornkamm conflict is misconceived from the start. Perhaps the choice between Jesus as social ethicist and Jesus as personal ethicist ultimately depends on a dichotomizing of individual and corporate, subject and object, which Kant and we post-Enlightenment folk today would recognize and approve, but Jesus would not. Surely in the resurrection, when the individual and Israel come fully into their own, when individual and corporate meet in perfect unity, that which is seen as irreconcilable now finally meets. Even if Tom Wright's Jesus in *Jesus and the Victory of God* may not have been fully consistent on the point, I am certain that the Tom Wright of today is.

I say this not only on account of what Tom writes about the resurrection, but also on account of the fact that he lives it. May the saga continue many years hence for the son of exile, the son of Aeneas. Speaking myself as a son of Ascanus, we continue to follow you on your epic journey. Until that journey ceases, the full end of exile awaits us one and all.

---

[30]Norman Perrin, *The Promise of Bultmann* (Minneapolis: Fortress, 1979), p. 87.

Response to Nicholas Perrin
N. T. WRIGHT

Never before have I been likened to a character from classical mythology. I am flattered—as I am by the close and careful attention Nick has paid to what I've written. I am especially grateful for Nick's exposition of and support for my work, and for his challenge to bring what I have written more recently into my picture of Jesus where it properly belongs.

I was glad to see Nick's analysis of why so many in Reformed and similar circles find my exposition of salvation controversial. He is exactly right: most Western Christians (sometimes even Roman Catholics!) have simply not wanted, as a matter of first principles, to think in terms of a corporate or covenantal orientation to their faith. So too with Nick's point about the relation between Jesus' life and the meaning of his death. Here the tradition has simply not helped centuries of Christians to understand what their own foundational texts had been trying to say.

George Caird, were he still alive, would be sorry to be typecast, as he was by W. D. Davies, as a collectivist who saw no personal challenge in Jesus' message. I suspect Davies seriously overdrew the contrast between Caird and Günther Bornkamm. That may have helped to bring an issue into focus, but I don't think it was fair to Caird at least.

That said, I fully accept Nick's point in relation to *Jesus and the Victory of God*. What he says chimes in with the questions raised by Brian and Sylvia. Both Jesus' critique of his contemporaries and his challenge to every single person needed to be drawn out more. I have been so used to seeing Jesus' commands and warnings being *reduced* to the rather trivial moral challenges faced by young people in comfortable Western homes that I was determined, if I could, to draw out the much larger picture. Start with the big picture and you'll get the details eventually. Start with the details and you may never know where you are on the map. I still think that the nationalist dream (of Israel becoming top nation by military conquest, restoring the ancient kingdom of David and Solomon) did function as a kind of meta-sin, but there was clearly plenty of ordinary, boring old sin going on too, and Jesus named and shamed it. I think of the warnings of the Sermon on the Mount, or of Mark 7, to look no further. The challenge to the rich young ruler, as Nick points out, is deeply personal, and not to be swallowed up within the larger national problem.

I am drawn toward Nick's suggestion that the events of A.D. 70 "were a kind of down payment of the eschaton." As I've agreed elsewhere, we can read Mark 13 on various levels. Once again my exposition has been tactical: faced with many Western Christians for whom Mark 13 *only* refers to "the second coming," I have found it necessary, following Caird, to point out that Mark at least thought it was about the fall of Jerusalem. But an event of that awesome significance is in any case likely to be paradigmatic as well as climactic.

So, yes: eschatology and kingdom ethics do indeed meet in the middle. But that only works if one grasps the strange complexities of an actual biblical eschatology, rather than the demythologized one of Bultmann or the false literalism of dispensationalism. Jesus wanted his followers, then and now, to be kingdom people in every department of their personal lives, just as he wanted them corporately to be the kingdom people whose life would shine out in the world. The fact that we can say this quite clearly today shows, I think, that we have come a long way since the debates between Albert Schweitzer and C. H. Dodd; perhaps, too, since the writings of Bornkamm and Caird. I wonder what people will be saying about all this, and about our own contributions, a generation or two from now?

5

Whence and Whither Historical Jesus Studies in the Life of the Church?

N. T. WRIGHT

IN EXPRESSING MY GRATITUDE—indeed, amazement—at the favor shown to me in having this conference devoted to discussion of my work, I suppose the best way I can demonstrate that gratitude is by trying to engage with at least some of the issues that have been raised. I am hoping to do so in more specific detail elsewhere, but I want now to speak about where the studies of Jesus in his historical context came from in the last century, how I became involved in that project, and where the major problems today seem to me to lie. These are problems both for the academy and for the church, and doubly so therefore for those of us who have tried to straddle the two.

The back story of the historical study of Jesus is by now almost as well known as the story of Jesus himself, but there are none the less one or two things that need to be said by way of reminder. When I was doing historical Jesus study, it seemed like the natural next thing to be doing in terms of what I'd done to that point. My story may be unusual in some respects, but we all in the Western world go back to the great historical works of the last three centuries. You can ignore them if you like, but that means you're going to be reinventing the wheel. Better to engage with them. But when we do engage with the scholarship and church life of the last few centuries, in much of Western Protestantism, and indeed Catholicism, we find that the church seemed to operate with a split-level Jesus. When reading the stories in the Gospels, everyone knew they referred to an actual man who lived and taught and died in the first century; but then there was this "Jesus" to whom they prayed, to whom they sang hymns, who they encountered in the sacraments. But this figure, though known as Jesus, seemed to float free of historical attachment, so much so that when Geza Vermes published his book *Jesus the Jew* in 1973, the very title came as a shock. Faith seemed to be confronted by history in a rather brutal fashion.

When we think of the dominant theological and biblical studies of the first half of the twentieth century, the point is clear: the neo-Kantian Lutheranism that had characterized Bultmann and his successors had set its face against history as such. Bultmann was indeed a great scholar, for all that I like many others disagree radically with him. He worked out a remarkably comprehensive picture of how early Christianity might have been; we need people who have big visions, even if they need to be corrected. In Bultmann's case, we are dealing with a particular kind of Lutheranism, and, while Lutheranism has great strengths, like all traditions it also has blind spots. For Bultmann, right through, history was a dangerous place because it encouraged people to think they could seize control of their own destiny. History thus became antithetical to grace; we must avoid doing too much history so that grace can still be grace. For Lutherans the framework is often that of the two kingdoms theology: the kingdom of this world and the kingdom of God are separate spheres. For all that Bultmann's tradition spoke of its work in terms of historical criticism, its aim was profoundly antihistorical: to use an imagined historical science to keep "history" well away from "faith": to keep the two kingdoms of God and the world well apart, to reinforce the perception of a three-decker universe which would keep heaven and earth at a safe distance from one another, and to prevent Christian faith from basing itself on history and so turning itself into a "work." It was not, in other words, the neutral, detached historical enterprise that many imagined, designed to discover "what actually happened."

There is a particular irony here. The German New Testament scholarship that gave itself to this antihistorical agenda was picked up by many in Britain and America who, despite Bultmann's insistence that presuppositionless exegesis is impossible, hailed his results and indeed his methods as though they were indeed neutral and objective, "the assured results of criticism." This was common coin when I was an undergraduate. When I was then teaching, my own students were expected to know all this, so I had to tell them about the whole tradition of scholarship, even though I was anxious about it from many angles, philosophical and cultural as well as theological and historical. The methods were not, after all, neutral. The source criticism of the nineteenth and early twentieth centuries, though asking a perfectly fair question (can we trace the route by which literary dependence among the Gospels traveled?), was done in such a way as to produce enough "historical Jesus" to sustain a kind of liberal Protestant faith, but to screen out some of the more sharp-edged aspects of the whole portrait. Similarly, Bultmann's method of form criticism, though asking a perfectly fair question (how did the early traditions of Jesus come to take the shape in which we find them in the Gospels?), was not neutral or objective, but was done in such a way as to produce the kind of results Bultmann and others were after within their philosophical, cultural and theological setting. Thus, in Germany after the First World War, there was a strong push to give up the idea of great, heroic leaders such as the Kaiser and Bismarck and to concentrate instead on *die Gemeinde*, "the community." The Weimar Republic did not, of course, last long, and indeed it gave rise to the most dangerous of all European "great, heroic leaders," but it was precisely at that time that Bultmann was arguing his view, that the Gospels do not give us a picture of Jesus as the big leader but rather of *die Gemeinde* at prayer, at witness and so on. Thus the Germany of the 1920s left a lasting intellectual legacy, a program of scholarly reading of the Gospels in which the quest was on, precisely not for Jesus himself but for *die Gemeinde*, the early community of Christian faith. The Gospels were therefore to be read as testimony, not to Jesus himself (why would anybody want that?) but to the church's life of faith. As for Jesus himself, it was obvious, from within the two kingdoms theology, that Jesus could not have been announcing a political message. He was obviously (to them) teaching something existential, something timeless, inculcating a spirituality, a conversion and ultimately a salvation, but not something that would impinge on this-worldly political and social reality. Once we locate Bultmann and his methods within the world of his own day, it all makes sense.

I might comment that this, perhaps, was what Bultmann and others really were called to say in their own day. It is not for us to comment too caustically on tough decisions taken by brave men in hard times. But we should not imagine for a moment that this was a neutral, objective, set-in-stone-for-all-time kind of scholarship. Anything but. (Any more than mine or anyone else's is neutral and objective!)

This was a step away from an earlier German scholarship in which serious history had flourished. Ancient historians have always protested against that kind of reading of the period. Ed Sanders, in a recent article, writes that up until the First World War German scholarship (he had Deissmann and others in mind) was producing some splendid and solid work on Jewish and Greco-Roman history which really did enable one to understand Jesus and early Christianity in its proper historical setting, but that the dominance of Bultmann after the war all but put a stop to that movement. It is now time, says Sanders, to get back to proper history. And I agree. But the legacy of this movement has been a nervous belief among many to this day: the belief that the New Testament can only tangentially, as it were, give us access to Jesus himself. I see this as like the pseudo-problem of the hare and the tortoise, according to which the hare can never actually overtake the tortoise, since all he can do is continually halve the distance between himself and his slower neighbor. But, just as we all know that the hare does in fact overtake the tortoise, so we should recognize not only that the four canonical Gospels were written in order to give the readers access to Jesus himself, not simply to the early Christian faith about him, but that they really do so in fact. The evidence, as I have argued at length elsewhere, is overwhelming. I do think that the sources tell us more than simply various things about the people who wrote them; they tell us about the things that were actually going on. It's not enough to say that "Matthew tells us about Matthew's community and his theology, so we can't be sure whether it tells us about Jesus." No: remember the hare and the tortoise. This is an optical illusion. Of course writers tell you a lot about themselves, whatever they're talking about. You have to read them critically, but you have to be a realist as well. So: critical realism.

This, I suggest, is enormously important for the church's mission and apologetic. Remember the slogan of Melanchthon in the sixteenth century: it isn't enough to know that Jesus is a savior; I must know that he is the Savior *for me*. I agree with Melanchthon, but I think we have to say it the other way round as well. We must today stress that it isn't enough to believe that Jesus is "my Savior" or even "my Lord"; *you must know who Jesus himself was and is*. Without that, merely saying that we have Jesus "within our heart" or that we "have a sense that Jesus loves me" or whatever can easily turn into mere fantasy, wish fulfillment. That has happened before, and it will happen again, unless it's earthed in actual historical reality. As a pastor, I am only too well aware of the problem of serious self-deception: more than one priest, defending indefensible actions, has said that he or she sensed the presence of Jesus, apparently endorsing his or her scandalous behavior. It's not enough to say you feel something, even the presence of Jesus, very strongly. Lots of people feel all sorts of things very strongly. In order to know that you're not just making it up, not fooling yourself—and if you don't think that's a danger, your skeptical friends ought to tell you—you must be able to say that this Jesus, who we know in prayer, this Jesus we meet when we are ministering to the poorest of the poor, this Jesus we recognize in the breaking of the bread, this Jesus is the same Jesus who lived and taught and loved and died and rose again in the first century. We must believe and confess that he did indeed inaugurate God's kingdom, die to bring it about and rise again to launch the consequent new creation. We must know who Jesus himself actually was and is. Generations of skeptics have swept Jesus aside in their efforts to prove that Christianity is a dangerous delusion. Richard Dawkins is only one of many examples. We have to be able to provide proper, well-grounded answers.

This is, if you like, the personal version of the larger point which Ernst Käsemann made in the 1950s: if we don't do historical-Jesus re-

search, difficult though it may be, we are helpless against the ideology
that manufactures a new Jesus to suit its own ends. When German
scholarship wasn't doing historical-Jesus study in the 1920s and 1930s,
Hitler's tame theologians were able to invent an Aryan Jesus, a non-
Jewish Jesus, and nobody in Bultmann's tradition could stop them. It
won't do to respond, as some have done, by saying: You ask me how I
know who he is? He is who he is in the tradition of the church! That is
precisely the point that has been radically challenged over the last two
hundred years, and to ignore that challenge, or wave it away as irrelevant, is to court disaster. You have to do the history, otherwise the
church can be dangerously deceived. As John Calvin said, the human
mind is a perpetual factory of idols. And one of those idols, those
homemade gods, can be named "Jesus"—not least by those who claim
to be canonical or orthodox Christians. How are we going to prevent
that happening?

    This personal point came home for me when I found myself, as a
young preacher thirty years ago, wrestling with texts in the quiet of my
study and wondering what to say about them. I was faced with the constant problem that most of the commentaries I had been given to study,
and many of the lecturers to whom I had listened, had made the rejection of this or that saying, this or that deed in the Gospels the touch-
stone of genuine, "sophisticated" scholarship. You had to be able to say
"Jesus didn't really say this or that," or "Of course Jesus never actually
walked on water," or "Jesus couldn't have thought of himself as divine
because he was a first-century Jewish monotheist"; these were your
passports to a world where you were taken seriously as a critical scholar.
The result was that many of my contemporaries in seminary and elsewhere, training to be preachers, simply shut off their critical minds
once they left college and went off to preach the old simple gospel they
had learned long before. That, I guess, may be better than nothing
when faced with questions to which one could not discover answers for
oneself. But how much better it would have been, and is, to engage with
the real questions and come through to real answers.

    For myself, I found myself incapable of saying in the pulpit, "As Jesus
said, . . ." without asking myself the question, *But did he?* And I found

myself unwilling to say in that same pulpit, "Some scholars say he said it, some say he didn't." I know that some young clergy in the 1960s and 1970s were only too eager to share their professors' doubts with their congregations, but that seemed to me profoundly counterintuitive. That isn't going to help most congregations most of the time. Should I then only preach from texts of whose historical value I had no doubt? Perhaps, but that could only ever be a stopgap. Nor was I prepared (despite what some of my own critics have said) to play the fundamentalist trump card: "The Bible says it." I have always had a very high theology of the Bible, but I have always regarded that as setting the questions, not establishing the answers. (On this, see *Scripture and the Authority of God*.) The stronger your theology of Scripture, I believe, the more the historical question ought to be pressed, precisely because Matthew, Mark, Luke and John do *not* appear to be saying "Welcome to our nonhistorical story-telling world" but "Here is a powerful lens through which to make sense of the events which actually happened in our midst."

I did not know, in the late 1970s and early 1980s as I was wrestling with these questions, how strongly Ernst Käsemann (whose commentary on Romans I had devoured, though not I hope uncritically) had mounted a protest, thirty years earlier, against the nonhistorical readings of the previous German generation. Käsemann, to be sure, saw the difficulties of offering a properly historical account of Jesus himself, but as I said a moment ago he saw equally clearly the problems that had been caused by not making the effort. Käsemann was (from my point of view) fighting this battle with at least one hand tied behind his back, not only because of the legacy of earlier German *Wissenschaft* and the academic imperative to build on it, but also because he too was operating within a theological framework in which the first-century Jewish notion of God's kingdom was more or less out of reach. Instead, he and his contemporaries imagined Jesus to be talking about "the near God" as opposed to a far-off deity, as though Jesus were trying to persuade his Jewish contemporaries not to be eighteenth-century deists. Käsemann's announcement of a program thus far exceeded his ability to launch it successfully. But his program remains important: without history there is no guarantee that the church will not reinvent yet more Jesus figures, which turn out to be projections or embodiments of this or that ideology.

That remains my main worry about the appeal to canon or tradition over against history. I believe in canon, and I believe in the Holy Spirit. But history has shown again and again that the church is well capable of misreading the canon, and that tradition can drift in many directions, some less than helpful, some decidedly destructive. To appeal to tradition and dogma as the framework for understanding Jesus is to say that not only the entire enterprise of biblical scholarship but also the entire Protestant Reformation has been based on a mistake. Some may find it strange to hear me defending either of these (critical scholarship and the Protestant Reformation!), but if the alternative is to say simply that tradition has got it mostly right I reply that the history of the church tells a very different story. It is that position, applied in moral and pastoral theology, that has landed the contemporary church (particularly, but not only, the Roman Catholic Church) in some of its worst current dilemmas.

Käsemann's agenda was thus always going to be held back by his own academic and intellectual context. But help was at hand from a quarter to which, even after the war, he and his contemporaries had not expected to look: the freshly studied world of first-century Judaism. This, from one angle at least, is where I myself came in.

I had first felt a flutter of excitement in Jesus himself as a real, human figure of actual history when I heard the rock musical *Jesus Christ Superstar* in 1971. I still think it contains among the best lyrics Tim Rice ever wrote, and for that matter some of the least banal music Andrew Lloyd Webber ever penned, but that wasn't the reason for the fascination. For the first time I realized that it was possible to ask the question, What was Jesus actually thinking about? I suppose that up till then I had taken it for granted that because he was the Son of God he went through life unreflectively, going off to die for the sins of the world as a kind of supernatural robot. The thought that Jesus might have struggled with vocational questions—What am I supposed to be doing? How ought I address this next problem? What is it going to be all about? These were fascinating possibilities. The musical evoked Jesus as a real person *who faced, and made, real and hard choices.* Some of those, I believed, were misrepresented (the idea of Jesus, tired after a long day's healing, suddenly losing his temper and having to be soothed by Mary Magdalene—this belongs in a Dan Brown novel, not in history), but others seemed not to be. Tim Rice caught the real dilemma of Gethsemane. He managed to express vividly, too, the clash between the disciples' expectations and Jesus' vision of God's kingdom, power and glory.

Haunted by all this, and by the fascinating questions it raised, I turned away into a decade of studying Paul, approaching questions of first-century Judaism through the lens of Romans 9–11 in particular. I recall a colleague in Merton College, Oxford, in the mid-1970s, asking me if there was a good recent book about Jesus in his historical context, and my having to confess that there didn't seem to be one. (Vermes's work seemed then, and seems to me still, best summed up in Henry Chadwick's verdict: "a rather pale Galilean.") But toward the end of that period, while completing my doctorate and teaching and pastoring in Cambridge, I read two books which rekindled my interest, one because it was massive and (mostly) wrong, the other because it was dense and (mostly) right. Schillebeeckx's *Jesus* projected a humanitarian Christology onto a fictive screen of source criticism and "discovered" the answer it started with. Ben Meyer's *The Aims of Jesus* possessed a philosophical sophistication and attention to first-century sources which was then without rival or peer, and has largely remained so. It was from Meyer that I learned critical realism, from Meyer too that I and many others learned that several Jesus-sayings that Bultmannian criticism had swept aside fitted like a key in a lock within the world of first-century Judaism. Once one had got over the obviously flawed "criterion of dissimilarity," which by itself would have rendered a Jesus who was merely a freak, the exploration of the Jewish world, in a way which left Vermes more or less standing at the starting gate, formed a rich context for exploring not so much "whether Jesus could have said this or that" but the question, Supposing Jesus said this or that, what would that have meant at the time? leading to the question, So what *did* Jesus mean at the time? What was he wanting to get across to his hearers? What was he trying to accomplish? What, in short, were his *aims?*

I think what was particularly liberating about this question was the recognition that Jesus was not simply telling people how to get to heaven. Most of Jesus' teaching, of course, doesn't look as though that's what he's saying, though his central slogan, "God's kingdom," had for so long been understood in that way that it was almost impossible for Protestants, whether conservative evangelicals or radical Bultmannians, to hear anything else. I suspect, in fact, I was the more prepared to listen to Meyer because, in the mid-1970s, I had come to believe, as a matter of exegesis, that Paul had been saying far more than "Here's how to go to heaven." The so-called New Perspective, which is the subject of a different session, was part of the same wave of studies as the Third Quest (which label, by the way, is justified particularly by Meyer's clear, detailed and sharp distinction between the post-Bultmannian New Quest and the kind of work he himself was doing, and which I picked up). Rather, I and others were becoming fascinated by the question, If Jesus' wasn't simply saying, "Here's how to go to heaven when you die," what was he saying? Why did some find his message utterly compelling, and why did others find it so dangerous and threatening that they determined to have him killed?

It was with those questions in mind that I arrived at McGill in the early 1980s and found myself, in late 1982, teaching an introductory course on the New Testament. I began, as you would expect with someone of my background (in classics and philosophy), with two streams of lectures, alternating between the ancient world of the Middle East from the Maccabees to John the Baptist and the modern world of critical scholarship from the mid-eighteenth century to the present. The two strands were designed to meet in the first chapters of the Gospels, and when they did I found that I at least had become fascinated (I can't speak for the students) by the sweep and power and frustration of the Jewish story of the period and the way in which the different movements (scribes, Pharisees, Essenes and so on) appeared not nearly so much as "religious" or "philosophical" teachers but as people with an agenda, a program about the national expectation and hope, a desire for God to act again and to do so decisively, a longing for a new Passover, a new exodus, a real "return from exile" (though I didn't appreciate the significance of that point until later). Whatever historical criticism might say about the Gospels themselves, the story up to the mid-twenties of the first century could be understood, from many sources and particularly of course Josephus, in a rich, multilayered unity of history, hope, faith, worship, scriptural reflection, political intrigue, empire, revolution, taxes and crucifixions. Herod the Great fitted extremely well into this world; so did Hillel and Shammai, Samias and Pollio, Judas the Galilean, and the other figures about whom we know far, far less than Jesus of Nazareth but whose motives, beliefs, aims and objectives we can study—*not* as figures who live only in a story, whether that of Josephus or those of the later rabbis, but as persons within actual history. The hare easily and obviously overtakes the tortoise: the historian really does know about Herod himself, not simply about "Josephus's narrative of Herod" or whatever. Nobody objects when people write books about Hillel that they are "constructing a Hillel behind the text" and thus falsifying some cast-iron principle either of literary criticism or Jewish faith. To be sure, Josephus does construct a narrative of Herod and the rest, and the wise historian takes full account of what Josephus is trying to do. To be sure, there are many points in all such historical work where the same historian admits that the conclusions are only tentative. But that it is possible to write *about Hillel*, not just about other people's ideas of him, the historian has no doubt.

My course reached John the Baptist. Here too there was no problem. Indeed, once we'd understood the Herodian legacy on the one hand, the Roman objectives in the Middle East on the other, and the ordinary Jewish aspirations in the middle, John fitted into the context exactly. Indeed, he came up in three dimensions, not just as a "voice in the wilderness," a disembodied prophetic word, but as a man with a mission and a hope. God was going to come and be king. Everything was going to be different. And by now we were treading on the sacred turf, not any longer of Josephus or the scrolls or the rabbinic traditions, but of the Gospels themselves. I remember thinking, when I got to that point in the lectures, *Is there any reason why we shouldn't go on doing the same kind of thing, in relation to Jesus and the Gospels, that we have been doing with the Jewish sources?* The answer was clear: Of course not. Jesus was a figure within history, and the sense that he made he made within that history. He wasn't floating free somewhere in mid-air. He was precisely living in the middle of it all. The Word became *flesh*. A canonical Christian is presumably committed to that point. Were we about to be warned off by the anxious thought police of the split-level world, insisting not only that one should not, today, allow one's faith to be sullied by history but also that the Gospels weren't committing that crime either? Were we only to be allowed to speak of Matthew's (or the others') *narratives about* John the Baptist or Jesus, rather than John or Jesus themselves? I saw no reason to give such objections any space. If we could read the Jewish story from the Maccabees to the Baptist by using all the available historical sources (including coins, archaeology and so on, as well as literary remains), why shouldn't we go on doing so? Could we not at least make the thought experiment of supposing that the story really *did* make historical sense—but not the historical sense of a Jesus telling people about a "near God" as opposed to a distant one, or about "how to go to heaven," but something that would be far more relevant and urgent to his Jewish contemporaries, something that actually enabled the parables and deeds of power to stand up straight at last, something that would be both compelling and crucifiable in that first-century world? That was the movement of my own thinking out of which, over a decade later, there emerged *Jesus and the Victory of God*.

As I stepped out of the boat of safe, sanitized, "critical" scholarship in answer to this strange summons, I had no sense at all of going "behind the text" to a Jesus the texts had falsified or skewed. Rather, I had, and still have, the sense of discovering *the Jesus the Gospels had been talking about all along* but whom the long tradition of Western misreadings (Catholic and Protestant, conservative and radical) had failed or even refused to see. As a scientific historian using the hypothesis-and-verification method, I was keen to include the data within the big picture. Only in a determinedly antihistorical world could it be supposed that *leaving out lots of evidence* could be a virtue in a historian. Of course, the post-Bultmannian picture of the early church as the cheerful factory for "fake" Jesus sayings has had a long inning, but the more we know about the early church the less, in fact, it appears that they made up Jesus sayings to suit their own new contexts. Nowhere in the Gospels does Jesus address the key problems we know from Paul to have preoccupied the early church. The obvious example is circumcision.

Reflecting on this false either-or (Jesus "within the Gospels" versus Jesus "behind the Gospels") led me, and leads me still, to reflect that the real-history Jesus was a *public* figure making a *public* announcement. To be sure, as Ben Meyer had rightly pointed out, the Jesus of the Gospels seems to have taught at two levels, speaking widely to the crowds and intimately to his close associates. But the content of his message was not private individual spirituality or salvation. It was about *what Israel's God was doing in history*, in real space, time and matter. I hadn't read much of Lesslie Newbigin at that point, but I think what I was stumbling upon was the emphasis that we now associate especially with him: Christian faith is *public truth*. Christianity appeals to history; to history it must go. It is about creation. It isn't a form of Gnosticism, escaping this wicked world of history and earth. It is a form of creational theology in which history and earth, space, time and matter, are *redeemed*. The Word became flesh, not vice versa. Matthew, Mark, Luke and John themselves are convinced that God's kingdom was inaugurated not when they picked up pen and ink to write their Gospels but when the living God took flesh and blood to inaugurate the kingdom, to live and die and rise again. In Matthew 28 the risen Jesus declares "all authority in heaven and on earth" is given—not to the books Matthew and the others would write, but to Jesus himself. If there is such a thing as scriptural authority, that is a shorthand for God's authority, through Jesus, exercised and put into practice through Scripture.

So I really do believe that the Gospels give us access to what Jesus was thinking, to his worldview and his mindset, as well as to what he did. This is not a matter of trying to psychoanalyze him. We're trying to get at the things which Jesus chose to do and say. We can ask the same question about John the Baptist: Why did he think it was a good idea to go down to the river and splash water over people? It wasn't an unreflective thing; it carried, and he must have intended it to carry, all kinds of symbolic resonances with the exodus and the entry into the land, in other words with the events that constituted Israel as God's people and might now reconstitute Israel as such. So with Jesus. He didn't just wake up one morning and decide, on a whim, that he might as well go and talk about the kingdom of God and see what would happen. He wrestled with it. According to the Gospels, he wrestled in prayer and fasting. We see in the Gospels the things he did, but those pose the question, to any intelligent reader: what did he think he was about? What was he hoping to accomplish? What did he hope would happen next? Is there a credible first-century Jewish mindset within which such actions make sense? Unless we can answer that, teachers and preachers are going to be left saying to themselves, *Well, Scripture says Jesus did this, or said that, but we can't be sure; there's a seed of doubt planted in my mind and my preaching will be affected by it.* And then what happens—which has happened for many generations now—is that the whole church shifts subtly, and decides that since we know "Christ died for our sins" that's all we need to think about. All the specific incidents in the Gospels can then just become little illustrations of this larger abstract theology. And with that not only is history lost but the kingdom of God, which is what the Gospels are all about.

This affects both the content of Jesus' message and the way we access it through the study of the Gospels themselves. Just as Jesus refused the protection of Peter and the others brandishing their futile swords in Gethsemane, so the Gospels refuse to be placed within a *cordon sanitaire* whereby, as the private property of "the church," they invite us into a world from which the muddled questions and muddy boots of the secular historian would be excluded. The Gospels speak of the kingdom coming in and through Jesus' own work, and of misunderstanding, opposition, threats both human and satanic, political danger of several different kinds, and finally an unjust trial and a horrible death—at which point, the same Gospels declare, Jesus is, however paradoxically, enthroned as "king of the Jews." The real falsification of the Gospels—the real "going behind the gospels to a different reality"— lies not in the attempt to understand, historically, the Jesus of whom they speak, but in the attempt to reconstruct the Gospels as sacred story *and therefore not also profane story.*

In particular, it seems to me radically counterintuitive to suppose that the Gospel writers themselves would support the nonhistorical reading that is often still proposed. The Gospels are not self-referential. They do not say, Come into our private world, and there you will find faith, hope and love. To be sure, as good story tellers they do indeed create what can be called a fictive world (not that the events they are describing didn't happen, but that all selection and arrangement of events is a human creation, a "fiction" in that sense), and they invite us to live in it. But they insist, on page after page, that this fictive world is one way of looking at *the real world of space, time and matter in which Jesus of Nazareth lived and died.* That, after all, is the point of Luke's careful placing of the story within the chronologies of world history and Jewish history. That, after all, is why Matthew's Jesus speaks of God's kingdom coming on earth as in heaven. It is, above all, what John meant when he spoke of the Word becoming flesh. The thought that they would be read as turning flesh back into word would have horrified the evangelists. They were Jews; creational monotheists; longing for Israel's God, the Creator, to act *within* space, time and matter, not to create another world, a "narrative world," within which certain things could be true in some Pickwickian sense whether they actually happened or not. To imagine that by invoking "story" we are somehow escaping the public, historical world is to forget what sort of "story" it is that the canonical Evangelists (as opposed, say, to "Thomas") think they are telling. Yes, it matters that we live within the story of Jesus as they have interpreted it. If the archaeologists came upon the court records of Pontius Pilate, that would of course be one of the most fascinating and important documents ever turned up by a spade. It would help us enormously in understanding what was going on. But we would not expect to construct our own worldview on the basis of the interpretation of the court proceedings that was offered by the official Roman stenographer. But recognizing that the canonical Evangelists invite us to see the events through their eyes and with their interpretation doesn't mean they are not inviting us *to see the events.* For them, the most important thing is that these things—the inauguration of the kingdom, and Jesus' death and resurrection—actually happened.

Within this, it made sense, and makes sense, as I said, to ask about the worldview and mindset of Jesus himself. Far too many Christians have been content to assume that because Jesus was and is the second person of the Trinity, he went about in a completely unreflective fashion, turning out those exquisite parables and engaging with people of all sorts in a richly human combination of severity and gentleness, of teasing and challenge, automatically and without thinking and praying through what the one he called "Abba, Father" was summoning him to do. To say this is not to claim to know more than we should. It is to ask substantially the same question we might ask not only (as we saw) about John the Baptist, but also about figures such as Hillel or Herod: why did they do what they did? And it seems to me, despite what is sometimes said, that when it comes to Jesus the Gospels themselves give us plenty of suggestions as to the answer: Jesus was "deeply moved"; "looking on him, he loved him"; "he gazed round, grieved at their hardness of heart." Creative fiction? I don't think so. This was Jesus as they had known him: a real human being, a historically available human being, not of course without mysterious depths (my closest and dearest friends, sharing my own culture and life, still remain mysterious), but knowable *by history as well as by faith*. That is what the Gospels offer; and, to repeat, any attempt to speak about Jesus as though the resurrection, and the fact of Jesus' being alive today, would enable us to have a "knowledge of him" which could enable us to bypass the knowledge which the Gospels offer is the real "going behind the gospels."

The canon itself, in fact, supports, indeed urges the kind of reading I have proposed. To appeal to the canon of Scripture over against the historical study of Jesus seems to me a category mistake. Rather, the real divide comes, alas, between the canon on the one hand and certain aspects (by no means all) of later church tradition on the other. I shall return to this point, but to make it briefly here: Matthew, Mark, Luke and John, all in their very different ways, insist that the full meaning of Jesus is to be found precisely as the climax of the canon, the point where the large and complex story of Adam and Abraham, of Moses, David and the prophets all comes rushing together. It won't do to say, "Oh, we can't go behind the text." It isn't a matter of setting up a "historical

Jesus" over against the "canonical" one. It won't do to claim that historians like myself are opting for the former, as a construct of our own, over against the latter. The whole point is that the canonical Jesus *is* the historical Jesus, in the sense that Matthew, Mark, Luke and John all intend to refer to someone outside their own thought world, the someone they knew as Jesus of Nazareth, and my judgment as a historian is that they are successful in that reference. The canonical story *is* the big story of Scripture. In fact, if I am accused of having in my head a "large narrative" which I then use as the template for interpreting the Gospels, I plead guilty—and summon the Four Evangelists in my defense. This demonstrably, is what they are urging us to do.

The real trouble is that for many centuries the church's tradition has refused to allow the Four Evangelists to say this to us, to allow the canon to be the canon. In fact, the church's perception of the canon has been very limited and distorted. This is the problem. The church has often colluded with shallow, one-dimensional readings of the canon and shallow, one-dimensional readings of who Jesus really was. For many traditional Christians it would be quite enough if Jesus of Nazareth had been born of a virgin and died on a cross (and perhaps risen again). But this leaves us with the baffling question, Why then did he go about doing all those things in between? Why did the canonical Evangelists take the trouble to collect and record them? Merely to provide the back story for the cross-based theology of salvation? Merely to show what the incarnate Son of God looked like and got up to? Simply to demonstrate, by his powerful deeds, that he was the second person of the Trinity? Was he, at that point, simply a great ethical teacher (and if so, how does that relate to his saving death?)? Or was he living a sinless life in order that his sacrifice, when eventually offered, would be valid? All these have been proposed within "the tradition" as ways of filling the blanks left by the great traditional omission of what the Gospels are actually talking about, namely, the inauguration of God's kingdom. If you appeal to the canon, then let the canon correct the tradition, not the other way around.

Actually, there is in any case no such thing as a reading of the canon without reference to extracanonical material. However much you may say you're a canonical Christian, we all depend on noncanonical material, on extratextual elements, even if it's simply the lexicon in which we look up the Greek words and find out what they meant at the time. Someone has constructed that lexicon from other noncanonical texts. Then there are archaeological finds, artifacts and so on, which help us understand how that world worked. You can't actually do a purely canonical reading. You can't actually do without history. Let us then embrace it and see where it takes us.

But I fear it is precisely the traditional church (I speak as a traditionalist!) that has invented another Jesus and superimposed that Jesus upon the canon, greatly diminishing what the canon itself was actually trying to say. As a result, the church has again and again tried to fit its "Jesus" into a different narrative, the story of how the second person of the Trinity revealed his divinity and saved people from their sins into a disembodied heaven. This, not surprisingly, has little continuity with the great canonical story into which the Four Evangelists hook their own work—not because Jesus is not indeed the second person of the Trinity, or because he did not indeed save people from sin, but because those theological shorthands are capable of being cashed out into many different narratives of which the genuinely canonical one is only one, and normally the ignored one. It is precisely the *canonical* Jesus who announces God's kingdom on earth as in heaven—something which "tradition" managed to screen out from quite early on. It is precisely the *canonical* Jesus whose death was, in his own intention, intimately connected with his kingdom agenda; again, one would not know that from later tradition. It is the Western tradition, coming to a particular climax (but not the only one) in Bultmann and his predecessors (Kähler among them) and followers (the New Quest in particular), that has insisted on inventing a Jesus "behind the gospels." Sometimes this has been "gentle Jesus meek and mild"; sometimes it has been the Preacher of the Word whose only real message is that he is indeed the Preacher of the Word, revealing simply that he is the revealer. Kähler's own famous protest about the danger of historians discovering a Jesus other than the one in Scripture turns out to be sheer projection. The tradition—the traditional church!—which Kähler embodied at that point did, and continues to do, exactly that. And the irony has been that the tradition has been so strong that nobody has even noticed. The Gospels have remained at the center of the church's life, but they have been muzzled and emasculated.

All of which leads us to the question, which looms up all the way from the medieval church onward: What then are the Gospels actually all about? I think that the Western church has simply not really known what the Gospels were there for. Here, at the heart of this paper, I have two main themes to explore. In both cases, rather than simply defending the project of the historical study of Jesus, I want to move to the attack, to expose and critique what seem to me demonstrable misreadings of the canonical Gospels themselves.

DIVINITY AND HUMANITY?

I begin with a point which may seem strange and even potentially heterodox, but which I believe is the high road to a genuine, canonical orthodoxy. The Gospels are not primarily written to convince their readers that Jesus of Nazareth is the second person of the Trinity. They are not talking about that. Rather, they are written to convince their readers that he really was inaugurating the kingdom of God—the kingdom of *Israel's* God—on earth as in heaven. That is front and center in the Synoptic Gospels, and not far behind in John (the rather few Johannine references to the kingdom (e.g., Jn 18:36) are none the less telltale). But it is almost entirely absent from "the tradition"—as witness the entire line of thought from the great creeds and the Chalcedonian Definition through to much dogmatic theology in our own day. Jesus as kingdom-bringer has been screened out of the church's dogmatic proclamation. The church has managed to talk about Jesus while ignoring what the Gospels say about him. That, indeed, is why there was a lacuna that liberation theology has tried to fill, sometimes with more success, sometimes with less. In fact, one might suggest sharply that it is the mainstream dogmatic tradition (arguing about the "divinity and humanity" of Jesus) that has actually falsified the canon by screening out the Gospel's central emphasis on the coming of the kingdom and by substituting for this the question of the divinity of Jesus, as though the point of the Gospels' high incarnational Christology were something other than the claim that *this is Israel's God in person coming to claim the sovereignty promised to the Messiah.* Psalm 2, front and center in the baptism narratives, says it all: but it is folly to abstract "you are my Son" from the psalm, or the baptism story, as though this were a proof of Jesus' divinity, while ignoring the conclusion of the psalm that Israel's God is giving to this "son" the nations of the earth as his possession. That, of course, is the context of the canonical account of Jesus' temptations: to gain the right end by the radically wrong means. And it is the full psalm, and the baptism story as resonating with the full psalm, that launches Jesus on a career—not of "going about explaining that he was divine" but of going about explaining what it means that Israel's God is present and active, in and through him and his work, to claim his rightful sovereignty over the whole of creation.

Seen in this light the particularly eighteenth-century apologetic reading of the miracles is shown up as the shallow thing it is. Instead of the deep biblical (canonical!) resonances which indicate that this is indeed the new age for which Israel longed, the "tradition" has read Jesus' mighty acts in terms of proofs of divinity. But this is an abstract divinity belonging more to the dry world of deism than to the rich world of Jewish faith and life. And, in any case, religious traditions, including the Jewish traditions, are full of strange stories about people doing surprising things, but, whether it's Elijah raising a child to life or Joshua making the sun stand still, nobody suggests that these things prove that they are somehow divine. That is an eighteenth-century diminution of what the ancient stories were actually about. The so-called miracles do sometimes point to the strange secret of Jesus' ultimate identity. But they do so within their primary emphasis, which is on the arrival of God's saving sovereignty within the world.

By the same token, the early church's proper insistence that Jesus was also fully human always tended to screen out what the canonical Gospels were saying, that the human Jesus was the Messiah of Israel, summing up Israel in himself and, with that, summing up the whole history of the human race. (Again, it is precisely the *canon* that would insist on this point, reading the Gospels in the light of Israel's Scriptures.) Seen from this angle the Chalcedonian Definition looks suspiciously like an attempt to say the right thing but in two dimensions (divinity and humanity as reimagined within a partly de-Judaized world of thought) rather than in three dimensions. What the Gospels offer is the personal story of Jesus himself, understood in terms of his simultaneously (1) embodying Israel's God, coming to rule the world as he had always promised, and (2) summing up Israel itself, as its Messiah, offering to Israel's God the obedience to which Israel's whole canonical tradition had pointed but which nobody, up to this point, had been able to provide. The flattening out of Christian debates about Jesus into the language of divinity and humanity represents, I believe, a serious de-Judaizing of the Gospels, ignoring the fact that the Gospels know nothing of divinity in the abstract and plenty about the God of Israel coming to establish his kingdom on earth as in heaven, that they know nothing of humanity in the abstract, but plenty about Israel as God's true people, and Jesus as summing that people up in himself. The Council of Chalcedon might be seen as the de-Israelitization of the canonical picture of YHWH and Israel into the abstract categories of "divinity" and "humanity." I continue to affirm Chalcedon in the same way that I will agree that a sphere is also a circle or a cube also a square, while noting that this truth is not the whole truth. Here, perhaps ironically in view of our ongoing conversation, Richard Hays's forthcoming work on the use of Scripture in the four Gospels bids fair to point to the rich heritage which the Gospels were evoking but which, I think, much of the tradition from the fourth century onward has screened out. The Gospels have a very high Christology; but this isn't about divinity in the abstract, but about *the God of Israel personally present and active.*

It is, in fact, the church's dogmatic tradition, through which the Gospels have been forced to give answers to questions they were not addressing, or not addressing head on, that has made the apologetic and historical tasks much harder. It is harder to retrieve the *canonical* Jesus (YHWH in person and Israel in person) because the whole church has taught itself to read the canon in ways that significantly diminish it, a problem that can only be remedied precisely by a fresh (however dangerous!) *historical* reading. But it is harder to retrieve a genuinely *historical* reading—the historical reading to which the canonical Evangelists were urging their readers, the history to which the canon gives access and was designed to give access—because of those same misunderstandings, which led people to say, with wondrous confidence, that the real Jesus "could not have said or thought" this or that "because he was a first-century Jew," while showing remarkably little knowledge of the rich world of actual Jewish discourse of his day. (The obvious example is monotheism: for generations, as I said before, it was a staple of historical criticism that no first-century Jew could think of incarnation, because they were all monotheists. Five minutes of serious study of Paul shows how mistaken this is.)

A further irony now emerges. It is precisely one of the founding principles of Protestantism that what Jesus did on the cross was unique, unrepeatable, *ephapax*, one-off. "He died for our sins once and for all," in a never-to-be-repeated sacrificial self-offering. But that principle, designed of course to ward off any supposed Catholic suggestion that Jesus might be recrucified in every Mass, is itself the proper root of a genuinely historical reading. That is why historical criticism, for all its ambiguity over the last three centuries, is from one point of view a natural outgrowth of Protestantism, however much then the various strands of Protestant tradition have introduced new quasi-Catholic distortions: because, classically in Bultmann but in all kinds of other ways too, the whole critical enterprise that has sought to read the Gospels as evidence not for Jesus but for "early Christian faith" was designed to highlight the words and deeds of Jesus not as part of a one-off, unique and unrepeatable event, but to turn them precisely into a repeatable, timeless statement of "the church's faith." Bultmann, in other respects so ultra-Protestant, was in this respect much closer to certain kinds of "catholic" reading. But it matters that these things *happened*. Without that, one would turn this specific statement into a general truth about theology, spirituality or extrahistorical salvation. That's not what the canonical writers were saying. They were saying that at one moment *in actual history* a great door swung open on its hinge, and the Creator of the cosmos declared that the way was now open into his remade creation. He was making all things new. The story of Jesus is about the real world, the actual space-time universe, not about the private spiritual experience of a specific group of people. The canonical story *is* the public story of the real Jesus and the real world, and to live within the gospel story—all that wonderful postliberal language about being the people of the story and so forth—is not to enter a private world, separated off from the rest of the space-time universe, but to enter the public world of space, time and matter, facing all its risks. To imagine that by entering the world of the Gospels, or by saying the magic word *story*, we are immune from the risks of living in the public world is to fail to realize *what story it is that the canonical Gospels are telling*. It is precisely the story of the *real world*, the world of space, time and matter, of actual events. My first real problem of not doing history properly is that we shrink the story of God and God's kingdom in Jesus, and the story of Jesus bringing Israel's story to its climax—which two stories are not two but one—to the thin, abstract categories of "divinity" and "humanity." It is much safer, less risky, to do that; much more in line with "the tradition" but much less like the real Gospels, or the real gospel.

This kind of reading could only be done, of course, once the unique event itself had become shrunk to one point: the crucifixion. This brings us to the second great point at which the entire Western tradition has not known what the Gospels are there for: the split, almost ubiquitous in tradition but never found in the canon, between Jesus' announcement of the kingdom and Jesus' pilgrimage to the cross.

KINGDOM AND CROSS

The split between kingdom and cross is not simply a scholar's construct. Nor is it simply one element in the Western tradition. It has radically shaped and colored church life and thought in many traditions and at many levels. In my own ministry it is not too much to say that I have met this split again and again, and have had to deal with its effects in the life and work of the church. It is sometimes, actually, seen as a division between the Gospels and Paul, with the Gospels offering a kingdom theology and Paul offering a *theologia crucis*. But actually it is better seen as a division within the gospel material itself. Schweitzer put it in terms of the stark question: Did Jesus go to Jerusalem "to work or to die"? Does the central message of Christianity concern the kind of things Jesus did, which other people must do as they follow him, or about his unique salvific death? If the former, why the cross? If the latter, why all the earlier material in the Gospels?

This problem is easily seen acted out in church life. Some Christians, some congregations and some whole multicongregational denominations have been grasped by the vision of Jesus announcing and inaugurating God's kingdom. Jesus went about doing good, healing people, feasting with sinners, bringing new life and hope in all directions. People today are still captivated by that Jesus, by that agenda. They sign on: *This*, they think, *is the man we want to follow!* And often they do wonderful things in his name. They really can, and sometimes do, make the world a better place. But then there comes a problem. How strange, how sad, that Jesus' public career was so brutally cut short! He was just getting going—he was on a roll! So much more needed to be done, so many more lepers to be healed, so many more people to catch his vision of a world set right. So what was the cross all about? And why do the Evangelists seem to highlight it in the way they do? Some, indeed, have suggested that, for some of the evangelists at least (Luke comes to mind), the cross has no real interpretation, no atonement theology attached to it: Jesus is simply putting into operation the agenda he announced at the start. Such a reading, of course, is bound to find Paul particularly opaque. It might be said that sometimes this has been convenient. "Kingdom churches," if we can call them that, have not always been happy with Paul's ethics. But actually the problem goes far deeper. Paul, obviously rooted in the death and resurrection of Jesus, and seldom mentioning the kingdom of God, has little appeal for those who glimpse Jesus at his kingdom work and find themselves called to join in.

For other Christians, of course, the cross of Jesus is at the very center of the faith. "Christ died for our sins according to the scriptures!" Nor is this simply a Protestant innovation. Medieval Catholicism produced a thousand pictures of the crucified Savior for every one image of Jesus healing, feasting or teaching. The Gospels then appear—as some would-be critical scholarship has argued they should be read—as "passion narratives with extended introductions." In Nick Perrin's phrase, the Gospels simply supply the "chips and dip," an optional hors d'oeuvre before we go on to the real main course, the real red meat, of Pauline theology. As we saw earlier, for many Christians it would have been quite sufficient if Jesus of Nazareth had been born of a virgin and died on a cross (and raised again afterward). They have no real use for anything in between. So why did Matthew, Mark, Luke and John spend such a long time telling us about it all? Purely out of antiquarian interest? Certainly not. The four Gospels are quite clear that the kingdom and the cross go together, but much of the later Western church has found that conjunction very, very difficult, and has often played kingdom theology off against cross theology, because it's had one vision of reality about God making the world a better place and another vision of reality about God saving people from their sins, and never the twain shall meet. But both in canon and in real history they do meet. They belong together. For some, indeed, Jesus' death looks more and more strange: a bizarre event in itself, with no apparent connection to his kingdom message (except insofar as the political power brokers misunderstood him). For Jesus in some sense to have *intended* his forthcoming death would make him, within our modern worldviews, simply "weird" (as one writer actually said), as though the whole thing was a kind of strange assisted suicide with some peculiar theology stuck on top of it. And unless we are going to diminish everything into that fog of misunderstandings, we are bound to ask, as a matter of history: how, within a first-century Jewish mindset, might Jesus of Nazareth have thought about, conceived, imagined as a matter of vocation, a vision of the kingdom which would be accomplished through such an event—this vision of his own forthcoming death as the climax, the key moment, of his kingdom program?

This can be asked as a matter of historical investigation. Such historical work is not designed to replace the canon with a historian's reconstruction, but to offer a hypothesis to explain what the church has manifestly not explained or understood. What then is it that the Evangelists are trying to tell us? They don't think there is a massive disjunction between kingdom and cross. How does it work for them?

Before answering the question, let us look at the same puzzle from the opposite end. For some traditional Christians, Paul is everything (at least, a particular reading of Paul is everything), and the kingdom of God (on earth as in heaven!) is nothing, or next to nothing. The dangerous possibility that Jesus might want us to *do* things and thereby justify ourselves by our works has led generations of cross-centered Protestants to be very wary of the Gospels with their detailed kingdom agenda and kingdom ethic. Think of the sheep and the goats in Matthew 25: Is "eternal life" and its horrid alternative really to be decided by what people *do?* Thus, in many churches the canonical Gospels, or rather their dismembered fragments, are relentlessly translated into narratives which are "really" about Jesus' salvific death. This of course is not a complete travesty, since the Evangelists do indeed recount many of the incidents in Jesus' public career in such a way as to point forward to Calvary. But the strong tendency in this cross-centered reading of the Gospels is to ignore, for instance, Jesus' bracing Jubilee agenda in Luke 4, or the striking commands about hospitality to strangers in Luke 14, or the cup of cold water in Mark 10, or (again) the "inasmuch" of the sheep and the goats in Matthew 25. At this point (ironically, considering the normal evangelical refusal of Bultmann and all his ways) the tradition that has focused on the cross to the exclusion of the kingdom adopts a more or less exactly Bultmannian hermeneutic: the stories about Jesus are really just reflections of different aspects of the cross-based kerygma—with the difference, of course, that whereas Bultmann thought they didn't actually happen, the evangelical tradition has insisted that they did. This, however, was not in order to explore their kingdom meaning but in order to shore up an endangered belief in scriptural infallibility, which was in turn serving two quite different agendas (modern rationalist apologetic against modern rationalist skepticism, and Protestant freedom over against the pope), neither of which were likely to send such readers back to the question of what Jesus might have thought he was doing when he announced that Israel's God was at last becoming king on earth as in heaven.

It is a question of history, as well as of canon, to ask how in fact, if at all, kingdom and cross belong together. History here (to repeat) is not a way of going behind the canon or falsifying it, but of asking the question the canon itself raises but the church has been very bad at even noticing, let alone answering. This question, I suspect, has been marginalized in much Western theology for a good deal longer than the five hundred years of Protestantism. The split has been instantiated in a variety of positions, both historical and theological. We might think, for instance, of the nineteenth-century picture of Jesus enjoying a successful "Galilean springtime" as he goes about healing and teaching and winning approval—only then to discover that people start to fall away, at which point he moves to "Plan B," going to the cross to force God's hand. Worse, there have been plenty of portraits (popular and would-be scholarly) of Jesus the social activist, launching a protest movement to show people a different way to live and then accidentally falling foul of the authorities, or Jesus the fanatic, with a complex (supposedly biblical) atonement theology in his head, going off to get himself crucified and somehow, inexplicably, healing and feasting and walking on water for a year or two before the moment came. These pictures have in their turn bred reactions in both directions, often picking up energy from the various social, cultural, ecclesiological and (not least) political contexts in which the story has been told, now this way, now that.

The second of those caricatures has been especially popular, all the way back to the great creeds. There, the virgin birth is followed directly by Jesus suffering under Pontius Pilate, and Jesus' endless kingdom is placed toward the end of the narrative, appearing to suggest that Jesus will only inaugurate this kingdom at the very end—which contradicts both the Gospels and Paul. The creeds, of course, record the results of the church's major early controversies. It is a kind of washing list: this is the laundry that we needed to clean up. But since the question of God's kingdom does not seem to have been among the problems to which an agreed solution seemed necessary, Jesus' kingdom inauguration during the course of his public career, and through his death and resurrection, finds no mention in them. That is the problem about taking what is essentially a list of resolved disputes and then using it as the agreed syllabus for the church's teaching. But, to say it one more time, there have been many Christians in the Western world who, with the apparent encouragement of the creeds, would be quite satisfied if Jesus of Nazareth had been born of a virgin and died on a cross and done nothing very much at all in between. That, they would assume, would be what canonical or traditional Christianity was all about. But the canon itself suggests otherwise.

Some, of course, have filled in this blank theologically. Some have claimed that Jesus was teaching us how to go to heaven, which as I've said hardly fits with most of the Gospel material. Some have suggested that he was leading a sinless life in order that his atoning sacrifice would be valid. This, though close to things which Paul and Hebrews both say, is not exactly highlighted in the Gospels themselves. Some have gone further, suggesting that Jesus was fulfilling the Mosaic law in a life of "active obedience," so that the righteousness which would accrue to someone who fulfilled the law might then be imputed to all his people. There are verses in Matthew which can be read that way (Jesus' "fulfilling all righteousness" in Mt 3, and "not coming to abolish but to fulfill the law" in Mt 5). But the particular theological construct implicit in this third proposal is, again, not something one would discover on the surface of the text of any of the four canonical Evangelists. It looks very much as though all such proposals are ways of papering over the very large crack between the (abstract) doctrines of incarnation (Jesus' conception and birth) and atonement (the cross and its saving significance). Once again, perhaps it is these abstractions that are causing the problem. The technical terms *incarnation* and *atonement* are, I believe, true signposts. But what is the reality to which they are pointing?

As far as the canonical evangelists are concerned, *there is no split between kingdom and cross.* The long kingdom narrative leads seamlessly up to the cross; the shadow of the cross falls on many kingdom announcing incidents; when Jesus dies, his kingship is proclaimed, with heavy irony, by the *titulus* over his head: "King of the Jews"! That, one might suggest, is actually a moment of real climax for the Evangelists: having portrayed Jesus as Israel's Messiah all through the narrative, now at last this royal status is proclaimed to all—but only from the cross. This is hugely profound and frequently ignored in the tradition.

For the Evangelists, *the kingdom is the project which is sealed, accomplished, by the cross,* on the one hand, and *the cross is the victory through which the kingdom is established,* on the other. Neither can be reduced to terms of the other, either by reading "kingdom" as the "heaven" to which we go because Jesus died for our sins, or by reading the cross merely as "the inevitable reaction of a wicked world and the 'domination system' against people who try to live differently." It is perfectly proper to ask the canonical Evangelists how the kingdom and the cross might go together—how they went together in the Evangelists' minds, as they clearly did, and how they went together in Jesus' intentionality, as the Evangelists imply they did. This, again, in other words, is not to advance a project behind the backs of the canonical Evangelists but rather to inquire whether their own vision of a single kingdom-and-cross reality corresponds to the aim and intention of Jesus himself. It is, in other words, to try to explain what the church for much of its life has manifestly not even begun to address, namely, what it is that the evangelists themselves are trying to tell us.

(We might note at this point, because it's out there in the media and popular culture, the massive and radical difference between the four canonical Gospels and those other documents, like *Thomas*, which have from time to time attracted the title "Gospel." These mostly Gnostic or semi-Gnostic texts have no interest in Jesus' death and resurrection, and for that reason alone have sometimes been hailed as more primitive or historical. But this is a complete misunderstanding. They offer a de-Judaized picture of a Jesus who was neither inaugurating the kingdom of Israel's God nor dying a meaningful—let alone salvific—death. They do not offer *news* about an *event*—something that has happened as a result of which the world is a different place—but *advice* about how to reorder one's private spirituality or to attain a disembodied salvation. Sadly, this is too close for comfort to some varieties of Protestantism and to some elements in post-Enlightenment culture. These two have sometimes made common cause and lurched toward the Gnostic "Gospels" as if they, rather than the canonical ones, rendered the genuine historical Jesus. Such a move fits well in a culture that has become cynical about any kind of traditional Christian faith and regards it as oppressive and self-serving, preferring instead some version of privatized self-help spirituality or soteriology. This is very like what happened in the middle of the second century, after the fall of the Bar Kochba rebellion. But it is a matter of history, not canonical prejudice, to see this as an utterly false move. Christianity from the beginning, as we know in Paul, was a gospel movement about the events in which Israel's God had acted decisively in the Messiah, Jesus.)

The question to be asked, then, is this: What sort of a kingdom is it that needs the crucifixion of the kingdom bringer for its completion? Or, conversely, what sort of meaning might one give to the cross—what sort of atonement theology might we envision—that effects the establishment of God's kingdom on earth as in heaven? The fact that this feels quite a strange question indicates worryingly that, as I have suggested several times, the entire Western tradition appears not to have allowed the canonical Gospels to make their full impact. Many kingdom theologies seem to have no place for the cross, and many atonement theologies, including "sound" evangelical ones, have no place for God's kingdom on earth as in heaven. Something is badly wrong with this picture. It appears that our contemporary division between kingdom work on the one hand and atonement on the other—which play themselves out in terms of the endless church debates between social ethics and saving souls—are radically misconceived. Our vision of social justice and of salvation have become cruelly detached from one another.

This is cognate with the problem I noted in *Evil and the Justice of God*, namely, that the philosophical problem of evil has been allowed to float free from the cross, while the cross, seen as atonement, has become quite detached from the massive and deeply troubling fact of evil, of all sorts, in the world. My working hypothesis is that the evangelists are reflecting a train of thought and prayer and vocation which was Jesus' own train of thought. Otherwise we'd have to suggest, once more, that Jesus was an unreflective sort of person who just went around doing odd things without really thinking them through or wondering where it would all lead, and that it was the evangelists who were the brilliant and innovative thinkers and theologians, the astonishingly versatile and innovative Scripture interpreters, who took these unreflective actions and put them together into a fresh coherent whole. Such a proposal ought to be counterintuitive, whether we approach the question from the tradition, the canon or from a warm but unthinking piety. That it is not counterintuitive is thus a reflection, not just of critical scholarship, but of the context of Western Christianity within which such scholarship could flourish.

In fact, the four canonical Evangelists insist that it was Jesus himself who did and said what he did in such a way as to generate a web of meaning, leading on from Israel's Scriptures, within which his kingdom inauguration and his forthcoming death would be mutually interpretative. The Evangelists intended to do what they in fact did, namely, to join up kingdom and cross and allow them to mean what they mean in reference to one another. They urge us not to enter into an ahistorical world of "story" in which we might live without ever raising the question of Jesus' own intentionality and mindset, but to allow ourselves to be impacted by the one-off historical facts of a particular human being believing certain things about his own place in the divine plan and acting in accordance with those beliefs. More specifically, I think the Evangelists are telling us on every page that Jesus of Nazareth believed that he was embodying Israel's God in launching his sovereign rule over Israel and the world, and that, as Messiah, he was embodying Israel's own destiny, and that this complex of beliefs would involve him (in fulfillment of ancient prophecy, psalm and story) in being himself apparently defeated at the hands of the pagans. The four canonical Gospels thus offer, I believe, from their four different angles, a compelling hypothesis, not about the abstract narrative world they are constructing but about Jesus himself. When the earliest post-Easter tradition says, as it does, "[He] loved me and gave himself for me" (Gal 2:20) or "Having loved his own who were in the world, he loved them to the end" (Jn 13:1), it makes sense—specifically *Christian* sense, not just post-Enlightenment historiographical sense!—to ask, but was that true of Jesus himself prior to the cross? Did Jesus really live and think and feel like that? Was Jesus himself passionately and compassionately motivated by love? Or is that only true of the way believers now encounter and experience the risen Jesus? The Evangelists themselves portray a Jesus who really was that sort of person and had that sort of impact on people.

That reflection is not simply an interesting fact about the Jesus conveyed by the canonical Gospels. It invites two further methodological elaborations. First, the Jesus of the canonical Gospels is both sovereign and vulnerable. The fact that we believe him to be the second person of the Trinity must not for one moment raise him above the vulnerability of being mocked, spat on, beaten and killed—or the vulnerability of being open to sharp critical historical investigation. Yes, he acts as if he's in charge, and he explains his actions by saying that this is what it looks like when God's in charge. But at the same time there are plots and schemes against him, which reach their head in his arrest, trial, mocking, beating and crucifixion. This is the Jesus the canonical Evangelists offer us, in line here with Paul who speaks of Jesus emptying himself and becoming obedient to the death of the cross. Later tradition (and some current proposals) appear to seek to protect Jesus from the historians' equivalent of the plots, trials, whips and nails, by removing him from the reach of those who ask the awkward did-it-really-happen historical questions, just as some of the Gnostic writings have Jesus being snatched away just before things get nasty, so he doesn't have to suffer and die on the cross. But this, it seems to me, is the scholarly/theological equivalent of Peter's flawed attempt to protect Jesus in the garden. It misses the point. The point is that the kingdom is inaugurated precisely by the vulnerable, canonical, historical Jesus, because the kingdom must come on earth as in heaven. He became vulnerable to the world of his day; is there any reason why we in the church should now take it upon ourselves to do what he forbade Peter and the others to do in the garden, that is, to defend him from attack and arrest? Is it not far more appropriate that we should respect him for who he is, rather than trying to make him into the sort of god with whom we would be able to live a lot more comfortably?

The second methodological elaboration highlights the meaning of love itself. Love does not sit still in safety and persuade the beloved to leap over a separating gap between them. Love goes to meet the beloved in the dangerous territory. Love is the highest mode of knowing, transcending the subject-object distinction which has formed the dilemma on which so much Western thought has been impaled. The canonical Gospels do not offer us a Jesus who can be grasped objectively, pinned to the page like a dead butterfly (to borrow Ben Meyer's graphic image from his discussion of D. F. Strauss).[1] Nor do they offer us a Jesus who is to be known only in the subjective appreciation and appropriation that comes when someone makes the narrative world of the Gospels their own, without reference to events and persons in first-century Palestine. They invite us to a different kind of epistemology, one which corresponds to the driving motive of their central character.

KINGDOM AND RESURRECTION

If it is problematic to put together the kingdom and the cross, there is also a problem about putting together kingdom and cross on the one hand with the resurrection on the other. There is much to say on this subject, but not here and not now. Of course I believe that the resurrection of Jesus is the vital moment in the story, the vital fact at the center of all history, the vital element in the Christian worldview. Of course the Gospel writers themselves, and their first readers, were writing and reading the story of Jesus as the story of one who was alive, who was known in Scripture and bread-breaking, in the *koinɵnia* of the Spirit and in the service of the poor. But the Gospels never forget, what much Protestant scholarship and popular thought, and much would-be orthodox or canonical Christianity has conveniently forgotten, that the resurrection is precisely the resurrection of the kingdom-bringer, the crucified kingdom-bringer, and that these elements are not left behind in the resurrection but rather fulfilled. It is vital in the New Testament that the risen Jesus is known by the mark of the nails and the spear thrust in his side, and that the resurrection is not simply about his being alive again but about his *ascension*, his new status as the world's true Lord—in other words, as the fulfillment of the kingdom agenda he began in his public career. This contrasts sharply with the notion, which has been popular in many so-called liberal circles, that all that the early

---

[1]Ben F. Meyer, *Aims of Jesus* (Pittsburgh: Pickwick, 2002), p. 99.

church really meant by resurrection was that the spirit or influence of Jesus somehow lived on, as a spiritual presence, even though his body was moldering in a tomb somewhere. The real objection to that is not simply, as conservative theology has responded, that this denies the great miracle, but rather that it makes no sense of the resurrection as the climax of Jesus' work of bringing God's kingdom on earth as in heaven. It deconstructs the narrative the Evangelists are at great pains to tell. The four canonical Evangelists see the resurrection and enthronement of Jesus as the conclusion of the story they had been telling all along. This, they are saying, is what it looks like when the agenda Jesus announced at the start is fulfilled.

Nor is the resurrection of Jesus seen by the Evangelists as a straightforward proof of Jesus' divinity in the sense people normally give that today. When Thomas makes his great confession, *kyrios mou kai theos mou*, the circle which is thereby closed with the Johannine prologue ("The Word became flesh. . . . No one has ever seen God, but the only begotten God has revealed him," literally *exegeted* him) indicates that we are therefore to reread the whole Gospel narrative as the story of God in human form, not simply to say, "Well! So he was divine all that time," but rather, "So that's what the incarnate God looks like; that's what he does; that's how he brings his kingdom and overthrows the ruler of the world." Otherwise the "proof of divinity" line leads only to a sigh of relief from the would-be orthodox Christian: There we are, the box has been checked, we're all right. Instead, in the Gospels the resurrection of Jesus leads to a quite different train of thought: Jesus really is God's Messiah (the verdicts of the courts have been reversed), and must have been Messiah all along; new creation has begun, and this must all along have been the point of God becoming king; all the forces of evil that stood in the way of God's rescue of creation and of Israel have been dealt with, and this must have been the meaning of the cross; Jesus is now to be enthroned as the world's true Lord, having done what in Scripture only Israel's God himself gets to do; and we, the witnesses of this event, are commissioned and equipped for the major task that lies ahead, establishing the fact of God's kingdom by the methods of God's kingdom. That is what the book of Acts is all about.

We must not short circuit the Israel dimension of the story the Gospels are telling. We will falsify it, forcing it into a different mold of our own making, instead of opening up our worldview to the possibility that it might itself need remaking by God, precisely through the process of reading and living the canonical story.

It will not do, then, to hold up the resurrection as a way of avoiding, or sidelining, the ongoing historical task. The resurrection means what it means because it is the resurrection *of this Jesus*, not of someone else. The church will constantly be tempted to use the resurrection itself as a way of avoiding the challenge of being the kingdom-bearing people. Rather, the resurrection establishes Jesus' people as people of new creation in themselves but also, as the sign of this, people through whom new creation happens. And one of the tasks of that new creation is precisely telling and retelling the story of who Jesus always was. This is the ultimate answer to the line of thought that ran from Bultmann through Gerhard Ebeling to Hans Conzelmann and others: writing the Gospels did not represent a failure of nerve on the part of the first or second generation of Christians. Rather, it represented a commitment to the new creation, to the kingdom of God on earth as in heaven, launched in the events to which the Gospels give us genuine historical access and now let loose into the world through Easter and Ascension themselves and through the gift of the Spirit to Jesus' followers. If Jesus was Messiah, and if his death was the kingdom-bringing event, then his resurrection means that new creation has begun. So often preachers at Easter say, "Jesus is alive again; therefore he's in heaven; therefore we'll go to be with him one day." That's not what the evangelists say. Rather, they say, "Jesus is alive again; therefore new creation has begun; therefore we have a job to do." And part of that job is precisely *to tell the story*, the story of Jesus as the climax of the story of Israel's God and the climax of the story of Israel, the means of the world's redemption.

PROSPECTS

Where might all these reflections lead us? There are many tasks still remaining. Biblical scholarship in the Western world has had a particular slant. It has not favored big-picture thinking; it's been much easier, for a long time, to earn a Ph.D. in biblical studies if you are an ISTJ on the Myers-Briggs scale than if your first letters are ENF. This has to do, not least, with the left-hemisphere dominance of Western culture, the propensity to privilege detail over insight, grasp over reach. (On this, see the remarkable work of Ian McGilchrist.)[2] But big-picture hypotheses are what we need just now. We need intuitive thinkers as well as details people. That, granted, is a problem when someone is doing a degree, for which accuracy in detail is an important requirement, but it's vital nonetheless. We need to look at the ways in which Jesus' kingdom proclamation broke open the molds of his day and perhaps of our day too. And there is plenty of room for this. The study of the Gospels in the light of all we now know about first-century Judaism positively cries out for exploration of big, new subjects: Jesus and the temple, Jesus and priesthood, Jesus and economics. There are literally thousands of exegetical and historical projects waiting to be undertaken from new angles of vision. I have no sense that my own previous work has solved all these problems. Think, as one example, of the meaning of the Last Supper: when Jesus wanted to give his followers the clue to the meaning of this forthcoming death, and how it related to the kingdom he'd been announcing and inaugurating; he didn't give them a theory, he gave them a meal, and a meal cannot remain an idea in your head. It feeds you, it strengthens and sustains you. You share it, you do it. It feeds you and other people too, and that is part of the meaning of the whole thing. We need to explore what all that might mean, in new ways. I hardly began to scratch the surface of all that in *Jesus and the Victory of God*, and it remains central and vital.

Work such as I am recommending, of course, is not exempt from the risk of being merely quirky. That's always the risk when you're reconceiving big ideas. But most of the supposedly leading Gospel scholarship of the last century has itself been quirky in the extreme, proceeding (if I am even a quarter right) from wrong premises, addressing wrong questions and coming up with answers which did no justice either to Jesus or to the Evangelists. We need, not least, a quite new form

---

[2]Ian McGilchrist, *The Master and His Emissary* (New Haven: Yale University Press, 2009).

criticism. It's a perfectly sensible question to ask why the traditions about Jesus got shaped the way they did. But Bultmann launched his form criticism of the Gospels on the basis of a hypothesis about early Christianity in which the earliest form of the faith was basically non-Jewish, so that reflection on Israel's Scriptures must have come in at a second stage. The Jesus Seminar, including Dominic Crossan, followed Bultmann down this blind alley. We now know—or should know—that this was absurd. It is far more likely to be the other way round, with Gospel traditions beginning with stories about Jesus that were initially told, by devout Jews with Scripture in their heads and their hearts, in such a way as to echo that Scripture, and developing into stories which, in a different context, were flattened down into something more like Hellenistic *chreiai*. But that is only one example; there could be many more.

If there are new worlds of scholarship waiting to be opened up, what about fresh readings of the Gospels in the service of the church? What is the "so what"? This, I believe, is not basically about apologetics—the older I get, the more I become suspicious of that project in at least some of its forms—but about *mission*. Somehow, the whole complex of kingdom, cross and resurrection must play out into a full-orbed gospel-rooted mission which will be significantly unlike the social gospel mission that forgot about the cross, or the "Jesus died for you" mission that forgot about the kingdom. One of the great breakthrough moments for me when I was first struggling with historical Jesus questions was John 20:21: *"As* the father has sent me, *so* I send you." That derivative correspondence—the "as" and the "so," with Jesus' own mission the source and template for that of his followers, as they receive the Spirit—suddenly opens up an entire hermeneutic world, demanding that the church again and again study the historical mission of Jesus not just to find out the back history of the crucified and risen One, but to realign itself with the shape and content of that mission in order to carry out its own. Jesus' own mission becomes the template and the energizing force for all that the church then has to do and be. We are to be for the world what Jesus was for Israel. You will only understand the mission of the church in the world if, instead of using the canon as a closed story, a charmed circle in which it means what it means but which you can't break into or out of, you go back to Jesus himself, which is what the canon is pleading with you to do, so that you can then see who he was and is and then discern, in the power of his Spirit, who we have to do and be. If you want to know what that looks like, read the book of Acts: a story of doing the kingdom, bearing the kingdom, suffering for the kingdom, and eventually announcing the kingdom under the nose of Caesar himself. That is what it looks like when the church goes out, with the breath of Jesus in our lungs, to tell the world that he is its rightful Lord. Sometimes people get hurt; sometimes a thousand people get converted; sometimes all sorts of things in between take place; and somehow the Gospel gets to Rome, to the center of human power and authority, to announce there that Jesus is Lord and God is king, openly and unhindered.

To do this, however, the church needs constantly to reconnect with the real Jesus, who the canonical Gospels give us but whom we have so badly misunderstood. The world will pull these things apart again, will lure us into the smaller worlds of *either* social work *or* saving souls for a disembodied eternity. Our various Western worldviews will force on us political agendas that are culled from elsewhere, which we can feel good about because they don't have the cross attached to them. Gnosticism is so much *easier* than Christian mission: easier epistemologically, especially in today's Western world, and easier socially and politically too. You don't have to worry about justice in the world if you go that route. Beware of atonement theologies that deliver a type of evangelical preaching which is actually detached from what Scripture actually says! (Two or three years ago a book was written which attempted to explain what the Bible says about the atonement. It had a lot of Old Testament, and a lot of Paul—but almost nothing about the Gospels. A travesty. The Gospels are not just the back story for Pauline theology.) And those who, in order to renounce Gnosticism, become glorified social workers will find all too easily that they are caught up in political agendas culled from elsewhere, which can be adopted with no need for the cross—the cross as the means of victory, the *only* means by which genuine kingdom victories are won. For this we need the whole gospel story, the whole story *as history*. History then; history now.

Once all that is in place, there is indeed an apologetic task. But this task is not (*pace* C. S. Lewis and others) to prove Jesus' divinity or anything like it, but to speak wisely and (historically) truthfully about Jesus and to show that the Gospels—as they are, not as the tradition has shrunk them into being!—really do make sense. Historically speaking, the case still needs to be made in public that the overwhelmingly best explanation for the rise of early Christianity is that Jesus of Nazareth really was and really did and said what the canonical Gospels say he was, did and said. It is no shame, in my view, to hear the questions of the skeptical historian and to answer them with all the first-century tools we can muster. It simply won't do to say, "Never mind the history; feel the power of this story": every sensible skeptic knows how powerful stories are. As Dom Crossan once said in my hearing, Mark's Gospel is a wonderful movie script, and because we all enjoyed the movie we all supposed it was true. Please note, I do not believe that historical research can compel faith. But, as I have said often enough in relation more specifically to the resurrection, genuine historical research is very good at cutting back the undergrowth behind which skeptical arguments had been hiding, and showing them up as worthless. This process, while not a full apologetic in the high modernist sense, can and should be a genuine *praeparatio evangelica*, clarifying and posing more sharply the ultimate challenge of the Christian message.

Otherwise—and this is my perceived problem with Karl Barth, or at least with those who have followed through some aspects of his thought—it really does appear to me that the gospel is presented as a closed, charmed circle, where we don't allow any natural theology, which protects itself against the ravages of negative historical scholarship at the massive cost of shutting itself off against any possibility of genuine inquiry from outside. There is no way out and no way in. It is all very well to say, "Come inside this circle, and you'll see it all makes sense," but that is no real argument to someone who says, "From outside I can see that you are living in your own deluded little world." And that isn't simply a matter of apologetics; it applies to politics and similar spheres as well. What good is it if I say to the government, "You ought to remit Third World debt," or "You ought to treat asylum seekers as vulnerable human beings, not as criminals," if they can retort, "That's all very well from within your charmed faith-based circle, but we live in the real world and you have nothing to say to us." No wonder Paul's speech on the Areopagus has had a bad press in neo-orthodox circles. Paul shouldn't have tried to build, they have said, on the signals of God in their culture. Isn't it bound to end up in compromise? But the whole point of Israel's tradition—of Abraham's vocation!—was that Israel should be the people *through whom* God would go out and address the world, in order to rescue the world. When Jesus said "You are the light of the world," he expressly warned against putting a bucket over that light. He presupposes that the world can and will see the light when it's shining and will be attracted to it.

And it is precisely the canonical Gospels which take us, not into a world simply suffused with the light of the resurrection, but into the pre-Easter world in which Jesus himself said such things. The fact that the Gospels are written from the perspective of Easter both does and doesn't mean that they tell things in that light. Yes, they wouldn't have bothered to tell the stories if they hadn't believed that Jesus was risen. But they explicitly encourage us to see things through the lens of the disciples' pre-Easter understanding. The Gospel writers themselves stress that the disciples did not, at the time, understand; they want us, their readers, to get inside the minds not only of Jesus' first followers, struggling to work out what he was talking about, but also of Jesus himself at that same time, frustrated at their lack of comprehension. They want us to understand what it was like beforehand, even though from time to time (Jn 2:22; Mk 9:10) they show that they, the storytellers, can see the longer end in sight. It matters to them that we hold that perspective at one remove and grasp what it was like in the days before they had even understood that Jesus really did have to die, let alone that he would rise again. Of course, without the resurrection there is no gospel. But it won't do to say that all the Gospels give us is the risen Jesus with some back story material attached. That's just back to Bultmann. Of course *we* know Jesus *as* the risen One who is with us today. But we only know the resurrection, in a canonical/biblical fashion, if we understand the resurrection precisely as the resurrection *of the crucified kingdom bringer.* To understand the resurrection in any other way is to misunderstand it, to snatch it out of its canonical and biblical context and make it serve some other set of agendas.

Thus, even though they are telling the whole pre-Easter story because they believe that Jesus was raised from the dead and is therefore the Messiah, the Evangelists are telling it in such a way as to insist that their readers need to know *what it was like then,* for the disciples and for Jesus himself. It is, after all, the pre-Easter Jesus who goes about doing and speaking the kingdom, and precisely if we say, with the letter to the Hebrews, that Jesus is the same yesterday, today and forever, we cannot use that as an excuse for imagining a docetic Jesus as today's Jesus and then projecting that back onto the pre-Easter world, as so much would-be orthodoxy has done. No: we know him today, if we know him truly, as the kingdom bringer, the crucified kingdom bringer, the crucified and risen kingdom bringer. We must continue to hold together what the Gospels refuse to split apart. We only know the meaning of the resurrection, and hence of present Christian faith, in the light of the kingdom and the cross. Without that, the very word *resurrection* loses its meaning and becomes merely a cipher for "the new spirituality." The point about resurrection is that the risen Jesus, though now immortal and beyond the reach of suffering and death, *is nevertheless the same Jesus who went about announcing God's kingdom and dying to bring it about.*

For all this we need to be, as Paul puts it, "transformed by the renewing of our minds." It is history as well as faith which enables us to say "he loved me and gave himself for me." It will not do to shun history, to declare it off limits, just because there is such a thing as skeptical historiography—any more than we should shun the use of money because there is a god called Mammon, or make ourselves eunuchs because of the goddess Aphrodite. There is a proper history and an improper history, and though they may sometimes look alike they need to be distinguished, and the former not rejected because of the existence of the latter. There is a large task still waiting here, namely, the fresh articulation of a historical method which will not be dictated to from within the shrunken world of post-Enlightenment epistemology, but will rather be open to genuine knowledge of the past and will not dismiss it on the spurious grounds that there is, after all, no real world outside the text. When faith says, "He loved me and gave himself for me," it can properly look to history to back it up. Otherwise we lay ourselves open once more to the obvious charge of fantasy—to which Western Christianity, alas, has so often been prone.

Time would fail me to tell of the meetings with the risen Jesus in John 20–21, where these epistemological issues are played out in terms of wonderful human drama. Here is Mary, who recognizes the risen Jesus through her tears and at the sound of her name being called. Here is Thomas, who wants to touch and see and is invited to do so (rather than being told off for coming with the wrong epistemology). Here is Peter and the challenge "Do you love me?" inviting Ludwig Wittgenstein's fascinating comment, "It is *love* that believes the resurrection." But here too are the encounters in the earlier parts of the Gospels: with Peter in Luke 5, Mary of Bethany in Luke 10, Matthew in Matthew 9 and so on. Jesus meets the disciples where they are, as we see in the wonderful exchange between Jesus and Peter, where Jesus finally comes down to Peter's level: "Simon, son of John, do you love me?" and then, when all Peter can say is "Yes, Lord, you know I'm your friend," phrasing his third question in Peter's terms: "Simon, son of John, are you my friend?" We need these stories; we need this historical Jesus. If these are just fantasies, they are no good to us; because we need the real Jesus, with the dust of the Galilean streets on his feet, to meet us in our dusty worlds, with the dust of today's streets on our shoes and in our souls, with the worries and weight of the world on our shoulders, with fears and suspicions and prejudices and misunderstandings in our hearts and homes. It is the real Jesus, the historical Jesus, the Jesus of yesterday who anchors our hold on the Jesus of today and tomorrow, who we know in the canonical Gospels, through the proper historical research which discovers what those canonical Gospels were really telling us rather than constructing a different Jesus behind or above them (as is done every time someone writes about Jesus without making front and center the fact that he was the kingdom bringer!)—it is this real Jesus who challenges the church, the scholar, the skeptic, the whole wide world, with the cross and resurrection as the kingdom-establishing events. He presents himself afresh through the multidimensional historical work which opens up what the Gospels were really trying to tell us, so that no one will imagine for a moment (as they are bound to do when listening to the antihistorical post-Barthian construct) that this message is the preserve and prerogative of the church, which so many have rejected. He is, and remains, the Jesus who comes to seek and to save the lost; to rescue sinners, not the righteous. To all alike he gives the same command, the command which draws together kingdom, cross and resurrection: "Follow me!"

If we are to obey that command, we need, not simply the knowledge of the post-Pentecost church that Jesus is alive and is with them in the present, but the knowledge the four canonical Gospels give us of who Jesus was and what he did. He is the same yesterday, today and forever; but we may be deceived, not least self-deceived, about who he is today, and only by regularly rerooting ourselves in the faithful stories of who he actually was can we be refreshed in faith and witness and enabled to avoid inventing an idol which, however much we call it Jesus, may be not quite the same person, and may serve our own ends. If the Messiah is not raised, said Paul, your faith is futile and you are still in your sins. And, we might add, if the Messiah who died is not the Jesus whose history we know through Matthew, Mark, Luke and John, our faith is groundless and we are still in our fantasies. We need the truly historical Jesus, not as a clever construct we can detect behind the canon or play off against it, but as the truly canonical and truly historical Jesus who (thank God!) we can still detect behind the later traditions that have screened out what the canon itself was trying to say. Scripture is the witness to Jesus. Woe betide us if, for whatever reason, we turn this round and make Jesus merely the presupposition of something we then call Scripture. You can always tell, because when Jesus takes a back seat things get out of balance: the kingdom out of balance with the cross, or the kingdom and the cross out of balance with the resurrection, or the kingdom, cross and resurrection out of balance with the life of the church. It is Jesus we follow, not (primarily!) Matthew, Mark, Luke or John. They are servants through whom we see Jesus, but Jesus is more than the sum total of their sense perceptions or our perceptions of their sense perceptions. And Jesus himself calls us to follow him, and calls us thereby into the wide open world, the world where God remains sovereign and vulnerable, the world of historical reality, the world of tomorrow's challenges: God's world, the world over which Jesus is already Lord and to which he will return to set all things right at last.

PART TWO

PAUL AND THE PEOPLE OF GOD

6

Glimpsing the Glory

Paul's Gospel, Righteousness and the Beautiful Feet of N. T. Wright

EDITH M. HUMPHREY

How, then, shall they call upon One in whom they have not believed?
And how shall they believe in One of whom they have not heard?
And how shall they hear of him without a herald? And how shall they
act as heralds, unless they are sent? As it is written, "How beautiful are
the feet of those who bring the good news of good things!"

ROMANS 10:14-15[1]

MY FIRST WEEK OF HIGH SCHOOL WAS TRAUMATIC. I had humiliated myself the first day by confiding to my mellow-yellow classmates of the late 1960s that I wanted to study Latin because it was the first step to reading the New Testament in its original Greek. That had evoked a titter of amusement, but it was nothing compared to what followed. I had ensconced myself, all 5'8" eager-beaver of me, in the front row. Spellbound by the British accent and the antics of my Latin teacher, I had forgotten about the length of my legs, sprawled out before me. Mr. Glazin was traversing the space between his desk and ours, waxing eloquent about Roman epic poetry (*Arma virumque canō,*

---

[1]Scripture quoted in this chapter is the author's translation.

Troiae qui primus ab oris); and how he would prepare us to read it. He made a sharp pirouette as he came to the side row, recommenced his pacing and tripped over my clodhoppers.

"McEwan," he intoned, "You have big feet: big *fat* feet!" I was undone: this was the cruelest blow, because—he could never have known it! Mine were size 11, width E, and at thirteen, with an adorable cheerleader to my right, that made for shame. My grandmother was not helpful when she recounted her youthful encounter with a man who had remarked, "Well, my wee gell, if ye fall doon, it won't be for want o' props to hold ye up!" I am much comforted that in Isaiah and Romans beautiful feet have less to do with size or shape than with direction and alacrity.

This insight was confirmed as I sat at the feet of my mentor and friend, the then Rev. Dr. N. T. Wright, during graduate studies at McGill. (Academics in Canada often wear sandals with woolen socks during the teaching season, so I have no acquaintance with Bishop Tom's feet per se!) As this audience knows, his proclamation of the gospel was (and is) beautiful, in both manner and content. He has directed numerous ears and hearts towards the One upon whom we should call. Into many fields his feet have ventured, and his trumpet has been carefully tuned to a variety of contexts, but always it gives a certain note: Jesus, the Messiah, crucified and risen, is LORD[2] of all!

Some scholars, when they produce two versions of their work, appear to be performing a kind of confidence trick. Usually the academic work comes first and then it is judiciously "dumbed down" for the nonspecialist: bottom-line decisions are emphasized, but the lines of argument obscured, with a verifying nod in footnotes to the earlier more academic tome. One can hardly blame academics for this procedure since arguments between specialists are notoriously hard to translate. By contrast, Bishop Tom has authentically walked in two worlds, sometimes begin-

---

[2]I here extend into the purview of the New Testament the practice of the English Bible in which the holy name of God is indicated by LORD spelled out in small capitals, signaling the Hebrew YHWH. My purpose is to capture the conviction of the New Testament writers (and Bishop Wright) that Jesus is to be identified in this way, as can be seen most clearly in 1 Cor 8:6 (cf. Deut 6:4) and Phil 2:5-11 (cf. Is 45:23). It is helpful to remember that punctuation and majuscules/minuscules are editorial decisions in transmitting the text of the New Testament.

ning the publication of his thoughts on the popular level because what he has to say concerns the general public as much as the academy. There are many who would disagree with the recent indictment of John Piper that the bishop's biblical analysis "leaves many ordinary folk not with the rewarding 'ah-ha' experience of illumination, but with a paralyzing sense of perplexity."[3] I have discovered that when students begin with Wright's presentation of the gospel, centered on God's action in Jesus, then his teaching on justification and righteousness (*dikaiosyn*™) fall into place, without vulnerability to this charge of abstruseness. To be sure, those with a particular formation find themselves perplexed, since they applaud his trenchant critique of certain liberal or revisionist arguments, but find themselves challenged in matters that contradict their earlier education. Consider a potential donor to our seminary who informed a bemused first-year student, "When you can tell me the difference between the active and passive suffering of Jesus, then I may consider a donation!" Alas, even if this student had mastered this in-house Reformed debate, her challenger had no intent to pursue the matter beyond using it as a shibboleth! For those not so confined, however, Wright's construal of *dikaiosyn*™ is "Not an Academic Question."[4]

So, where do the feet of N. T. Wright go? First, they enter the ancient world, and especially the Scriptures, which this herald invokes as a lamp for his feet and a light to mark the path. Second, they have gone into the camp of the faithful, into debate among other New Testament scholars (including those who also bear the label "New Perspective") and into the tangled field of the public arena. These multivalent feet show the bishop's conviction that though the Scriptures are the library of the church, they are also open to public reading and discussion: the incarnate Word has come into our space-time world.[5]

There is, however, a particular set of questions that emerges when the community of faith reads his work. We will begin with his treatment of the gospel and the righteousness of God, move on to apocalyp-

---

[3] John Piper, *The Future of Justification: A Response to N. T. Wright* (Wheaton, Ill.: Crossway, 2007), p. 24.
[4] Trevin Wax, "The Justification Debate: A Primer," *Christianity Today* 53, no. 6 (2009): 34-36.
[5] N. T. Wright, *Justification: God's Plan and Paul's Vision* (Downers Grove, Ill.: IVP Academic, 2009), p. 39.

tic language, especially as it relates to the doctrine of the ascension, and close with his stance as scholar and leader. Throughout, we will see how Bishop Tom moves beyond his brief as historian, literary critic and wise church leader, assuming the role of "psychopomp," encouraging us, like C. S. Lewis's energetic Reepicheep, "further in" (if not "further up") to catch a glimpse of glory. If, at a few points, I endeavor to point out where these beautiful feet may have misstepped or halted, please interpret this as a clumsy service to "wash the feet of the saints" or to further our bold concourse as siblings in Christ.

RIGHTEOUSNESS

I was, when I met Bishop Tom, a young Salvation Army officer, trained to share the gospel by using booklets such as "The Four Spiritual Laws." But I was also a newly minted and avid pro-lifer, impressed by the spiritual vitality of Roman Catholic friends. I was chagrined that I had learned about this urgent response of the gospel from those who "did not have assurance of their salvation because they believed in works-righteousness." Their love for Jesus and their fruit was manifest: what sense was I to make of all this? Given the "bridge" characteristics of Anglicanism, it is hardly surprising that my dilemma was addressed by a then youngish Anglican priest-scholar. He was like the Levites in Joshua who marked where the river bottom was firm so that God's people might take memorial stones celebrating the saving act that God himself had wrought (Josh 4:3). We must "let Scripture be Scripture," he insisted, permitting the Bible to retain its mystery even when it opposes our neat interpretive schemas.[6]

Bishop Tom discerns that the Pauline gospel is the proclamation of Jesus as Lord, and that the "righteousness of God" is God's very own righteousness, not a statement about us (whether by imputation, impartation or infusion). This very One is himself the LORD, who has shown forth the magnificent righteousness of God—a God faithful to his covenant, as we hear in Daniel 9, and consistent in all that he says and does. Here was the answer to my dilemma concerning Catholic friends:

---

[6]Ibid., p. 40.

salvation is by the actions of God in Jesus, whom we recognize as the LORD who has died and has been raised. It is the LORD who saves, not our knowledge: we are Christians, not Gnostics.

But some have worried that N. T. Wright has compromised the gospel in building upon insights of James Dunn and Ed Sanders. Astonishingly, one critic complains that Bishop Tom does not spell out what he means by the Lordship of Jesus. He seizes upon a paragraph in the bishop's work that he considers to be a "summary description" of lordship. In this passage, however, Bishop Tom is describing the result of the proclamation about the Lord—the liberation of men and women, and the formation of a community of love.[7] Having confused the result of the gospel with its content, it is no wonder he complains that Bishop Tom emphasizes ecclesiology over soteriology. But he has missed the point. In fussing about the reconfiguration of justification, many miss that the first plank in Wright's reading of St. Paul is neither ecclesiology nor soteriology, but Christology and theology! Bishop Tom demonstrates by way of 1 Corinthians 8 and Philippians 2 that to say "Jesus is LORD" means that the Son, with the Father, is worshiped and accorded "the Name."[8] St. Paul's gospel is about this very identification of Jesus with the Old Testament LORD: the crucified and risen Messiah is far greater than Israel could have imagined, and to him every knee must therefore bow.

Critics also fail to see how Wright combines the insights of Dunn and Sanders without following their views slavishly. Moreover, they do not follow the Bishop's arguments through, for example, Romans 9–11. There we are shown how Israel tried to establish her own righteousness by means of the works of Torah (Dunn interprets these as circumcision, Sabbath and kosher laws) and so missed out on the great incarnation of God's own righteousness among them in Jesus. Because such critics do not carefully follow the lines of Wright's own exegesis, they do not see the use that Bishop Tom makes of these other scholars: they are helpful

---

[7]Cornelis P. Venema, "What Did Saint Paul Really Say," in *Answering the Challenges to the Doctrine of Justification By Faith Alone*, ed. G. L. W. Johnson, David Wells, and G. P. Waters (Wheaton, Ill.: Crossway, 2006), pp. 42-43. Venema quotes N. T. Wright, *What Saint Paul Really Said* (Grand Rapids: Eerdmans, 1997), p. 61.
[8]Wright, *What St. Paul Really Said*, pp. 66-68.

in establishing the character of Judaism at the time of Jesus so that the righteousness of God can be seen in all its glory. The proclamation of the gospel—Jesus, the crucified and risen Messiah is LORD—illumines God's righteousness and faithfulness toward his people. In Bishop Tom's understanding of God's righteousness and justification, we find two great treasures: first, a sturdy defense of the distinction between God and the creation; second, a robust sense of reality.

Point one is key to worship. Protestants need to be reminded that if we are saved on the basis of our own faith, then faith becomes a "work"—the very trap they have sought to avoid has ensnared them, as they become captive to fideism. Moreover, if the gospel is all about righteousness credited or imparted to me, then the scriptural narrative is really about *me*, not about a mighty God whose arm has saved. We need, in this individualistic age, a sturdy defense of the difference between God and me. We are not evangelical Marias, singing, "I have confidence in confidence alone!"

The second factor, his robust sense of reality, has made some nervous, thinking that Bishop Wright is importing works righteousness through the back door. He insists that we have to read the *whole* of Romans, including bits that talk about a future judgment based on our deeds. Scripture must be heard to say what it actually says, even when there are some puzzling paradoxes. We cannot excise the statement "God will render to each according to his [or her] works" (Rom 2:6) in order to highlight the declaration that a person "is justified . . . apart from works of Torah" (Rom 3:28). The works of Torah do not justify; but the fruit of our lives (continuous perseverance in well-doing) is to match what God has said in acquitting us. What God declares about us in the present (that we are "righteous") must cohere with what is actually true of us in the future, or he is not a righteous judge. In the last days, what is known within the household of faith will become "public knowledge"—clear for all to see because we will share in the glory of Christ.[9] But this comes by way of Jesus, not by way of the Torah. God is not engaging in make believe: what he says actually will come to pass.

---

[9]Ibid., p. 119.

We are indebted to Bishop Tom for putting righteousness, faithfulness and faith in their proper places. Those who take the time to read through his treatment of various passages will see that he is not dismissing the importance of human faith but giving it content—we are called to faith *in the God who raised Jesus from the dead.* Nor will we be led back to thinking that we can earn God's favor—for God is the righteous one who shows his faithfulness in Jesus and calls us into new life. Bishop Tom's insistence that we let God be God and Scripture be Scripture is salutary both for a church community that has devolved into sentimentality and for Christians who have, all unwitting, made doctrinal knowledge or human confidence into a work that avails with God. It is because of what God has done in Christ that we have, in Bishop Tom's own words, been "enable[d] to become . . . the truly human beings that [we] are meant to be."[10]

We glimpse the glory! But here I must pause, stopping for a brief moment to ask whether we might have glimpsed even more had our theological Virgil not been quite so rigorous in maintaining his very important distinctions. Yes, we must maintain the difference between the righteousness of our divine Judge and his declaration that we may be, because of Jesus, "in the right." Yes, a judge never gives his own justice to the defendant, even when that pleader is declared innocent. But there are hints in the Gospels and the Letters that we are not in any ordinary courtroom. For God's courtroom is also his throne room and temple, and where the glory of the Lord abounds, strange things happen. The astonishing nature of these goings-on is intimated in that perplexing verse, "For us he has made him sin, who knew no sin, that we might become the righteousness of God in him" (2 Cor 5:21). Does this constitute an Achilles' heel for the beautiful feet of N. T. Wright, and his argument about *dikaiosyn™ theou?* I do not believe so—rather, this is the exception that proves or demonstrates the rule.

In virtually every case of Paul's letters God's righteousness remains his very own. But here St. Paul associates the righteousness of God

---

[10]Ibid., p. 43.

with humanity (the "we"). Bishop Tom mitigates the shock by reference to apostolic activity: St. Paul and the others "incarnate" or embody God's *dikaiosyn*™ as they proclaim God the Reconciler. After all,
2 Corinthians 2–5 has mounted a defense of Paul's apostolic mission.[11]
But the bishop's reading, I think, does not heed all the rich nuances of
this extended passage, nor does it fit perfectly with the immediate
argument in chapter 5. Certainly, the apostle has had need to defend
his apostleship among the Corinthians. However, the situation in
2 Cor 3–5 is similar to that other more impassioned oration in chapters
11–13. There, Paul asks the rhetorical question "Do you think that all
along we have been defending ourselves?" (2 Cor 12:19)—and the answer that he wants to hear is "No!" His foundational purpose has not
been to mount an apology but to build up the Corinthians. Similarly
here: Paul has indeed compared himself to Moses, dubbed the Corinthians his own "letter of recommendation," alluded to his vulnerability, reminded them of his suffering. But he has also spoken of "the
unveiled faces" of "all," of the transformation of all, of the light shining
in "our hearts" (over against the blindness of unbelievers), of "all of us"
who must appear before the judgment seat and who hope for the resurrected life. Indeed, in the verses just prior to the one in question, Paul
has been talking about Christ dying for all (2 Cor 5:14), about "anyone
in Christ" and about all things becoming new (v. 17). We must remember that the "we" in Paul is notoriously difficult and sometimes
unstable—here, as in Ephesians. In the context of statements about
"all" and "all things," it is not likely that this phrase can be tamed by a
plea of extravagant language concerning apostolic proclamation. Could
the same Paul who has contrasted old covenant and new by juxtaposing Moses' privileged illumination over against the transfiguration of
the whole church really intend to limit incarnational language to the
apostolic ministry?

Also, consider the lack of congruity: Christ was *made sin*—simply

---

[11]Wright formulates this interpretation of 2 Cor 5:21 with different degrees of complexity in
What St. Paul Really Said, pp. 104-5; "New Perspectives in Paul," in *Justification in Perspective:
Historical Developments and Contemporary Challenges*, ed. B. McCormack (Grand Rapids: Ru-
therford House, 2006), pp. 252- 53; and *Justification*, pp. 158-67.

so that *[hina] the apostles* could show forth God's righteousness (2 Cor 5:21)! In such a construal the shock of the first part of the sentence (Christ made sin) does not match the functional quality of the second. No, if Christ was made sin it could hardly be *for the purpose of* the apostolic charism. Instead, Paul indicates a miracle that makes its impact on all in the new creation. To read 2 Corinthians 5:21 as a mystery does not undermine all that has been argued rightly about God's very own righteousness. (The logic is much like that of our Christian story: the incarnation can only overwhelm those who have firmly grasped the distinctness of a holy God. It would be ho-hum for a polytheist.) It is the God-man who assumes death and sin in order to win life and righteousness for God's people. It is this one who stands as judge, as advocate and as defendant. What life is there except that of God, the giver of life? What righteousness is there but God's very own? God does not give grace: he gives his very self! In continuity with the theme of glory in 2 Corinthians 2–5, here in 2 Corinthians 5:21, we encounter *in nuce* the doctrine later known as *theosis*.[12] We glimpse the glory of what human beings are "meant to become" at that very point where the exception proves the well-taken rule of Wright. Indeed, this interpretation sets us up perfectly for chapter 6, which speaks about our call to light, holiness, righteousness and fellowship.[13]

One is holy, one is righteous, one is the LORD Jesus Christ. Yet, holy things are for the holy. It isn't contractual; rather, it is a mystery, going beyond theories of righteousness—imputed, imparted or infused. We anticipate a deepening communion with the holy Trinity, our full transformation into the likeness of that One who is the very image of the

---

[12]I do not, in suggesting this, follow the line of argument set out by Stephen Finlan, who takes exception to Wright's reading of 1 Cor 15, by caricaturing Wright's distinction between *sōma psychikon* and *sōma pneumatikon* as "forc[ing] simplistic choices . . . between physicality or ghostliness" ("Can We Speak of Theosis in Paul?" in *Partakers of the Divine Nature: The History and Development of Deification in the Christian Traditions*, ed. M. J. Christensen and J. A. Wittung (Grand Rapids: Baker, 2007), p. 71.

[13]Some have queried particularly 2 Cor 6:14-18, considering this passage to be incoherent with St. Paul's theology and redolent of Essene dualism. This is absurd, for the call to be God's holy temple is found elsewhere in the Corinthian correspondence, as is the divide between light and darkness.

Father. Who could have envisioned the "large room" (Ps 31:8) in which God intends to set our feet? This is what

> no eye has seen,
>> nor ear heard, [nor feet traversed!],
> nor the human heart conceived,
>> what God has prepared for those who love him. (1 Cor 2:9)

"APOCALYPTIC"

Apocalyptic language is one way in which the unimaginable is conceived.[14] As a student of G. B. Caird, Bishop Tom has been both hailed and critiqued for his approach, especially with regards to the historical Jesus.[15] Here, he follows the strategy of the Master Debater, who accepted, for argument's sake, the foundations of the Sadducees, and still confounded them. (In Mt 22:31-32, Jesus argues from Torah, rather than the rejected book of Daniel, that there was a resurrection of the dead.) Bishop Tom crushes the lion of literalism and the adder of skepticism, using the canons of literary and historical criticism. Jesus was no failed apocalyptic visionary, but used apocalyptic "metaphor with teeth," investing what seemed to be ordinary political and historical events with theological meaning.[16] By means of historical method, Bishop Tom also boldly goes where most historians have never gone before. He asks pointed questions concerning that apocalyptic event occurring in mid-time, the crucifixion and resurrection of Jesus, which left imprints in time that need to be considered. His cogent argument in *The Resurrection of the Son of God*, that "cognitive dissonance" cannot account for the proclamation of the earliest Christians, is welcome.[17]

---

[14]I put *apocalyptic*, this adjective-qua-non, in inverted commas in order to signify that it is a term used frequently by scholars (indeed, by Wright himself) but that it is an ambiguous term, which I prefer myself to avoid. Instead, it seems more useful to talk in terms of the genre "apocalypse," or to modify the adjective so that readers will be aware of what feature associated with apocalypses is being considered: apocalyptic imagery, apocalyptic eschatology and so on.

[15]G. B. Caird, *The Language and Imagery of the Bible* (London: Duckworth, 1980). See especially chap. 14 (pp. 243-71) on eschatology.

[16]N. T. Wright, *The New Testament and the People of God* (Minneapolis: Fortress, 1992), p. 652.

[17]N. T. Wright, *The Resurrection of the Son of God* (Minneapolis: Fortress, 2003), p. 697. Since no Jewish first-century thinker was expecting a Messiah to be crucified and raised, the disciples' proclamation of this cannot have been a fantasy they clung to after the dark hours of Good Friday and Holy Saturday.

In Wright's accounting, Jesus' vocation as Son of Man qua Suffering Servant is vindicated in Jesus' own resurrection and in the destruction of the Jerusalem temple. The "Son of Man coming with the clouds" *to* the Ancient of Days is not, therefore, an expectation of the end of the space-time universe, nor even a reference to Jesus' future parousia, but a symbolic way of saying that Jesus expects to be publicly vindicated. Bishop Tom faces the challenge of Albert Schweitzer, mooring Jesus firmly in his Jewish environment, but not agreeing that Jesus was therefore mistaken. Instead, the great future event of resurrection is brought into the midst of human history. "Apocalyptic" is part of the repertoire, the arsenal of the prophetic Jesus.

All this is enormously helpful! Yet, I remain uncomfortable with the reductive definition of "apocalyptic." What does apocalyptic language actually do? Bishop Tom's explanation assumes a kind of rhetorical artifice rather like his own masterful vision in that wonderful tale about "Michelle" that he told against Dominic Crossan.[18] In the *New Testament and the People of God* he speaks of the necessity of judging each apocalypse individually to determine whether it reflects a mystical vision or has a literary quality.[19] While he seeks to appreciate the polyphony of apocalyptic passages,[20] he describes Jesus as "encoding (or decoding) an entire theology" by means of his words and actions.[21] My own work with apocalypses makes me uneasy about his suggestion that we are to defang apocalyptic symbols as merely political, and not also to receive them as pointers to heavenly or future realities interconnected with our own lives. It is a matter of the direction of the reference and the taming of the symbol.

Sometimes, it is clear, apocalypticists did write literary facsimiles of visions for theological and political purposes.[22] But other passages bring us into touch with the mystical, the inexpressible: the apocalypse medi-

---

[18]"Taking the Text with Her Pleasure," *Theology* 96 (1993): 303-10. See also N. T. Wright, "Taking the Text with Her Pleasure," NTWrightPage.com <www.ntwrightpage.com/Wright_Text_Pleasure.htm>.

[19]Wright, *NTPG*, pp. 290-92.

[20]Ibid., p. 282.

[21]Ibid., p. 652.

[22]See the Animal Apocalypse in *1 Enoch* and Similitudes in *Shepherd of Hermas.*

ates another world, another time, another reality, and *thereby invests this world with meaning*. Our lives, Israel's life, the church's life take on importance in that they partake of a larger-than-human-life reality. "More is happening than seems to be happening," as Father Patrick Reardon puts it in his little book on Job.[23] I want to affirm what Bishop Tom affirms, without denying what he denies.

Consider C. S. Lewis's words on Jesus' ascension, in which he argues that we cannot be certain where the metaphor leaves off and reality begins. Until we have been there, it will not do to say that a physical "going up" has nothing to do with returning to God. We cannot be certain which part of the picture is sheer window dressing and which part partakes of the reality that we have not yet seen.[24] Yes, Jews of Jesus' day did speak of the sun and the moon being darkened in reference to historical events; Ezekiel also used resurrection imagery to refer to the return from exile. But we know that resurrection was not conceived of simply symbolically in Jesus' own day. And what sense does resurrection make without death? Similarly, if one is expecting a cosmic remaking (as Paul does in Romans 8:18-22), and a new heavens and new earth (Hebrews, Peter, Revelation), then one surely expects a cosmic death first. Try as I may, I cannot symbolize the language found in 2 Peter 3:10: "But the day of the Lord will come like a thief, and then the heavens will pass away with a loud noise and the elements will be dissolved with fire, and the earth and the works that are upon it will be burned up." The Petrine vision squares with Jewish visions such as those found in *1 Enoch* 1:6 and *4 Ezra* 7:30. It looks, after all, as if some Jews in Jesus' day did anticipate the actual end of the world.

However, there is, within Bishop Tom's argument, a clue as to the appropriate connection of the Son of Man who comes to the Ancient of Days and the Son of Man who will return: this is the resurrection of Jesus himself. Just as the resurrection of Jesus took everyone by surprise, so the judgment of Israel and the fall of the temple may be seen as the judgment of God on this world put back into history. The Jews

---

[23]Patrick Reardon, *The Trial of Job* (Chesterton, Ind.: Conciliar Press, 2005), p. 46. This is Father Reardon's definition of "the Bible's apocalyptic principle."

[24]C. S. Lewis, *Miracles: A Preliminary Study* (New York: HarperOne, 2001), pp. 231-43.

looked for a general resurrection: Jesus' resurrection is God's own confirmation of that hope. Similarly, the events of A.D. 70 are God's prints on history, assuring us of the reality of final judgment. But after judgment, resurrection, and so, in history, after Israel, after the flesh cedes to the new Israel, there is Christ's body, which includes Jew and Gentile. Yet we still await a heavenly city, when God's bride, completely purified and fulfilled, is revealed.

I am, of course, using typological interpretation, a method that coheres with the unusual elasticity of apocalyptic language. Jesus spoke of the coming historical trial of Israel in apocalyptic terms; but these events participated in cosmic events that we have not yet witnessed, just as Jesus' own resurrection is bound up with God's final purposes of resurrection for his people. Jesus saw Satan fall from heaven, symbolized in the successful mission of the seventy disciples, but an indication also of the final defeat of that one who has been bound by the first parousia of the Son. The first referent in Jesus' apocalyptic word (Mk 13; Mt 24; Lk 17; 21) was the coming ordeal in Judea, no doubt—but that does not exhaust its meaning. The redirection of this language to speak of the return of the One who called himself Son of Man did no violence to the original teaching. Rather, it was latent in the language itself. So, Paul already echoes Jesus' words when he anticipates Jesus being revealed with the angels "when he comes on that day" (2 Thess 1:10). By the time of Justin, Matthew 24 was being read as a promise of the second coming (*Apology I*, 51). And in the sermons of the Golden Mouthed, we see common-sense Antiochian interpretation that applies Matthew 24 to the events of A.D. 70, but that appeals to Act 1:10 as the link which helps us to read these verses in terms of Jesus "coming on a cloud as he was taken up" (*Homilies on Matthew* 76). These events are conceptually linked because they are pictures of the ruling King, vindicated and acting for his people.

Besides, there are interconnected comings and goings. Though the Son of Man comes in Daniel *to* the Ancient of Days, Bishop Tom reminds us also about the owner of the vineyard returning to his land. There is, then, an upward *and* a downward direction, one attributed to Son of Man, the other to the Almighty. Jesus personifies both as the ascending Son of Man and as "the embodiment of YHWH's return to Zion."[25] Assurance of God's visitation remained with the church through the Holy Spirit, yet there is also in the New Testament a strain of exile, retained in the Apocalypse, in the angelic word of Acts 1 and in those poignant redirected words about the coming of the Son of Man. The powerful polyvalence of apocalyptic language offers not simply a sign of past judgment (though it does this) but a powerful word for the church today: and it does this without robbing the words of their historical power.

ASCENSION

Let us turn to the ascension and to Christian hope. In *Surprised by Hope*, Bishop Tom emphasizes resurrection over heaven, insisting on the importance of the body. In dealing with Jesus' ascension, he follows Douglas Farrow, distinguishing between the resurrection and ascension of Jesus, highlighting the taking of the human body by Jesus in the ascension event (he doesn't simply disintegrate or "go back" to being a bodiless God), and emphasizing the absence of Jesus as well as his presence in the Holy Spirit. The ascension prevents us from visualizing Jesus' victory as merely spiritual, and thinking of the incarnation in temporary terms. ("Beam me up, Scottie!") It prevents us from imagining the Christian hope in terms of immaterial existence and thereby devaluing the body. And it prevents us from confusing God the Son with a spiritual presence or confusing the church with Jesus. To understand the ascension properly reminds us forcibly of our status as creatures, and yet also hints that heaven and earth are "not so very far away from each other."[26]

In dealing with the scandal of the ascension story for our skeptical generation, the bishop follows this rule: "Part of Christian belief is to find out what's true about Jesus and let that challenge our culture."[27] When we trace Jesus' journey, we catch a view both of what makes Jesus

---

[25]N. T. Wright, *Jesus and the Victory of God* (Minneapolis, Fortress, 1996), p. 639.

[26]N. T. Wright, *Surprised by Hope: Rethinking Heaven, the Resurrection and the Mission of the Church* (New York: HarperOne, 2008), pp. 114-16.

[27]Ibid., p. 111.

unique, but also of what God intends for us, since Jesus is the true Israel, the new Adam.

What, then, of the ascension? Doug Farrow makes two important
points, helpfully picked up by the bishop. First, there are two divergent
histories the church must keep in tension—the history of the world and
the history of Jesus. Second, we must see our life in terms not only of
an ascension of the mind or spirit, but in terms of Jesus' bodily resurrection and ascent, which brought human history to a climax and allowed
for the giving of the Spirit. To think only of mental ascent is to allow
"the doctrine of the ascension . . . to dissolve Jesus' humanity."[28]

Farrow does not dismiss outright the human ascent of mind and
spirit—how could he, given the injunctions of New Testament letters to
set our minds "on high" (Eph 2:6; Phil 2:5; Col 3:1-3; Heb 12:22)?
However, he does view talk of spiritual ascent as suspect, because it can
dilute the robust Christian hope for bodily resurrection and the return
of Jesus. Bishop Tom agrees. I want to heed the caution of my friends,
without minimizing this venerable tradition that goes back to the New
Testament. There are both present *and* future implications of Jesus' ascension. Because the Son has assumed our human nature, it is no mere
fantasy that we are presently "seated in heavenly places" (Eph 2:6).
Thus, we are enjoined, "Set your mind on things above" (Col 3:2). We
are quite right to be disturbed about the human tendency, even among
believers, to try to seize power, to "bring down Christ" by means of
spiritual prowess or institutional claims. There are certainly cases where
individuals or ecclesial institutions have blurred the distinction between
Christ and themselves by appealing to the Spirit. But that is not spiritual or noetic ascent in its Christian shape.

There remains for the Christian the call to "seek the face of the God
of Jacob" so that we might "ascend the hill of the Lord" and stand with
feet in his holy place (Ps 24:3, 6). This yearning is appropriate because
a new ladder has been given—the Son of Man, who by his own ascension has "taken upon [his] shoulders our nature, which had gone astray
. . . and bring[s] it unto God the Father."[29] When and how does our

---

[28]Douglas Farrow, *Ascension and Ecclesia* (Grand Rapids: Eerdmans, 1999), p. 141.
[29]Orthros (Eastern Orthodox Matins), Canon for the Ascension, Ode 7.

ascent take place? It takes place by ascesis, the carrying of the cross alongside Christ, as each of us plays Simon of Cyrene to the One who alone can bear this burden for us. It also takes place in prayer and in worship, as (to use the words of Cyril of Jerusalem) we bring to the presence of God "heaven, earth, oceans, sun, moon and the entire creation."[30] This is not an ascent that leaves behind the world or that hopes to escape it; instead, we offer all up to the Creator and Redeemer of all.

How is Jesus' ascension a pattern for us? It transforms what would have been merely a fall and restoration (a V-shape story) into a story of mending-plus-glory (a story with check-mark contours). Jesus' ascension shows that all of what we are has been assumed, and so it is not our bare redemption but our entire hallowing and exaltation that God has in mind. Now, we ascend in mind and spirit to where we are, by virtue of our union with Christ, already seated, and as we make this ascent together and enabled by the Spirit, even our bodies and this world are not left unchanged. "Soar we now where Christ has led, following our exalted head."[31] Now—in worship! In our reading of the Word and especially in our partaking of the Eucharistic mysteries, we are caught up into the heavenly places—not so as to escape the world but to present it before the risen, slaughtered Lamb who can unseal the scroll. There is a present aspect to our ascent. Is there a future one, as well? Bishop Tom is right to castigate those who posit from a single verse (1 Thess 4:16) the doctrine of a rapture, and he is, I believe, exactly right to envision this meeting as the church rushing to greet Jesus as he returns to judge and to remake! But does nothing happen when we greet our beloved? Is our "ascent" simply for his benefit, a human vanguard on his way to match the angels "rank on rank" who watched the "Light of lights" descend?[32] Is this ascent not also a fulfillment of our destiny, a sign of our own glorification? Is it a bodily answer to the longing of our souls, minds and spirits to "enter

---

[30]Cyril of Jerusalem *On the Mysteries* 5, lect. 23, "On the Sacred Liturgy and Communion," p. 6.

[31]This line is from Charles Wesley's "Hymn for Easter Day" (1739), also known as "Christ the Lord is Risen Today!"

[32]The allusion Is to Gerald Moultrie, "Let All Mortal Flesh Keep Silence" (1864), a hymn inspired by the Anaphora of the Liturgy of St. James.

into his kingdom" (cf. Jn 3:5), that is, "to rule with him" (cf. 2 Tim 2:12)?

There are clues to this great climax (the Greek word *klimax* literally means "ladder!") in the Scriptures and in Christian tradition. Revelation 11 strangely retells the story of God's two faithful, who seem to be Moses and Elijah. Elijah, you will remember, was assumed and did not die. About Moses, there are conflicting stories: the canon speaks of his death and hidden tomb, whereas the pseudepigraphon suggests that he was assumed. Here, the two faithful follow the very path of Jesus— they are martyred during their *martyria*, they are mocked and lie dead for about three days, then they are raised and invited, "Come up here!" And they ascend in a cloud of glory, sharing in the victory of the one true witness, Jesus. Of course, there is another one of whom the historic church has had similar things to say, though her familial glory has sometimes been misunderstood or confused with the One who alone defeated death and sin. Stories like these should not undermine the uniqueness of our Lord. Rather, they underscore the greatest truth about ascension: "When You fulfilled your plan of salvation for us and *united earth to heaven*, You ascended in glory, O Christ our God, never leaving us, but remaining ever-present. For You proclaimed to those who love You: I am with you and none else has power over you."[33]

I think fewer Christians today need the lessons emphasized by Farrow and Bishop Tom, that Jesus is absent from us, and that the church is not identical with the Holy Spirit. Rather, we need assurance that Jesus is present with us in the Eucharist and in the proclamation of the Word. In worship we are not simply practicing but being taken up into all this! In our individualistic age we are less tempted to make false mediators and mediatrixes than to assume that "I can do this myself." The ascension sets our imagination on heavenly things and fixes our wills on the One who will show us, while we wait for his final return, what he has for us to do, not separately, but together with the Church in every time and place. In this Church, every member points, though some more luminously than others, to the One who is the only God-man.

---

[33]Kontakion for the feast of the Ascension, Orthodox tradition (emphasis added).

This vision harmonizes with Bishop Tom's understanding about the continued significance of this world. God intends to unite earth to heaven, so that the holy Trinity is ever present with us. Our hope is not that we should be unclothed but further clothed, that there should be a renewed heaven and earth, though death should intervene. So shall we ever be with the LORD. If Bishop Tom says more about the further clothing, the cosmic union and the renewal than about the purging effect of ascesis, death and judgment than many ancient fathers of the church, that is perhaps excusable. All of us long to look beyond the valley to the heights where our feet itch to go: better yet, we yearn for the valleys to be exalted so that they too can feel the wind bringing newness of life. In the end, this is where the righteousness of God will lead: though there is a dark side too, portrayed in the apocalypses, that ought not be glossed. "At last our feet are standing at your gates, Jerusalem! Jerusalem, built as a city, in one united whole, there the tribes go up, the tribes of Yahweh, a sign for Israel to give thanks to the name of Yahweh. For there are set the thrones of judgement" (Ps 122:2-5 Jerusalem Bible).

CONCLUSION: THE BEAUTIFUL FEAT

I have one longing: that the feet of Bishop Tom would venture more deliberately into the world of the church fathers and more completely into the strange terrain of the Eastern Church. (I would say that, wouldn't I?) Certainly, he has done this more in his *Surprised by Hope* than in previous works[34] and there are rumors that the bishop is using the language of *theosis* these days too! But there are points in his "surprised" book that surprised *me*—I did not always recognize the spin that he put on Orthodox teaching. This is, I think, because at the foundations our friend remains a Protestant. In his own words, "My only agenda . . . is to be as close as I can possibly get to what Paul actually says. And I really don't care too much what different later Christian traditions say."[35] Here, the bishop probably is referring to

---

[34]Though he emphasizes here the *earliest* church fathers, as though the later ones may have lost the glory, or their way! See Wright, *Surprised by Hope*, pp. 172-73.

[35]For a full transcript see "Trevin Wax Interview with N. T. Wright," *Kingdom People*, Novem-

much later traditions, but it is telling that he also cheerfully ignores early church fathers, in (for example) his Cairdian interpretation of Matthew 24 or in his neglect of the purgative cosmic "day" that precedes the new creation.

Consonant with this approach is also his strong emphasis on "freshness," as though this were the measure of scholarship and proclamation. Our age, of course, is oriented toward the novel, and we must speak so as to be heard. There is also the factor of Bishop Tom's multiple readership. Sometimes what the bishop says is no doubt intended for one set of ears and for a certain context. In assigning his little book *Who Was Jesus?* over the years to students, several times a few have stumbled over the phrase "it is . . . highly likely, that the Church has distorted the real Jesus"[36] and assumed that the bishop is a revisionist. He is not, of course. But his solution to distortion is "only no-holds-barred history," as though the historian alone, and not the witness of God's people as a whole, were the authoritative voice as to reality.[37] Some of these moves may be apologetic and missional. But they are vulnerable to the charges of professionalism and rank individualism—characteristics that do not match the humility of our dear friend. Asked by one of my students, "Where is your reading of Matthew 24 upheld by any of the church fathers?" Bishop Tom responded with simplicity, "I don't know." It would at the very least be an exercise in Christian *koin₵nia* for this shepherd to seek out more deliberately the counsel of his siblings of ancient days, where he will indeed find emphasis on God's own righteousness, on Jesus' engagement with Israel and on the importance of the body—and perhaps some challenges as well! Indeed, many of those with whom he is in conversation are intent to "go back to an ancient future": such a move on his part would be welcomed by them, and not suspect, as it might have been in the past. The call to freshness and *semper reformanda* is salutary for God's people: so too is the reminder that God's Holy Spirit has never abandoned his people, and that he has promised to "make the place of [our] feet glorious" (Is 60:13).

---

ber 19, 2007 <http://trevinwax.com/2007/11/19/trevin-wax-interview-with-nt-wright-full-transcript>.
[36]N. T. Wright, *Who Was Jesus?* (Grand Rapids: Eerdmans, 1992), p. 18.
[37]Ibid.

By means of Bishop Tom Wright our generation has glimpsed the exalted One whose feet alone are all-glorious, and who in humility submitted to their washing and their piercing at the hands of those whom he loved. The critique and the adulation which the bishop's vigorous work has evoked are not easy burdens to bear, and our brother continues to respond to both with balance, equanimity and grace. Salty persons like Bishop Tom retain the admiration and the affection of both friends and opponents. In all this, he has not lost his footing, and his actions and words have served as "signposts of hope, pointing back [to Jesus] and on [to the hope of glory]."[38] And that is no mean feat!

Response to Edith Humphrey
N. T. WRIGHT

In her opening pages Edith Humphrey insists on a clear and full understanding of complex arguments I have advanced, which is a welcome antidote to various one-sided readings. We seem to be on the same page in a great deal of our reading—and perhaps our praying too.

I remain, though, impenitent about my reading of 2 Corinthians 5:21. I do indeed think that the picture of transformation in 2 Corinthians 3:18 may be still in Paul's mind at this point, but as so often I want to insist on what Paul actually says, as opposed to what any larger frameworks—Reformational in some cases, Orthodox as here—may wish to find. In the whole passage (2 Cor 4:7–6:13) Paul repeatedly refers to his own ministry, presumably because the Corinthians had objected that his undignified suffering undermined his apostolic claim. Almost every verse is about "we" and "us" in this restricted sense. In particular, note 2 Corinthians 5:11-21. We know the fear of the Lord, so we persuade people; we are manifest to your conscience; we are not commending ourselves again but giving you an opportunity to boast about us; and so on. Then, in an ascending climax (all right, a "ladder," but one of argument no less than spiritual exaltation!), he writes that God, reconciling us to himself through the Messiah, has given *us* the message of recon-

---

[38]Wright, *Surprised by Hope*, p. 295.

ciliation (v. 18) and the word of reconciliation (v. 19). *We* are ambassa-
dors for the Messiah; God is appealing through *us; we* beseech people,
on behalf of the Messiah, to be reconciled to God (v. 20). The most
natural way of reading verse 21 is then similarly focused on "we": the
apostolic ministry, exactly as in verses 18 and 19, is rooted in the death
of the Messiah on behalf of sinners. The cross is the platform for the
apostolic ministry of embodying God's covenant faithfulness. This leads
exactly into 2 Corinthians 6:1-13, Paul's passionate and brilliant exposition of the paradoxical apostolic lifestyle. I am perfectly happy to say
that we might, from this point, reason or speculate that Paul might want
to say the same kind of thing on a wider canvas too, leading us toward
those heights of mystical union of which Edith, here and elsewhere, has
written so movingly. But the exegete's primary task, however much he
or she enjoys such further work, is to explain the primary, surface meaning of the text—not, to be sure, in the narrow, dry-as-dust way to which
many have rightly reacted, but recognizing that the human mind can
imagine all sorts of appealing and helpful things which need the re-
straining anchor of genuine historical exegesis.

For the same reason I am wary of opening the door too far to an
unfettered world of supposedly apocalyptic theology. Here Edith
moves out, way beyond Paul (it is odd, perhaps, that she does not mention 2 Thessalonians, which might be more germane) and into the
tricky worlds of 2 Peter, Revelation and of course the so-called apocalyptic discourse in the Gospels. As Nick Perrin suggests in his paper,
I am not averse to contemplating ways in which Jesus' prediction of the
fall of Jerusalem might provide a template for the larger questions
raised by Romans 8, 1 Corinthians 15 and so on. The danger, as I see
it, is that many Christians, not least in North America, are only too
eager to say, "There you are; it really is about the end of the world; so
let's forget all this irrelevant stuff about Jerusalem and read the text
the way we always did." I am eager to affirm that in biblical theology
heaven and earth overlap, interlock, collide, challenge one another and
are finally brought together as in Ephesians 1:10 or Revelation 21. It
may well be, and Edith may be one of the people who has most clearly
alerted us to this, that the language of what we loosely call "apocalyp-

tic" is a peculiarly good vehicle for bringing this worldview into expression, since its particular gift is to denote earthly events and connote their heavenly significance, and perhaps vice versa. But after several generations in which the earthly referent was marginalized or straightforwardly ignored, leaving us with liberal exegetes quietly triumphing over the delay of the parousia ("There you are! Jesus got it wrong!") and conservative exegetes eager for the rapture, we must pay attention to the solid rock of the first layer of meaning before we build nearby on what may be sand.

This leads naturally to the ascension. Here Edith writes with a poetic and evocative quality which doesn't always give me a steer as to what, as a Pauline exegete, she wants me to do differently. I don't think I have neglected the notion of a coming "day," and I am in principle happy with *theosis* as part of an account of Paul's soteriology or anthropology. But here we meet once more with the problem of Scripture and tradition. It's rather fun to be accused, for once, of being a Protestant. Yes, I insist that the first meaning of the text is what it actually says; I honor later writers but I know that they, like me, are capable of distorted and partial readings. The theologians and exegetes of later centuries, while right about so much, had important blind spots which we correct best by rereading the texts. Tradition is important, but I will drink to Paul first and to tradition afterward.

7

The Shape of Things to Come?

Wright Amidst Emerging Ecclesiologies

JEREMY S. BEGBIE

FASHIONS IN CHRISTIAN PUBLISHING can be short-lived.[1] But the flurry of recent writing on the theme of the church shows no signs of abating. In an environment marked by declining denominational membership, and many who may be attracted by the person of Christ and a broadly based "spirituality" but who shrink at the idea of joining a local congregation, the shape of an effective missional engagement of the church with our culture has become an acute issue. Not surprisingly, ecclesiology is very much on the agenda.

In the last twenty years or so, especially in the United Kingdom and the United States, some of this rethinking of the church has been happening in the midst of and in relation to a diverse cluster of networks dubbed "emerging church."[2] Concerned with finding forms of corpo-

---

[1] I am very grateful to the following for their perceptive comments on earlier drafts of this paper: Paul Weston, Steve Walton, Richard Hays and Dona McCullagh.

[2] Following F. LeRon Shults, I shall take "emerging churches" to refer to new forms of church life arising in late-modern Western societies, "emergents" to the practitioners within this movement. The term "Emergent" is best reserved for the network set up in 1997, sometimes known as "Emergent Village" <www.emergentvillage.com>. For representative voices, see Brian D. McLaren, *A Generous Orthodoxy: Why I Am a Missional, Evangelical, Post/Protestant, Liberal/Conservative, Mystical/Poetic, Biblical, Charismatic/Contemplative, Fundamentalist/Calvinist, Anabaptist/Anglican, Methodist, Catholic, Green, Incarnational, Depressed-Yet-Hopeful, Emergent, Unfinished Christian* (El Cajon, Calif.: Youth Specialties, 2006); Doug Pagitt and

rate Christian life that can embody and promote an effective missional engagement with late- or postmodern society, especially with the unchurched, it constitutes a kind of crucible of questioning and experimentation—raising, often in very concrete ways, the kind of questions and issues being raised more widely in the church at large, and far beyond Europe and North America.[3]

For any who delve into the literature of this inchoate movement, especially noticeable among the theologians recommended for fruitful *ressourcement* is N. T. Wright.[4] Certainly in New Testament scholarship

---

Tony Jones, eds., *An Emergent Manifesto of Hope* (Grand Rapids: Baker, 2007); Tony Jones, *The New Christians: Dispatches from the Emergent Frontier* (San Francisco: Jossey-Bass, 2008); Doug Pagitt, *A Christianity Worth Believing: Hope-Filled, Open-Armed, Alive-and-Well Faith for the Left Out, Left Behind, and Let Down in Us All* (San Francisco: Jossey-Bass, 2008); Ian Mobsby's website <http://ianmobsby.net>; and Peter Rollins's website <www.peterrollins.net>. See also the Emerging Church Info website <www.emergingchurch.info>. For discussion, see F. LeRon Shults, "Reforming Ecclesiology in Emerging Churches," *Theology Today* 65 (2009): 425-38; Eddie Gibbs and Ryan K. Bolger, *Emerging Churches: Creating Christian Community in Post-modern Cultures* (Grand Rapids: Baker Academic, 2005); Steven J. L. Croft and Ian Mobsby, eds., *Ancient Faith, Future Mission: Fresh Expressions in the Sacramental Tradition* (Norwich, U.K.: Canterbury Press, 2009); Louise Nelstrop and Martyn Percy, eds., *Evaluating Fresh Expressions: Explorations in Emerging Church* (Norwich, U.K.: Canterbury Press, 2008).

Common in the United States are emerging churches that are disaffected with their previous church experience (especially fundamentalist, evangelical and charismatic), and have become relatively independent Christian groups. More typical of the United Kingdom are initiatives that arise from but continue to relate closely to traditional denominations, such as the "fresh expressions" initiatives of the Church of England, which followed the report *Mission-Shaped Church: Church Planting and Fresh Expressions of Church in a Changing Context*, ed. Graham Cray (London: Church House, 2004). See John Drane, "Editorial: The Emerging Church," *International Journal for the Study of the Christian Church* 6, no. 1 (2006): 3-11. Using similar categories, Scott Bader-Saye believes much can be gained from a conversation between what he calls "post-evangelical emergents" (those who consciously react against evangelical theology and culture to form independent communities) and "mainline missionals," who, although pursuing their initiatives out of a certain dissatisfaction with denominational churches, are generally keen to retain close ties with them (Scott Bader-Saye, "Improvising Church: An Introduction to the Emerging Church Conversation," *International Journal for the Study of the Christian Church* 6, no. 1 [2006]: 12-23). There are those who want to make a distinction along theological lines between two groups of emergent churches: in Mark Devine's words, between "doctrine-friendly" and "doctrine-wary/doctrine-averse" groups. See "The Emerging Church: One Movement—Two Streams," in *Evangelicals Engaging Emergent: A Discussion of the Emergent Church Movement*, ed. William D. Henard and Adam. W. Greenway (Nashville: B & H Academic, 2009), pp. 4-46.

[3]See Alan Jamieson, "Post-Church Groups and Their Place as Emergent Forms of Church," *International Journal for the Study of the Christian Church* 6, no. 1 (2006): 65-78. Scot McKnight states: "At its core, the emerging movement is an attempt to fashion a new ecclesiology (doctrine of the church)" ("Five Streams of the Emergent Church," *Christianity Today* 51, no. 2 [2007]: 37).

[4]On one prominent "emerging churches resources" website, top of the list under the heading "A

he is very much an "approved" name, quoted at length in the emerging blogosphere. In some respects this is odd. For here is a movement largely led by those at the younger end of the age spectrum, typically challenging long-running assumptions and forms of church life and mission deemed to be inadequate to the postmodern condition—top-down professional management, centralized organizational structure, control through tight hierarchies, strong ties to places and buildings, and so forth. And many of its leaders believe they will be effective just to the extent that they are not weighed down by the inherited roles and structures of official leadership.[5] Yet here is an Anglican bishop, well past his first flush of youth, a powerful figurehead in an ancient institution many would regard as highly bureaucratic, indeed, as the epitome of a top-down social arrangement, a major land-owner with a huge commitment to buildings, able to move only with glacial slowness down antediluvian ecclesiastical valleys.

In this paper I want to explore what it is about Wright's ecclesiology that is proving attractive to so many at work in the "emerging" movement, especially in his writings on the apostle Paul. But we will go on to ask: what elements in Wright does the new movement choose to neglect, underplay or even wholly ignore, and why? Further, we will ask: might it be that some of these neglected elements could be of considerable benefit to the emerging ecclesiologies of emerging churches, and not only to them but to other visions of the church currently on offer in the ongoing ecclesiological ferment?

FIVE FEATURES OF WRIGHT'S ECCLESIOLOGY

To begin with, then, what is it about Wright's ecclesiology that appeals

---

List of Important Names for the Movement" is N. T. Wright; see the Gathering in Light website <http://gatheringinlight.com/2006/06/07/emerging-church-resources-a-beginners-reference-guide>. See also the Open Source Theology website <www.opensourcetheology.net>; and "N. T. Wright on the Post-Emerging Church," Emergent Village Weblog <www.emergentvillage.com/weblog/nt-wright-on-the-post-emerging-church>. Other prominent figures include Walter Brueggemann, David Bosch, Lesslie Newbigin, Dallas Willard and LeRon Shults.

[5]"There is surely some irony here. Those who have the most freedom to do what the church is allegedly called to do are those who are not officially authorized to do so" (F. LeRon Shults, "Tending to the Other in Late Modern Missions and Ecumenism," *Swedish Missiological Themes* 95, no. 4 [2007]: 432).

to those wrestling with the shape of the church missiologically in the current climate? I highlight five features.[6]

1. Integral. The first and most obvious is simply that, as with Paul, the church is both integral and central to Wright's theological vision. To a movement for whom finding the shape of "the church to come" is such a major concern, this is bound to prove appealing.

For Wright, to be more specific, ecclesiology is intrinsic to the fabric of salvation. God's deliverance, God's saving action to "put the world to rights," involves at its heart the formation of a community. Here we need to reckon with powerful currents, especially in Protestantism, that would construe the salvation-church link as merely extrinsic, currents that Wright has often found himself resisting, as have the emerging church networks.[7] In a book sadly out of print, Oliver O'Donovan astutely pinpoints a weakness in the architecture of the Thirty-nine Articles of Religion, a key Anglican confession of faith. The first article on the church (19), echoing the Augsburg Confession, defines the church as "a congregation of faithful men, in which the pure Word of God is preached, and the Sacraments be duly ministered according to Christ's ordinance in all those things that of necessity are requisite to the same." Leading up to that is a robust series of articles on salvation. But conspicuous by its absence is any organic link between the two theological spheres: any acknowledgement that salvation by its very nature is ecclesiologically directed, oriented to the formation of a new community with Christ as its head. And, hardly less problematic, immediately following we are given a lengthy series of articles on ecclesiastical organization: the church's institutional arrangements (its governance, ministers, modes of discipline and so forth). In a rare burst of un-English bluntness, O'Donovan remarks: "The ecclesiastical theory

---

[6]This is not an exhaustive list. For reasons of space, I have not dwelt on Wright's stress on story, the arts (and imagination), and his engagement with the postmodern condition, all of which find a ready hearing in emergent circles.

[7]There is little doubt that, especially in the United States, a large part of what goes under the heading of "emerging church" constitutes a "reactive subculture"—that is, its norms and values respond to, or oppose perceived failings in, established churches: whether congregations, denominations or (very commonly) evangelicalism (Luke Bretherton, "Beyond the Emerging Church?" in *Remembering Our Future: Explorations in Deep Church*, ed. Andrew Walker and Luke Bretherton [London: Paternoster, 2007], pp. 35-36).

of the Reformation was tacked on as a large and overgrown appendix to an evangelical theology which had no real place for the Church."[8]

All sorts of qualifications need to be made here, about the circumstances of the Thirty-nine Articles, its concern to steer clear of Roman ecclesiology and so forth. But O'Donovan nonetheless signals a dichotomy, a doctrinal breach between salvation and church that has never really been properly healed in Protestant thought. The resultant ecclesiology can be institutionally heavy (as we have just seen), or institutionally light (as in forms of pietism and much evangelicalism, when the external forms of the church become a matter of indifference). It can be fed by a diversity of intellectual streams. For example, behind much of the evangelicalism that shaped Wright's background, and the background of many in the emerging church networks, is what we might call "voluntarist contractualism," a philosophically and politically shaped individualism still very much alive in our culture, fueled by the liberal ideology of choice.[9] In this scheme individuals secure their identity prior to being part of a church by exercising a wholly unconstrained act of will in response to the gospel, a cognitive and conscious decision for Christ that ensures salvation and a place in heaven. Subsequently, and through a quite distinct act of the will, the saved person joins a church, understood in purely visible and localized terms, and as an aggregate of individual believers, related to each other (solely?) by virtue of their resolution to commit to Christ and to this particular group. Thus relationships within the church are seen as merely instrumental to the strengthening of each member's "relationship with the Lord." Those reared in such a climate will only scratch their heads when they encounter Wright, who refuses to succumb to the Protestant hiatus between gospel and church (some would call it a hiatus hernia), and who maintains a strong ecclesiological current through most of what he writes.[10]

---

[8]Oliver O'Donovan, *On the Thirty-Nine Articles: A Conversation with Tudor Christianity* (Exeter, U.K.: Paternoster, 1986), p. 92.

[9]Stanley Grenz, "Ecclesiology," in *The Cambridge Companion to Postmodern Theology*, ed. Kevin J. Vanhoozer (Cambridge: Cambridge University Press, 2003), p. 257.

[10]Some might suspect this to be a recent development in Wright, a symptom of his steady promotion to episcopal office. Not so. It was three decades ago that I encountered a Wright essay

Wright's ecclesiological cantus firmus is maintained in no small measure through *a refusal to think of the church in abstraction from the story of Israel.* This, he believes, is pressed upon us not least by Paul, for whom the lordship of Jesus that the gospel announces is that of Israel's Messiah.

In various ways, against the background of idolatrous human rebellion against the Creator God, whose good creation is multiply marred and fractured by sin and death, Wright charts the manner in which God, beginning with Abraham, covenants to himself a community to undo Adam's sin and renew the human race as God's image-bearers in creation; a community called to be *in* and *for* the world to gather up the praises of creation toward God, and share the wise and loving rule of God toward the world.

Through Israel's idolatry a second-order crisis arises, bringing calamitous judgment, such that Israel itself needs to be redeemed.[11] In keeping with the prophetic promise of a new covenant, Jesus is anointed by the Spirit to be Israel's rightful Messiah, who, as the representative Israelite, takes on the task Israel was unable to accomplish. Israel's destiny of vicarious suffering reaches its climax in the Messiah, who takes on the weight of God's wrath on Israel, and representatively of the whole world, suffering and dying under its load. In him, Adam's sin is at last reversed and its consequences borne away. Humanity is renewed in this one nonidolatrous person, and God's purposes for creation through the human race can be set in motion again. A fresh community is made possible, not the replacement or displacement of Israel, but

---

for the first time, when he was chaplain at Downing College in Cambridge, and I an ordination candidate down the road. It was in the form of a pamphlet with a revealing subtitle: *Evangelical Anglican Identity: The Connection Between Bible, Gospel and Church,* Latimer Studies 8 (Oxford: Latimer House, 1980.) Addressing the Church of England's evangelicals, he insisted that they had no business sidelining the church in the name of Scripture and the gospel: those committed to the Bible's *euangelion* (properly understood) will ipso facto be committed to the ecclesia.

[11]As is well known, and somewhat controversially, Wright holds that although the majority of Jews by the time of Jesus believed that their geographical Babylonian exile had ended, they believed that the exile—perceived as a historical period and marked by suffering and oppression, and brought about through national sin—had not. For his response to critics on this issue, see "In Grateful Dialogue: A Response," in *Jesus and the Restoration of Israel: A Critical Assessment of N. T. Wright's* Jesus and the Victory of God, ed. Carey C. Newman (Downers Grove, Ill.: InterVarsity Press, 1999), pp. 258-60.

a renewed "Israel of God" (Gal 6:16), brought back from exile and reconstituted, and indeed redefined, around Jesus Christ.[12] To belong to Christ's church is thus to belong to Israel's true Messiah, and thus to Abraham's seed.

This way of framing ecclesiology, without premature abstraction from narrative, means that many of the dichotomies that have arisen in the Christian doctrinal tradition are avoided from the start. Take, for example, the dichotomy between atonement and ecclesiology, one that

---

[12]This, of course, raises the vexed issue of "supersessionism," a less than helpful term for what is in fact a range of positions. See Bruce Longenecker, "On Israel's God and God's Israel: Assessing Supersessionism in Paul," *Journal of Theological Studies* 58, no. 1 (2007): 26–44. The most notorious exegetical battleground text is Romans 9–11. Wright tells us: "I take the word *[supersessionism]* to refer to that which Paul is manifestly opposing in Romans 11: the belief on the part of Gentile Christians that Jews have been cast off irrevocably, so that the church, albeit founded on the Jewish Messiah and with an early base of Jewish members, was now an exclusively Gentile family. Over against that, the natural reading of 11:11ff. is to have Paul say: that is the kind of belief that the Jews themselves had, the attempt to confine grace to race—and if you make that kind of presumption God will deal with you in the same way! (11:21)" ("Romans 9–11 and the 'New Perspective,' " in *Between Gospel and Election: Explorations in the Interpretation of Romans 9–11*, ed. Florian Wilk, J. Ross Wagner and Frank Schleritt (Tübingen: Mohr, forthcoming), n.p. He thus clearly rejects a supersessionism that would suggest that God had irreversibly spurned ethnic Israel (as in so-called replacement theologies), that the Abrahamic covenant has been abrogated. But he also avoids a "two-ways" or "two-covenant" scheme (one for Jews, one for Gentiles) which would suggest that the Jews could be "grafted in" by some means *other* than Christ. Rather, for Wright, "Paul believed Jesus to be the fulfillment of the covenant and the promises, so that the community of those who believe in Jesus is, for him, the single family promised to Abraham, able to be referred to in a shockingly straightforward manner as *Ioudaioi* (2:29), "sons of Abraham" (Galatians 3:29), "the circumcision" (Philippians 3:3), "sons of God" (8:12-17) and similar Israel-titles." Later he writes: "for Paul, the community of those who believed in Jesus as the risen Messiah and Lord were the true inheritors of the promises God made to Abraham." In his commentary on Romans, he interprets Paul as claiming that "Abraham's family, Israel, the Jews, the circumcision, are neither reaffirmed as they stand, nor 'superseded' by a superior group, nor 'replaced' with someone else—that is what he is arguing against in 11:13-24—but transformed, through the death and resurrection of Israel's own Messiah and the Spirit of Israel's own God, so that Israel is now, as was always promised, both less and more than the physical family of Abraham: less, as in 9:6-13; more, as in 4:13-25" ("The Letter to the Romans: Introduction, Commentary, and Reflections," in *The New Interpreter's Bible*, ed. Leander E. Keck [Nashville: Abingdon, 2002], 10:690). This, of course, must never be confused with anti-Semitism, or being anti-Jewish (Longenecker, "On Israel's God and God's Israel," pp. 40-42).

Douglas Harink has criticized Wright severely on these matters (Douglas K. Harink, *Paul Among the Postliberals: Pauline Theology Beyond Christendom and Modernity* [Grand Rapids: Brazos Press, 2003], chap. 4) but has misunderstood (even misrepresented) him in quite serious ways. For a pointed response to Harink, see Richard B. Hays, "Review of *Paul Among the Postliberals: Pauline Theology Beyond Christendom and Modernity*, by Douglas Harink," *Interpretation* 58, no. 4 (2004): 399-402, also available at <www.interpretation.org/reviews/oct-04/index.htm>.

is often tacitly assumed by many who oppose Wright. It is supposed that atonement, Christ's work on the cross, concerns the act by which God deals with sin, wrath and death, and reconciles the individual sinner to himself for eternity, while ecclesiology attends to something radically distinct: in some popular forms, the way in which individuals commit to a society in which they can, among other things, hear and rehear the message of Christ's atoning act for individuals, believe it, celebrate it and share it with others. Given Wright's adoption of some aspects of the New Perspective on Paul, many suspect he neuters atonement with ecclesiology, or at least sidelines it drastically. Rather, without denying its impact on the individual, he is urging that we do not extract atonement from its corporate embeddedness, its Israel-rooted past and its church-shaped future. The healing of interhuman relations is intrinsic to what God is about at the crucifixion. He writes: "the cross of Jesus Christ not only rescued sinful human beings from their eternal fate but also rescued fractured humanity from its eternal antagonism."[13] It is this corporate sense of atonement which many in the emerging church have been trying to recover (no doubt clumsily at times), raised as many of them have been on individualistic and ahistorical accounts of the cross.[14]

Another dichotomy avoided is that between justification and the church. Classically, justification has been construed in individualized and ahistorical terms. Wright comments in one place: "If you take the old route of putting justification, in its traditional meaning, at the centre of your theology, then you will always be in danger of sustaining some sort of individualism."[15] By contrast, for him, justification is inseparably related to Israel's story, and thus part of the larger narrative of God's vindication of the righteous, extending to God's eschatological justification of those who belong to Jesus the Messiah on the last day.[16]

---

[13]N. T. Wright, *Justification: God's Plan and Paul's Vision* (Downers Grove, Ill.: IVP Academic, 2009), p. 148.

[14]It is significant that Wright criticizes a recent influential defense of "penal substitution" as ignoring the story of Israel (N. T. Wright, "The Cross and the Caricatures," *Fulcrum*, Eastertide 2007 <www.fulcrum-anglican.org.uk/news/2007/20070423wright.cfm?doc=205>).

[15]N. T. Wright, *What Saint Paul Really Said* (Oxford: Lion, 1997), pp. 157-58.

[16]Ibid., chap. 7.

2. Eschatological. A second feature of Wright's ecclesiology that is naturally appealing to emerging churches is its eschatological flavor, its orientation to the future, something again he believes is central to Paul. Significantly, when asked to speak to an "emerging" group on the shape of the church to come, Wright speaks of "doing ecclesiology backwards," from the future.[17] This does not signal a mere restlessness with the present (and past) in the name of an entirely "open future," a fixation with novelty riding on an eschatology without content,[18] but rather a plea for attending first to the new creation—the eschaton promised in the resurrection of the crucified Jesus, with God's redeemed people at the center—and in that light struggling to discern the shape of the church in our time.

With this goes a vibrant sense of the Spirit as the one who brings a provisional yet visible and concrete anticipation of that future.[19] "Just as the resurrection of Jesus opened up the unexpected world of God's new creation, so the Spirit comes to us from that new world, the world waiting to be born."[20] Through the Spirit the church is given to be an embodiment of the day when God will do for the cosmos what he has already done for Jesus at Easter, a prototype of the community of the age to come. The church groans in the midst of the old creation (Rom 8), but enjoys through the Spirit's agency a foretaste of the new.[21] This outlook is bound to be welcomed by emerging church circles, eager as they usually are to avoid both the kind of despair and resignation that denies any direct involvement of God with the church, and the presumption that the eschaton is ours to grasp fully now.

It is in the light of this directional thrust, energized by the Spirit, that Wright reads Paul's understanding of the church's mission. God's

---

[17]N. T. Wright, "God's Future for the World Has Arrived in the Person of Jesus," *Open Source Theology*, September 20, 2004 <www.opensourcetheology.net/talks>.

[18]Some, it should be admitted, would see this as a danger of some emerging church initiatives; see, e.g., Martyn Percy, "Old Tricks for New Dogs? A Critique of Fresh Expressions," in *Evaluating Fresh Expressions: Explorations in Emerging Church*, ed. Louise Nelstrop and Martyn Percy (Norwich, U.K.: Canterbury Press, 2008).

[19]See, e.g., N. T. Wright, "The Holy Spirit in the Church," *Fulcrum*, April 29, 2005 <www.fulcrum-anglican.org.uk/events/2005/inthechurch.cfm>.

[20]Ibid.

[21]The church is a "place" where heaven and earth meet (ibid.).

people are sent to announce to the world that Jesus is Israel's Messiah and the world's true Lord, that God's project of putting the world to rights has climaxed in Jesus and will one day be completed for the whole cosmos. But this declaration is to be enacted through human agency: the church is called, after the pattern of Jesus, to be a vehicle of the promised new world, a Spirit-propelled agent of the world's liberation. Expanding on this, Wright employs the concepts of *achievement* and *implementation*: what has already been achieved in Christ is now to be implemented in the world at large through the Spirit.[22] This means the character of mission is inescapably Christ-shaped—something of enormous importance to the emerging church movement. As Wright is fond of saying, "As Jesus is to Israel, so the Church is to the world."[23] The Father's sending of the Son to Israel is now transposed into the Son's sending of his Spirit-empowered people into the world. In his latest book, *After You Believe*, this is expounded through a sustained treatment of virtue, the patterns of life embodied in Christ and now characteristic of his royal priesthood, a life of pain-marked servanthood, identifying with the condemned, misunderstood and misrepresented, vindicated through dying, always bearing in the body the death of Jesus, so that the life of Jesus may also be displayed (2 Cor 4:10).[24]

3. Cosmically situated. Third, especially resonant with the emerging church's ecological alertness is Wright's insistence that we maintain the connection between God's purposes for and through his people, and God's purposes for the whole of created reality. God's "putting-to-rights" entails rescuing the entirety of creation from the corruption, decay and death, which, through human sin, has defaced its goodness and reconfiguring it in divine splendor as the new creation. This has already been effected in Christ, and in the meantime is to be enacted in and through his community, the community of the liberated children

---

[22]Thus Wright can speak of mission as the outworking of the resurrection of Jesus, anticipating the time when God will transform all things as he once transformed the body of Jesus (N. T. Wright, *Surprised by Hope: Rethinking Heaven, the Resurrection, and the Mission of the Church* [New York: HarperOne, 2008], p. 277).

[23]Cf. "As the Father has sent me, so I send you" (Jn 20:21).

[24]N. T. Wright, *After You Believe: Why Christian Character Matters* (New York: HarperOne, 2010).

of God, in which humanity's true calling to be "wise stewards" of the earth can be rediscovered. Such is the perspective opened up by texts such as Romans 8.[25] In this context we should note the enormous importance Wright attaches to passages such as Colossians 1:15-20, where the church is pivotally situated amidst Paul's vision of creation-wide christological reconciliation (v. 18).[26]

4. Material. Bound up with all this is a resolute stress on the church's materiality—again, something that resonates strongly with "emergents." Just as there is a refusal to downplay or marginalize the inherent value and goodness of all things created—affirmed in the incarnation and resurrection, and to be finally sealed in eschatological re-creation—so there is a resolute concreteness about Wright's ecclesiology. Indeed, his theology as a whole, and his interpretation of Paul not least, is marked by a certain impatience with abstractions and a notable allergy to Platonist and Idealist philosophies—at least of the type that would subordinate the particular to the general, the contingent to the universal, the material to the immaterial. He draws extensively on philosophical writing, to be sure, but rather more from language theory and ethics than metaphysics. He employs narrative theory, but is deeply distrustful of distilling universal patterns from biblical narratives—as if a story's meaning is best understood apart from its historical situatedness or its relatedness to intrinsically sequential, publicly observable events. He draws on historical theology but is suspicious of dogmatics that has not done its historical homework.[27] (Arguably, he is oversuspicious of doctrinal history; in particular, there would seem to be tremendous possibilities in bringing Wright's work into fruitful conversation with much current trinitarian theology, especially that of the Reformed

---

[25]See his exegesis of Romans 8 in, e.g., "Letter to the Romans," esp. pp. 590-608.

[26]It is worth noting that this text played a key and decisive part in reordering Wright's early thinking on the relation between redemption and creation (N. T. Wright, "My Pilgrimage in Theology," *Themelios* 18, no. 2 [1993]: 35), also available at NTWrightPage.com <www .ntwrightpage.com/Wright_My_Pilgrimage.htm>. For his exegesis of the passage, see his *The Climax of the Covenant* (Edinburgh: T & T Clark, 1992), chap. 5. A similar creation-church integration is evident in Ephesians; see N. T. Wright, *The Resurrection of the Son of God* (London: SPCK, 2003), pp. 236-40.

[27]In this he joins hands with a range of writers of recent years who insist that doctrinal language cannot be abstracted from the physical, embodied, corporate and political practices of the church (e.g., Sarah Coakley, John Milbank, Lewis Ayres).

tradition in the line of Karl Barth, the Torrances, Colin Gunton and others, a tradition which shares so many of the same passions and concerns as Wright, and [properly read] would not weaken Wright's insistence on empirical grounding in history, and the need for effective engagement with nonchurch culture.)

In the same circle of ideas Wright eschews the all too common contrasts between one's "relationship with the Lord," understood as internal, private, invisible and physically unmediated, and one's membership of a church—external, public, visible and mediated physically. He is wary of accounts that treat the authentic church as a disembodied ideal or imply that to speak of the church as a reconstituted Israel without temple or land means we can dispense with the notion of the church as materially embedded in space and time.[28] Concomitantly, the anthropology serving his ecclesiology shuns all suggestions of divisions between body and soul, material and nonmaterial, physical and nonphysical, in which the latter of each pair is valorized at the expense of the former. For example, he is especially keen that we do not misexegete passages such as 1 Corinthians 15: the *sōma pneumatikon* of the age to come is not a dematerialized body in a dematerialized world but a Spirit-animated, hyper-physical body, inhabiting the new creation, flooded with the glory and immortality of God.[29]

As we might expect, Wright is not slow to draw out the political dimensions of this. There can be no confining the church to some purportedly private zone, as if salvation removes the church from the complexities of power, either in its own life or the life of its surrounding society. Again, this dimension is taken up by the more politically aware in the emerging church movement. In Wright it finds particular focus in his account of Paul's counterimperial theology, with the church set in opposition to the pretensions of Caesar's empire,[30] a political orientation he believes is also demonstrably present in the

---

[28]Wright, *Surprised by Hope*, pp. 269-76.
[29]Wright, *Resurrection of the Son of God*, pp. 347-56.
[30]See, e.g., N. T. Wright, *Paul: Fresh Perspectives* (London: SPCK, 2005), chap. 4; and "God and Caesar, Then and Now," in *The Character of Wisdom: Essays in Honour of Wesley Carr*, ed. Martyn Percy and Stephen Lowe (London: Ashgate, 2004), pp. 157-71.

Gospels.[31] The proclamation of the crucified Jesus as Lord announces to the principalities and powers that "their time is up," dethroning every other would-be king, and the church is the embodiment of that very *kerygma*, God's own justice. By its very nature it is a *polis*, a visible social arrangement with a quite specific set of power relations configured supremely in the light of the cross and made possible by the Spirit, and as such an advance sign, instrument and foretaste of the world to come.

All this makes Wright highly attractive to those struggling "on the ground," so to speak, struggling to find visible, tangible and embodied expressions of the church that can engage and transform the material particularities and complexities of this or that place and time.[32]

Similar concerns are evident in Wright's account of worship, which again he understands in a widescreen format: creation at large worships the Creator, and humans are called to focus and gather this praise to the Creator's honor. Humans have fallen into idolatry, but in Christ, nonidolatrous worship has at last been offered by a human in the midst of creation, making possible the song of the church evoked in Revelation 5. His accounts of baptism and Eucharist are set against this canvas. Wisely avoiding a priori definitions of *sacrament*, he steers clear of rifts between material and nonmaterial, and Procrustean theories of signification. Physical water and Spirit baptism are not driven apart, any more than they are clamped together by some externally imposed necessity; both are related to the narrative of new life and new creation stretching from creation, Israel's exodus deliverance, Jesus' own baptism, through to entrance into his body, the church. The Eucharist is likewise given a multilayered reading, earthed in Israel's history and anticipating the feast of the new creation through sharing by the Spirit in the life of Christ, crucified, risen and ascended; a sharing that takes

---

[31]See, e.g., N. T. Wright, "Kingdom Come: The Public Meaning of the Gospels," *Christian Century* 125 (2008): 29-34, also available at "The Public Meaning of the Gospels," Religion-Online.org <www.religion-online.org/showarticle.asp?title=3559>.

[32]By the same token, Wright will not impress those in the movement who are still captive to what he calls a "popular-level Protestantism," exemplified in a knee-jerk suspicion of buildings, of any attachment to places and spaces, along with a reaction against special days, seasons, occasions. See Wright, *Surprised by Hope*, pp. 271-72.

place through physical elements and bodily, corporate, symbolic action.[33] What emerges is an account of the Eucharist that refuses to be constrained by what Wright sees as inherited metaphysical cul-de-sacs, an account strikingly close to that of John Calvin (an influence he readily acknowledges).[34]

Baptism and Eucharist are thus approached from a perspective that many in the emerging churches will naturally warm to—one which is unashamed about God's investment in the physical order but retains a sense of God's eschatological freedom, thus preserving the subtlety and openness of the biblical witness to these practices, and remaining relatively free from what he sees as the loaded and unnecessarily divisive rhetoric of much sacramental controversy.

5. Improvisatory. A fifth area of resonance: Wright's employment of the model of improvisation. Admittedly, he uses this primarily to elucidate the nature of the authority of the New Testament,[35] but it includes a particular way of understanding the church's active responsibility vis-à-vis the biblical text. The scenario is that of a Shakespeare play, most of whose fifth act has been lost, and of a group of actors immersing themselves in the first four acts and improvising the fifth act accordingly. Analogously, Wright speaks of creation, fall, Israel and Jesus as the foci of the first four acts respectively; the first scene of act 5 is the writing of the New Testament, which of course hints at the ending of the drama. The remainder of act 5 is an improvisatory performance by the church, with that finale in view, an improvisation that needs to be faithful to the first four acts—fitting and appropriate—but not a mere repetition or imitation of them. The improvisation is fallible and risky, free of necessity; that the playwright's spirit has been given to the actors does not "validate in advance all they do or say."[36]

A vision begins to open up, then, congruent with Wright's eschato-

---

[33]See N. T. Wright, *The Meal Jesus Gave Us: Understanding Holy Communion* (London: Hodder & Stoughton, 2002); and Wright, *Surprised by Hope*, pp. 285-88.

[34]Speaking of his years in Montreal, he writes: "My view of the Eucharist, which had started at a rock-bottom low as an undergraduate, had received an upward jolt through reading Calvin (yes, try it and see), and had been nurtured through my early years as a chaplain. It finally came together and started to approach that of Paul" (Wright, "My Pilgrimage in Theology").

[35]N. T. Wright, *The New Testament and the People of God* (London: SPCK, 1992), pp. 139-44.

[36]Ibid., p. 143.

logical and pneumatological thrust, of the church being faithful to a God-given script that climaxes in the presentation of Jesus Christ, and, in line with Scripture's witness, being enabled by the Spirit to improvise in contingent ways that are appropriate to diverse circumstances.[37] It is not hard to see how such an understanding resonates with the concerns of many in the emerging church networks, especially those keen to retain a strong sense of the authority of the scriptural text while also being aware of the need to be light-footed, engage nimbly with the social and cultural particularities in which they find themselves, and avoid imposing fixed schemes and importing grand plans.[38]

To sum up: Wright offers an ecclesiology that is christologically grounded and pneumatically enlivened. He opens up a vision of the church as integral to salvation, grafted into the story of Israel, eschatologically charged and situated amidst God's space-time order. Its worship and mission are materially and socially embedded, and its life is marked by a Spirit-led improvisatory interplay of faithfulness and contingency.

All these themes are music to the ears of the emerging churches on both sides of the Atlantic. However, there are other themes in Wright's repertoire that are not heard so often in the cyberspace of the emerging networks. Quite why is not always clear. But they are arguably crucial if a movement which at its best offers promising new life is not to be routinized into sterility or evaporate into the air, and crucial not only for theologically alert emerging leaders but for the many others currently struggling to articulate an ecclesiology for our time. I highlight three of these easily forgotten themes.

FORGOTTEN THEMES

1. Ascension. The first is the ascension—at first blush, a curious, perhaps even arcane matter to mention. Wright makes much of it; indeed, he devotes half a chapter to the ascension in *Surprised by Hope*,[39] draw-

---

[37]Wright comments that "among the actors' tasks would be to decide, for instance, whether the production was to be 'safe' or 'relevant,' 'authentic' or 'contemporary,' and so forth—and also to take proper account of the context in which the production was to take place" (ibid., p. 141, n. 28).

[38]See Bader-Saye, "Improvising Church."

[39]Wright, *Surprised by Hope*, pp. 120-28.

ing especially on Douglas Farrow's *Ascension and Ecclesia*, as well as the work of T. F. Torrance.[40] The issue at stake is this: in the proper concern to recover a central place for ecclesiology, it is perilously easy to inflate it to the point where the integrity of the gospel—the announcement of the lordship of Christ—is relativized or even smothered. The core theological difficulty would appear to be articulating the relation between Christ and his church, and it is here that the ascension proves critical. Wright insists that the ascension cannot be collapsed into the resurrection—to claim Jesus is risen from the dead is quite distinct from saying he ascended to heaven.[41] However, the distinctive significance of the ascension cannot be resolved into the claim that Christ is now present everywhere, nonmaterially ubiquitous. Even less can it be linked to a nonmaterial understanding of the resurrection. Rather the ascension speaks of a fully human, representative Messiah going ahead of us to be enthroned as Lord over heaven and earth, to share in God's eschatological authority and rule, and as such, not now being localizable in any particular place or space within creation but universally accessible in any place through this Spirit. The ascension is about "Jesus going ahead into God's sphere, into God's future, against the day when heaven and earth become one, and he is once more personally present in the new, combined, heaven-and-earth."[42]

As Wright sees it, if this view of the ascension is downplayed or forgotten, "the church expands to fill the vacuum,"[43] for we lose a sense of Christ standing over against the church as Lord and High Priest. Christ thus becomes so closely identified with the church that the gates are opened to strident triumphalism on the one hand (no need to illustrate that!) or painful disillusionment on the other (when the church's abysmal failures become all too apparent).[44]

---

[40]Douglas Farrow, *Ascension and Ecclesia: On the Significance of the Doctrine of the Ascension for Ecclesiology and Christian Cosmology* (Edinburgh: T & T Clark, 1999); Thomas F. Torrance, *Space, Time and Resurrection* (Edinburgh: Handsel Press, 1976), chaps. 5-7. See also Wright's discussion in *Resurrection of the Son of God*, pp. 653-56.

[41]With special reference to Jn 20:17 and Lk 24:51; Wright, *Resurrection of the Son of God*, p. 654.

[42]Wright, "Holy Spirit in the Church."

[43]Wright, *Surprised by Hope*, p. 123.

[44]The difficulties here are only compounded by assuming the Christ-church relation is parallel

To maintain Christ's simultaneous absence and presence, set in motion by the ascension, Wright points to the work of the Spirit who *both* links heaven and earth, granting access to the risen and ascended Jesus Christ, *and also* ensures the "space" between Christ and his church, the proper ontological and eschatological distance pending the final union of heaven and earth. The Spirit, actualizing God's future here and now, enables a genuine union with Christ, but never in such a way that Christ becomes the possession of the church (recall Jesus to Mary Magdalene—"do not cling"). This is another place where Wright comes very close to Calvin.[45]

I would suggest that emerging ecclesiology, and indeed some others currently on offer, might be prevented from going astray by revisiting the ascension and exploring the perspectives opened up by Wright. If some contemporary Roman Catholic ecclesiologies *are* to be questioned as unduly inflated, it might be wiser to engage them at this critical point, where the determinative issues are raised with great clarity, than to proceed directly to matters of authority, ecclesial organization and so forth.[46] Similar things could be said of the "Radical Orthodoxy" movement, which shows, I think, a less than health tendency to resolve the continuing identity and agency of Christ into the identity and agency of the church;[47] or of Robert Jenson's extreme Lutheran ecclesiology, in which Christ's personal will and action comes close to disappearing entirely amidst the will and action of the church.[48]

---

to the hypostatic union of divine and human in Christ (as when the church is described as the "extension" of the incarnation).

[45]"If . . . you have to choose between Luther and Calvin in New Testament theology, in my judgement you should normally go with Calvin" (N. T. Wright, "Communion and Koinonia: Pauline Reflections on Tolerance and Boundaries," NTWrightPage.com <www.ntwrigh tpage.com/Wright_Communion_Koinonia.htm>.

[46]Michael Scott Horton, *People and Place: A Covenant Ecclesiology* (Louisville: Westminster John Knox Press, 2008), pp. 155-61.

[47]Ibid., pp. 161-64; John Webster, "The Church and the Perfection of God," in *The Community of the Word: Toward an Evangelical Ecclesiology*, ed. Mark Husbands and Daniel J. Treier (Downers Grove, Ill.: InterVarsity Press, 2005), p. 85.

[48]Horton, *People and Place*, pp. 166-68; Webster, "Church and the Perfection of God," pp. 85-86. See Robert W. Jenson, *Systematic Theology: The Triune God* (New York: Oxford University Press, 1999), 2:211-15. Arguably, a Christology that is careful to distinguish divine and human natures needs to be held along with an appropriate grasp of the "fundamental asymmetry" between divine and human action (Christoph Schwöbel, "The Creature of the Word: Recovering the Ecclesiology of the Reformers," in *On Being the Church: Essays on the Christian*

2. Israel. Second, there is the matter of Israel. An uncompromising stress on the christological heartland of ecclesiology is ubiquitous in emerging church literature, and often with it a trinitarian enthusiasm. But what of the grounding of all this in the Abrahamic covenant, in election, exodus, exile, Second Temple hopes and expectations, not to mention the "praxis," "questions" and "symbols" that, along with Israel's story, constitute its worldview?[49] These very Wrightian emphases are rarely considered at length. As history shows, however, without immersion in this matrix, ecclesiology quickly falls prey to quite alien habits of thought and action—philosophies of the corporate good, ideologies economic and political, reductionist social theory, and more—whose effects can be ruinous because they have not been shaped by characteristically Jewish currents. On a wider front also, other currently fashionable ecclesiologies have a distressing propensity to hoist the anchor out of Jewish soil, so to speak.[50]

3. Catholicity. Third, there is the matter of catholicity. Given the fluidity of this concept, we should make a working distinction between "qualitative" catholicity and "extensive" catholicity: qualitative catholicity speaking of the church's transcending all social and cultural divisions, as well as natural divisions such as age and gender; extensive catholicity speaking of the church's spatial extension, its comprising all professing Christians in all places.[51]

Community, ed. Colin E. Gunton and Daniel W. Hardy [Edinburgh: T & T Clark, 1989], p. 120; cf. Webster, "Church and the Perfection of God," p. 76).

[49]Wright, *New Testament and the People of God*, chap. 5.

[50]The call by Bruce Marshall and others for theological attention to be given to what it means to speak of the "Christological inclusion of Israel's election" can only bode well for ecclesiology. For extended discussions of these issues, see Bruce D. Marshall, "Do Christians Worship the God of Israel?" in *The Work of the Spirit in the Practices of the Church*, ed. James J. Buckley and David S. Yeago (Grand Rapids: Eerdmans, 2001); Bruce Marshall, *Trinity and Truth* (Cambridge: Cambridge University Press, 2000), pp. 169-79; R. Kendall Soulen, *The God of Israel and Christian Theology* (Minneapolis: Fortress, 1996); Peter Ochs, "Judaism and Christian Theology," in *The Modern Theologians: An Introduction to Christian Theology Since 1918*, ed. David Ford and Rachel Muers (Malden, Mass.: Blackwell, 2005), pp. 645-62. See also Reinhard Hütter, *Bound to Be Free: Evangelical Catholic Engagements in Ecclesiology, Ethics, and Ecumenism* (Grand Rapids: Eerdmans, 2004), esp. pp. 210-14.

[51]In a reply Wright made jointly with David Stancliffe to Cardinal Kasper's address to the Church of England's House of Bishops in 2006, the authors, following John Zizioulas, comment on a semantic shift in the notion of *catholic:* "The Augustinian understanding of Catholicity as universal overtook the more ancient Pauline and Ignatian understanding of

Qualitative catholicity. Wright never tires of stressing that in the apostle Paul's view, because of the victory sealed on Good Friday and the ascended Christ's outpouring of the Spirit, the church cannot be in thrall to social divisions based on differences of race, gender and socioeconomic standing. "When Jesus Christ died and rose again," he writes, "he transformed the covenant people of God into a single, worldwide family for whom the only defining badge is faith, . . . the very specific faith that Jesus is risen from the dead as Messiah and Lord of the world."[52] He presses this home forcibly with respect to ethnic division, a matter about which he believes the so-called New Perspective is highly instructive: "when Paul appeals for 'tolerance' in the church, the issues over which he is saying there should be no quarrels are precisely the issue[s] where there were cultural boundary-markers, especially between Jewish and Gentile Christians."[53]

In and through the humanity of the new Adam, then, a mode of relating has been made possible that is not ruled by the alienating boundaries that so easily come to determine our social worlds. In our own day perhaps the greatest threat to this is the ideology of consumerism, allied to forces of social segmentation, when the church is reduced to a "lifestyle enclave,"[54] each local assembly becoming an homogenous affinity group catering for a particular profile of preferences (or grievances!), and as such, clearly differentiated from other such groups. Here lurks a critical danger for emerging church initiatives, virtually all of

---

Catholicity as inclusive" (N. T. Wright and David Stancliffe, "Women Bishops: A Response to Cardinal Kasper," *Fulcrum*, July 2006 <www.fulcrum-anglican.org.uk/news/2006/20060 721kasper.cfm?doc=126>). That is, the earlier sense of *catholic* meant something like "transcending all social, cultural and natural divisions," but later it came to mean "universal"—the catholic church is geographically extended over the whole earth, and is greater in number than any other. Here I am treating the former sense as fundamental.

[52]Wright, "Communion and Koinonia."

[53]Ibid. Wright says of Romans 14: "[Paul] wants Christians to stop thinking of themselves as basically belonging to this or that ethnic group, and to see the practices that formerly demarcated that ethnic group from all others as irrelevant, things you can carry on doing if you like but which you shouldn't insist on for others." He makes similar comments about Galatians 2 (ibid.).

[54]"A lifestyle enclave is formed by people who share some feature of private life. Members of a lifestyle enclave express their identity through shared patterns of appearance, consumption, and leisure activities, which often serve to differentiate them sharply from those with other lifestyles" (Robert N. Bellah, *Habits of the Heart: Individualism and Commitment in American Life* [Berkeley: University of California Press, 1996], p. 335).

which are culture-group specific. Many such initiatives find it hard to
mature to that further stage when the Word of the cross and the power
of the Spirit disrupt homogeneity to forge an infinitely profounder
unity, one possible only through Christ crucified and risen. The point
has been put very sharply by critics of emerging churches, such as John
Hull and John Milbank.[55] What is not always provided in such critiques is a pinpointing of the christological root of qualitative catholicity. Wright's work can serve to push us back to those awkward New
Testament texts that refuse to speak of the church as bound by any
unity except that which originates in the *ephapax* of the cross, as well
as to the supporting themes of election and covenant, which will subvert the propensity to allow consumer choice to become the de facto
foundation of the church's oneness.

Related to that, is not a similar reorientation needed among those
who naturally warm to relational ecclesiologies supported by highly
social doctrines of the Trinity—"communion" ecclesiologies, as they
are sometimes dubbed, associated especially with Henri de Lubac,
much post-Vatican II Roman Catholic ecclesiology, John Zizioulas,

---

[55]See their critique of emerging church initiatives within the Church of England: John M. Hull,
Mission-Shaped Church: A Theological Response (London: SCM, 2006); John Milbank, "Stale
Expressions: The Management-Shaped Church," *Studies in Christian Ethics* 21, no. 1 (2008):
117-28. Milbank speaks of projects such as "fresh expressions" and "mission-shaped church" as
an "evangelical-liberal collusion," propelled by the instrumental reason of a capitalist, manage-
ment-obsessed ideology, amounting to a "blasphemous denial" of the church. "The Church
cannot be found amongst the merely like-minded, who associate in order to share a particular
taste, hobby or perversion. It can *only* be found where many different peoples possessing many
different gifts collaborate in order to produce a divine-human community in one specific location" (Milbank, "Stale Expressions," p. 124). (The phrase "collaborate in order to produce a
divine-human community" is unfortunate, given what Milbank wants to oppose.)
    For a perceptive discussion of emerging churches in relation to the "homogenous unit prin-
ciple" (HUP; what is in essence the observation that people like to become Christians without
crossing racial, linguistic or class barriers), see Tim Dean, "FX, EC and the DNA of HUP:
Homogeneity and Heterogeneity in Emerging Churches: A Problem Explored" (available online at <www.fulcrum-anglican.org.uk/page.cfm?ID=457>). Dean defends the Church of
England report *Mission-Shaped Church* (2004) against Hull's critique, but writes: "Despite my
concluding that Hull's critique is wrong on all counts, there is one important implied criticism:
the means and strategies of mission, themselves need to embody the radical demands of the
Gospel." Later, he says: "HUP's great flaw is taking an *observational* truth, and making it into
a *programmable mission strategy* without due regard for the transformational aspects of the
gospel based on the reconciling nature of God which see diverse communities acting as one in
the cause of justice and love for all, irrespective of ethnicity, culture, gender, wealth, etc."
(Dean, "FX, EC and the DNA of HUP"). See also Percy, "Old Tricks for New Dogs?" p. 38.

Nicholas Sagovsky, Stanley Grenz, Miroslav Volf and others?[56] This fashionable outlook often appears in emerging church writers, but, significantly, rarely in Wright. Doubtless it has opened up immense possibilities, and few would deny that intrahuman relations in the church must in some manner reflect and share in the intratrinitarian relations. But questions have to be asked if we are presented with a vision of interweaving divine and human communion with little if any mention of the cross, and with it the sheer, unspeakable horror of what God's reconciliation in Christ exposes and heals. We can enjoy being relational with those we have chosen to be relational with, and it is gratifying to think we might even be enjoying the Trinity in the process, but we are much less happy when someone we would never choose to spend a Sunday morning with is thrown alongside us simply by virtue of their baptism into Christ. At that point, what Robert Bellah calls "the narcissism of similarity" needs to be cracked apart by cruciform realism.[57] In John's Gospel, we recall, Jesus' prayer for his disciples' unity—that they would be one as he and his Father are one—is spoken in the shadow of crucifixion (Jn 17:22). The late and great Lesslie Newbigin used to make that point repeatedly. (Indeed, it is worth noting how close to Newbigin so much of Wright's vision of the church is.) If the church is built on any unity other than what has been achieved at Golgotha, we are declaring that the principalities and powers still rule the world, and the church is powerless against them. Sadly, this is a seam in Wright and Newbigin that is very often ignored by emerging bloggerati.[58] Hence Martyn Percy observes (overcyni-

---

[56]See, e.g., John D. Zizioulas, *Communion and Otherness: Further Studies in Personhood and Church* (London: T & T Clark, 2006); Henri de Lubac, *Catholicism: A Study of Dogma in Relation to the Corporate Destiny of Mankind* (New York: Sheed & Ward, 1958); Nicholas Sagovsky, *Ecumenism, Christian Origins, and the Practice of Communion* (Cambridge: Cambridge University Press, 2000); Stanley J. Grenz, *Theology for the Community of God* (Nashville: Broadman & Holman, 1994); Dennis M. Doyle, *Communion Ecclesiology: Vision and Versions* (Maryknoll, N.Y.: Orbis, 2000); Miroslav Volf, *After Our Likeness: The Church as the Image of the Trinity* (Grand Rapids: Eerdmans, 1998); Miroslav Volf and Maurice Lee, "The Spirit and the Church," in *Advents of the Spirit: An Introduction to the Current Study of Pneumatology*, ed. Bradford E. Hinze and D. Lyle Dabney (Milwaukee: Marquette University Press, 2001), pp. 382-409.

[57]Bellah, *Habits of the Heart*, p. 72.

[58]Essentially the same considerations apply to the common pressure from emerging church circles that a wide variety of traditions and practices should be recovered and promoted—Celtic,

cally, perhaps) that although the emerging church movement in the United Kingdom may use the "rhetoric of extensity"—outreach, inclusiveness, engaging the surrounding culture and so forth—it is in fact composed largely through "intensity" and "in-reach," resulting too often in groups of the like-minded that are relatively disengaged from local communities (what he calls "dispersed intensity").[59]

Extensive catholicity. If we turn to the second sense of catholicity—the spatial extension of the church, the totality of the church worldwide—the specter of institutionalism quickly appears, for in order to embody and ensure some degree of church unity on a large scale, institutional arrangements will inevitably come into play. The temptation here is twofold: on the one hand, to regard visible unity as exclusively an institutional matter, and on the other to collude with a naive anti-institutionalism.

THE CATHOLIC CHURCH AS VISIBLE

We return to O'Donovan and the Church of England's Thirty-nine Articles, for what happens in this sixteenth-century text is indicative of much Protestant ecclesiology. We saw that O'Donovan laments the lack of a properly theological account of the church. Expanding on this, he notes the lack of any account of the invisible church; we hear only about the church in the realm of appearances. Also, the visible church is defined in terms of its activities or practices, and, what is more, these activities are understood largely in relation to the church's institutional

---

charismatic, Russian Orthodox, labyrinths, whatever—and combined in ways that eschew the binary oppositions and exclusiveness of the past. At its best, this encourages "a generous orthodoxy," to adopt Brian McLaren's term. At its worst, it fosters an unprincipled bricolage or pastiche (see Bretherton, "Beyond the Emerging Church?" pp. 46-47). Part of the weakness here is a failure to take account of a tradition as something that matures in and through time, through apprenticed immersion, and in response to particular circumstances. The danger is that a particular church never learns to develop its own particular tradition but becomes merely a site where other traditions are accommodated in juxtaposition. With this goes a tendency to adopt ancient traditions and practices without the benefits that come from attending to the growth of that tradition, and its embeddedness in quite specific social and cultural contingencies. The deeper problem concerns the issue of unity we have just been speaking about: the ease with which a tradition or set of traditions becomes a new center around which the church gathers, once again making a merely human preference not only a missional provisionary but an ecclesial ultimate.

[59]Percy, "Old Tricks for New Dogs?" esp. pp. 30-35.

structures. O'Donovan argues that however we understand the visible-invisible distinction, "we must be careful not to be seduced by [it] into thinking the only thing left to us in the realm of appearances is an *organization*."[60] In other words, we need a sense of the visible, catholic (extended) church, and to insist that its visibility is a larger matter than the visibility of the institutions that express it. For the church consists of all who are baptized into Christ, an "observable social reality" that belongs to the realm of appearances in its own right.[61] And—we might add—we will not be helped here if we overpress what some are keen to call "the primacy of the local church," *this* or *that* particular gathering of the baptized meeting regularly in a specific place.[62]

What has this to do with the emerging church followers? Like many modern Protestants, they will tend to snort at any whiff of institutional expansion—oversized ecclesiastical bureaucracies, swollen theologies of the ordained ministry, denominational idolatry. And many (though by no means all) will suspect much of the "unity talk"

---

[60]O'Donovan, *On the Thirty-Nine Articles*, p. 89.

[61]Ibid.

[62]In support of a document by Rowan Williams, Wright comments: "The key point then is this: . . . though some things can indeed be decided by a local church, the decision as to which things can be decided locally is not itself one that can be taken locally" (N. T. Wright, "Rowan's Reflections: Unpacking the Archbishop's Statement," *Fulcrum* <www.fulcrum-anglican. org.uk/page.cfm?ID=453>). The fundamentally *theological* grounding of the one church in Wright's eyes is made very plain in the course of the Wright-Stancliffe response to Cardinal Kasper (see n. 51): "The question of Cardinal Kasper bringing a distinctively Roman perspective to Anglican affairs is also revealed in his remarks about unity, and about the role of the ordained ministry, and particularly of bishops, in engendering communion within that. The Anglican tradition takes its role as a 'bridge' seriously, and we too believe that we must work for, discern and enhance that unity for which Jesus prayed. But *we do not believe that eucharistic unity ('communion' in that sense) is only attainable when there is full recognition of ministries, and all are in communion with the see of Rome.* In Anglican theology, unity is achieved by our saying yes to God's gracious invitation to his table. It is because we are one with God through being caught up in Christ's one perfect self-offering to the Father that we have unity with one another, rather than communion with God being a consequence of our union with one another. We, in other words, are inclined to see eucharistic sharing not as the goal at the end of the ecumenical pilgrimage where God is waiting for us, but as the path of that pilgrimage itself, along which he accompanies us on the way. *We would base our theology of union within the Godhead on a dynamic incorporation into the divine life of the Holy Trinity, rather more than on a sacramental theology based on the validity of the sacrament confected by one who has the authority to do so*; and we would prefer to see debates about orders within the frame of mutual eucharistic hospitality, rather than the other way around. In this regard, *we would look to Galatians 2, with its clear teaching that all who believe in Jesus Christ belong at the same table*, no matter what their cultural background" (Wright and Stancliffe, "Women Bishops," italics added).

that comes from the ecumenical movement. Pursuing church unity on the large scale, after all, becomes quickly tarnished by the oppressive interests of the powerful, by centralized, hierarchical management systems, and thus by deadening uniformity (a uniformity that is often profoundly insular).[63]

Fair enough. But O'Donovan's critique of Protestant institutionalism bites deeper than this. Put bluntly, the Protestant error is to see visible unity as merely an institutional matter, whereas visible unity is a *gospel* matter—and this is something Wright repeatedly declares. To be baptized into Christ is to be intrinsically linked to all baptized persons, that worldwide body of the catholic church, who at the most fundamental level have been pulled together by virtue of the cross, resurrection and Pentecost. This should generate a sense not only of all we can receive from countless others we may never have seen or met, but also a sense of costly obligation, of the sort we find Paul urging in connection with the Jerusalem collection—which Wright describes as "a major element in [Paul's] practical strategy for creating and sustaining the *one family of God redefined around the Messiah and in the Spirit.*"[64] Further, a gospel-driven conception of unity will always work against homogeneity, for it is energized by a cruciform reconciliation of the unlike and a Spirit-driven flourishing of difference within the body.

Without this sense of "extensive" catholicity, we are left with a church made up of a constellation of homogenous groupings, whose relatedness to each other is seen as entirely an institutional matter, best left to middle-aged clerics who like committee meetings. It is not obvious that the emerging church movement has headed off this danger sufficiently.

NAIVE ANTI-INSTITUTIONALISM

If staid institutionalism is one danger, naive anti-institutionalism is another. Wright is clearly not one who shirks institutional immersion. Anyone trying to keep pace with his ceaseless activity at diocesan, na-

---

[63]See Shults, "Reforming Ecclesiology in Emerging Churches," pp. 428-30. The more philosophically minded in the movement will commonly warm to the "turn to alterity" (otherness) associated with writers such as Emmanuel Levinas and Paul Ricoeur, where the preservation of irreducible difference is contrasted with the pressure to conform to some ideal of "sameness."

[64]Wright, *Paul: Fresh Perspectives*, p. 167 (italics added).

tional and international levels will testify to this. And this is not *despite* his commitment to the church as the one people of God brought into being by the Messiah through the Spirit, but *because* of it. I cannot help notice overkeenness to dismiss institutions among some of my friends in the emerging movement (and in myself). (Similar things could be said about the way power is portrayed.)[65] It is one thing to urge that the catholic church is not institutionally founded, quite another to pretend that the church can somehow be "exempted from ordinary and mundane patterns of human association"[66] and thus from "stable structures of social interaction."[67]

Significantly, Wright's heavy institutional involvement is largely ignored by the young ecclesiologists drawing on his work. Along the same lines, Newbigin's claim that the local congregation is "the hermeneutic of the Gospel" can be quoted enthusiastically in emergent writing,[68] but his decades of work for visible church unity (sometimes in the most barren institutional settings) receives rather less attention.[69]

There may be interesting changes afoot in the United States in this regard, where emerging church initiatives have generally been far more distanced from established denominations. Following up their earlier research covering the period 2001-2004, Eddie Gibbs and Ryan Bolger note that in the last few years "much has changed": they believe that "emerging initiatives within traditional churches" are the "next horizon for the spread of emerging church practices in the United States."[70]

---

[65]Kester Brewin, a teacher and founder of Vaux, a group of artists and city lovers based in London, is representative of many: "I believe in leadership. People need direction. But we need to find models of it that have nothing to do with power" (quoted in Gibbs and Bolger, *Emerging Churches*, p. 199). For discussion of the complexities of power, theologically conceived, see Stephen Sykes, *Power and Christian Theology* (London: Continuum, 2006).

[66]Bretherton, "Beyond the Emerging Church?" p. 37.

[67]Volf, *After Our Likeness*, p. 234.

[68]Lesslie Newbigin, *The Gospel in a Pluralist Society* (Grand Rapids: Eerdmans, 1989), chap. 18.

[69]As a commentator sympathetic to emerging church initiatives has said, "Emergent leaders would do well to consider the ways in which order, oversight and connection can foster relationship, mutual growth, humility and accountability" (Bader-Saye, "Improvising Church," p. 14).

[70]Eddie Gibbs and Ryan K. Bolger, "The Morphing of the Church: Emerging Churches within Denominational Structures," *Theology News and Notes* 55, no. 3 (2008): 3.

CONCLUSION

This has mainly been an exercise in what the ecclesiology of Wright has offered and could offer to the emerging church movement. It might well be asked: Is there anything the emerging church movement has to offer Wright as far as ecclesiology is concerned? If ecclesiology is understood as an account of the nature and character of the people of God that seeks its determinative grounding in the biblical texts, then in terms of the exegesis of Scripture, it is hard to find in the writings of the emerging church instances where a correction of Wright is required, or where a biblical emphasis or theme developed by the emerging church is ignored or seriously underplayed. It may be, however, that where emerging church writers wish to push Wright further is with respect to his loyalty to the particular institutional arrangements to which he is inevitably committed as bishop, notwithstanding what I have said about "naive anti-institutionalism." Where the emerging movement is perhaps most probing is when it reminds us of the frailty and proneness to corruption of any authority structures in any church. Many in the emerging churches are there because they have been wounded by institutional heavy-handedness. No one could accuse Wright of this, but has there appeared in his output enough critique of the extraordinarily elaborate apparatus that a contemporary diocesan bishop has to negotiate, or of the ways in which such apparatus has on occasion inadvertently injured those in the body of Christ? This is to raise questions far beyond the scope of this essay, but perhaps they are worth asking, not despite but precisely because of the vibrant and inspiring ecclesiology that Wright has given us.

Response to Jeremy Begbie
N. T. WRIGHT

Like the man in Moliere who discovered he had been speaking prose all his life without realizing it, Jeremy Begbie has made me realize that I have been developing and expounding an ecclesiology for the last few decades without being aware of it. I am enormously grateful to him for ferreting out several recondite bits and pieces of my writings, making interesting connections between them and my exegetical work, and drawing them into a clear and fair synthesis.

In particular, I have been as fascinated as he has with the question of why the emerging church should have taken such interest in the work of a middle-aged Anglican bishop, like a pack of greyhounds taking their lead from an old, heavy elephant. One obvious answer falls outside Jeremy's (Pauline) remit: the emerging church has been busily recovering the theme of the kingdom of God from its earlier obscurity within evangelical thinking. Since I have highlighted the same theme, they regard me as an ally. I strongly agree with Jeremy's emphasis on the way in which my treatment of Paul draws out the integrated nature of theology and politics, and on the necessary historical rootedness of the whole enterprise both of exegesis and of Christian discipleship.

When it comes to the ascension (it is fascinating to see how significant this topic has become in our present discussions), I should draw attention to my little guide, *Acts for Everyone*. There I explored further the double notion which I think Acts takes for granted: first, heaven is the "control room" for earth, so the one who is now installed there is not removed and irrelevant, but is seated on the throne from which earth, as well as heaven, is now run. Second, when Jesus is exalted to heaven he is portrayed as the reality of which Caesar, with his sham apotheosis, is just a parody. I would now go further and suggest that all four Gospels, in their different ways, tell the story of Jesus as *the story of how Jesus became King of Israel and Lord of the world*, with the ascension as one way of emphasizing this outcome.

I agree with Jeremy that there are real dangers in the cultural homogeneity of the emerging church—as there are with all denominations, whose attractions to the postmodern church-shopper may have more to do with "feeling at home with people like myself" than with anything more spiritual or theological. This is endemic in denominationalism as a whole; Anglicans suffer from it as much as anyone. But the closing pages of this remarkable paper lead me to reflect on the way in which the words *institution* and *power* still carry such negative resonance. I believe this is part of the legacy of the Romantic movement, which privileged *spontaneity* and *authenticity* over anything that required hard work, and the supposed free movement of the Spirit over against anything requiring structure. The rejection of power ascribed to one "emerging" leader (n. 65) is telling, and to my mind naive. One might as well say one was going to have a substantial community in which there would be no sex and no money. No doubt some are called to live in poverty, abstinence and obedience as a sign of contradiction. But relationships, resources and responsibilities are part of the God-given structures of creation, and to imagine one can do without them is to invite them to return, dangerously, by the back door.

Many churches, including my own, have wrestled with the ambiguities and puzzles of power and weakness over a long period. No doubt if we were inventing ourselves from scratch we wouldn't do it quite the same way. But we have to start where we are, not where we aren't. It doesn't do to long for a blissful romantic idyll where everything somehow happens without anyone thinking, planning, leading, teaching, rebuking or warning. Or why would God have given such a variety of gifts to the church? That, indeed, is a further topic we might consider. Certainly, I regard both the Anglican Communion and the emerging church movement as gifts from God to the wider Christian family. I suspect that living with that paradox is no harder, in fact, than it was for first-century Christians to come together across the boundaries of Jew and Greek, slave and free, male and female.

8

Did St. Paul Go to
Heaven When He Died?

MARKUS BOCKMUEHL

NEW TESTAMENT ESCHATOLOGY IS ONE of many areas of biblical scholarship on which Tom Wright has left his characteristically bracing and original mark. In this essay, which is intended as a constructively critical tribute to his extraordinarily fertile and prolific contribution, I propose to engage his approach to certain Pauline aspects of the traditional Christian belief in life after death. Wright's approach has been spelled out in recent years in works including his large book on the resurrection, *For all the Saints?* and *Surprised by Hope.*[1]

The broader concerns of Tom Wright's eschatological scheme seem to me wholly laudable, perhaps above all in his argument that the bodily resurrection of Jesus is the fundamental pillar of the Christian story of salvation, without which little or nothing that is distinctive about Christianity makes any sense. As Wright puts it, "early Christianity was a 'resurrection' movement through and through."[2] Indeed, and notwithstanding two centuries of the so-called historical Jesus industry and all its works, the first and last question that matters for the New Testament witness to Jesus is quite simply this: "Is he dead or alive?"[3]

---

[1]N. T. Wright, *The Resurrection of the Son of God* (London: SPCK, 2003); *For All the Saints? Remembering the Christian Departed* (London: SPCK, 2003); and *Surprised by Hope* (London: SPCK, 2007).

[2]Wright, *Resurrection of the Son of God*, p. 210.

[3]Cf. Beverly Roberts Gaventa and Richard B. Hays, eds., *Seeking the Identity of Jesus: A Pilgrimage* (Grand Rapids: Eerdmans, 2008), pp. 20-21.

What sets Jesus apart from the historical Caesar or any other historical figure is that neither Paul nor any other early Christian writer ever speaks of him as anything other than alive in the present. On this matter, Wright has rendered an invaluable service to the task of freshly comprehending and articulating the New Testament for the twenty-first-century church and academy.

Wright quite rightly highlights too that the New Testament's affirmation of the resurrection (and ascension) of Jesus in turn underpins the Christian hope for the resurrection of believers, when God will "fill the earth with his glory, transform the old heavens and earth into the new, and raise his children from the dead to populate and rule over the redeemed world he has made."[4] In that day the "veil" will be lifted as "heaven and our world will be integrated completely, and be fully visible to one another."[5]

Few careful students of the New Testament would find significant fault with these affirmations. Even one of Wright's more combative critics of recent years agreed: "As Wright likes to put it, we need to recover the biblical focus on 'life after life after death.' I believe Wright is right about that. As he is also on target when he insists that the resurrection is 'not the story of a happy ending but of a new beginning.' "[6]

These are matters on which Tom Wright and I have exchanged amicable views in print.[7] The large area of shared exegetical and theological common ground in our reading of Pauline and New Testament eschatology makes it seem more interesting for present purposes to single out an aspect that appears to offer particularly fruitful scope for further discussion and debate. As is perhaps the case for some other topics discussed in this volume, we shall see that the fuses of controversy tend to be lit less by Wright's eloquent and laudable affirmations than by some of his concomitant denials.

---

[4]Wright, *Surprised by Hope*, p. 277.

[5]Ibid., pp. 147-48; similarly *Simply Christian* (London: SPCK, 2006), p. 147, citing Col 3; 1 Jn 2–3. For the "veil" language see p. 187.

[6]Richard John Neuhaus, quoting an unidentified passage in Wright, "The Possibilities and Perils in Being a Really Smart Bishop, etc.," *First Things* 182 (2008): 57-72.

[7]Markus Bockmuehl, "Compleat History of the Resurrection: A Dialogue with N. T. Wright," in *Journal for the Study of the New Testament* 26 (2004): 489-504, and in the same issue, N. T. Wright, "An Incompleat (but Grateful) Response to the Review by Markus Bockmuehl of *The Resurrection of the Son of God*," pp. 505-10.

Here, more specifically, my focus is on his conviction that an affirmation of the bodily resurrection necessitates a denial of the traditional Christian belief that the faithful "go to heaven" when they die. I shall examine Wright's Pauline exegetical and theological basis for this view and argue two main points: (1) Paul's own writings, although difficult and ambiguous in some respects, appear in fact to entail a compatible belief both in a future bodily resurrection and in the departed believer's immediate and permanent entry into the presence of the exalted Christ in heaven; (2) the apostle's earliest known readers, from the inner-canonical (e.g., deutero-Pauline) to the late second century and beyond, sense no contradiction or compromise in affirming that Christians, including Paul himself, go permanently to heaven when they die and that this abiding heavenly presence with Christ is compatible with being resurrected bodily when God creates his undivided new heaven and earth. The exceptions to this twofold conviction appear almost exclusively among certain Gnostic Christians who affirmed only a heavenly afterlife.

On Not Going to Heaven When You Die

Tom Wright believes traditional Christianity to be fundamentally mistaken where it affirms that believers in some meaningful sense "go to heaven" when they die. He regards this position as dangerously subversive and profoundly incompatible with orthodox faith in the resurrection. Whatever interim situations the departed might experience, in describing the ultimate destiny of believers "resurrection" and "going to heaven" are mutually exclusive alternatives:

> The use of the word *heaven* to denote the *ultimate* goal of the redeemed . . . is severely misleading and does not begin to do justice to the Christian hope. . . . The ultimate destination is (once more) *not* "going to heaven when you die" but being bodily raised into the transformed, glorious likeness of Jesus Christ.[8]

Far from any sort of heavenly afterlife, rapture into outer space or end of history, Wright believes biblical eschatology envisions instead

---

[8]Wright, *Surprised by Hope*, p. 180.

the resurrection of the body in the likeness of Jesus, who returns to Zion to gather his restored people not into heaven but to be with them on earth.[9] In his own concise summary of his position,

> "Resurrection" does not mean "going to heaven when you die." It isn't about "life after death." It's about "life after life after death." You die; you go to be "with Christ" ("life after death"), but your body remains dead. Describing where and what you are in that interim period is difficult, and the New Testament writers mostly don't try. Call it "heaven" if you like, but don't imagine it's the end of all things. What is promised after that interim period is a new bodily life within God's new world ("life after life after death").[10]

In seeking to exegete passages like this, we have the benefit of a series of high-profile media interviews in which Wright restates and annotates his arguments of *Surprised by Hope* with admirable clarity. Such comments were offered to *Time* magazine, ABC's *Nightline*, Canada's *100 Huntley Street* and others. In *Time*, he explains that when the time comes for God to complete his saving plan, "you won't be going up there to him, he'll be coming down here."[11] He goes on to claim, "Never at any point do the Gospels or Paul say Jesus has been raised, therefore we are all going to heaven. They all say, Jesus is raised, therefore the new creation has begun, and we have a job to do."[12]

While serious students of the New Testament will surely resonate with the affirmations in the second sentence, some may stumble over the denials in the first. While Scripture is hardly systematic on this point, a number of texts ranging from the Gospel of John (e.g., Jn 3:14 with Jn 12:32; 14:2-3; 17:24) via Ephesians (e.g., Eph 2:6) to Hebrews (e.g., Heb 12:22-24) do seem at least prima facie to imply what Wright

---

[9]Ibid.

[10]Wright, *Simply Christian*, p. 186.

[11]David Van Biema, "Christians Wrong About Heaven, Says Bishop," *Time*, February 7, 2008 <www.time.com/time/world/article/0,8599,1710844,00.html>. This turn of phrase appears prima facie to subvert his confidence elsewhere (e.g., as cited above in n. 5) that in the eschaton the distinction between heaven and earth will be no more. (For this reason it may be relevant to acknowledge that when this material was first presented at the 2010 Wheaton Theology Conference, Wright appeared to distance himself from this quotation.)

[12]Ibid. Cf. the similar but markedly less hyperbolic language of Wright, *Surprised by Hope*, p. 56.

denies: it is precisely because of Christ's resurrection and ascension that Christians too gain access to the heavenly Jerusalem as the eternal dwelling place of the exalted Christ which in the new creation will be universally revealed, redeeming and subsuming the old.

Wright's strong resistance to the idea of a heavenly destination seems at times compelled as much by understandable fears about Christian ecological and political escapism as by the biblical texts themselves (whose own interest in heaven does have deeply political implications, as he rightly points out).[13] In an online interview with an interfaith blog, he castigates the fact that

> Somehow, though, the evangelical movement turned toward a sort of disembodied piety and got out of the business of social justice. And evangelicals picked up this idea that there is no use doing anything in this world. . . . There's an inscription that says, "Heaven is Home." But that simply is not biblical language. That's not something Wilberforce ever would have said.[14]

Here too Wright's infectious positive commitment to social justice has great merit. The invocation of William Wilberforce, by contrast, would seem to demand on the one hand a more candid acknowledgment that quietist avoidance of social justice is of course hardly characteristic of "evangelicals" *tout court*, either then or now. But conversely, and perhaps more importantly, it is again at the point of his sharpest denial—certainly about Wilberforce on "Heaven Is Home" and possibly about "biblical language" too—that Wright seems least persuasive.[15]

---

[13]E.g., Wright, *Simply Christian*, pp. 192-94; *Surprised by Hope*, pp. 224-33. He told *Nightline* that the implications of God's new heaven and new earth motivate him "enormously" (see Martin Bashir, "Bishop's Heaven: Is There Life After the Afterlife? Bishop Tom Wright Offers New Perspective on Heaven and Hell," *Nightline*, February 26, 2008 <http://abcnews .go.com/Nightline/FaithMatters/story?id=4330823&page=3>).

[14]N. T. Wright, "157: Conversation With 'Tom' Wright on Resurrection, Heaven and Hope on Earth," *Read the Spirit*, 2008 <www.readthespirit.com/explore/2008/4/30/157-conversation-with-tom-wright-on-resurrection-heaven-hope.html>.

[15]Although patently no passivist, Wilberforce was deeply motivated by the sentiment of the inscription Wright rejects: he laments the church's and society's "utter forgetfulness of its being the great business of life to secure our admission into heaven, and to prepare our hearts for its service and enjoyments" (William Wilberforce, *A Practical View of the Prevailing Religious System of Professed Christians in The Higher and Middle Classes in This Country, Contrasted with Real Christianity*, 14th ed. [London: Cadell & Davies, 1820], pp. 187-88; cf. p. 56). "A Christian is to regard himself a stranger and a pilgrim, and to have his portion, his conversation, his

Resistance to polarizations of piety over against social justice—or for that matter of heavenly over against resurrection life—has marked sound Christian theology, evangelical or otherwise, in every age.

This much may suffice, perhaps, to establish the background to Tom Wright's denial that Christians "go to heaven" when they die. We now turn to explore this question on a somewhat smaller Pauline canvas: what did Paul himself believe about the experience of life after physical death—and what did his early readers think he taught?[16]

WHAT SAINT PAUL REALLY SAID, ACCORDING TO N. T. WRIGHT

It is in 2 Corinthians that we first find Paul employing eschatological language of entering one's true home that is not physical but "a house not made with hands, eternal in the heavens" (2 Cor 5:1).[17] While "at home in the body" he is "away from the Lord" (2 Cor 5:6), but he clearly prefers the opposite, that is, to be at home with the Lord (2 Cor 5:8). So also in Philippians Paul reflects on the possibility of his death, which would be a matter of "setting forth to be with Christ" (Phil 1:23).

These passages just cited do not receive sustained attention either in *Surprised by Hope* or even in the big *Resurrection* volume,[18] because for Tom Wright they fall under the heading of the believer's intermediate state of "restful happiness." This is the situation in which disembodied

---

treasure, his country in heaven. Be these my habitual feelings, through Thy grace, O Lord!" (Journal entry April 22, 1804, quoted in Robert Isaac Wilberforce and Samuel Wilberforce, *The Life of William Wilberforce* [London: J. Murray, 1838], 3.154). John Newton too, himself hardly blind to Wilberforce's political struggle, wrote to him more than once of going "home" to heaven (so, e.g., *Letters* dated April 21, 1797; June 3, 1797).

[16]Limitations of space here preclude an engagement with the debate about whether Paul changed his mind on eschatology, e.g., between 1 Cor and 2 Cor, see C. H. Dodd, "The Mind of Paul: Change and Development," in *Bulletin of the John Rylands Library* 18 (1934): 69-110; for later discussion cf., e.g., Murray J. Harris, "2 Corinthians 5:1-10: Watershed in Paul's Eschatology?" *Tyndale Bulletin* 22 (1971): 32-57; idem, "The New Testament View of Life After Death," *Themelios* 11, no. 2 (1986): 47-52; Richard Longenecker, *Studies in Paul, Exegetical and Theological*, New Testament Monographs 2 (Sheffield: Sheffield Phoenix, 2004). Most interpreters today (including, e.g., Wright, *Resurrection of the Son of God*, p. 370) would agree that Paul perhaps does not change his mind so much as his perspective (but contrast the more roundly skeptical view in Paul Woodridge, "Did Paul Change His Mind? An Examination of Some Aspects of Pauline Eschatology," *Themelios* 28, no. 3 (2003): 5-18.

[17]Scripture quoted in this chapter is the author's translation.

[18]But see pp. 219-21 of this chapter for Wright's view of Phil 3:20 and the idea of colonial "citizenship."

Christians find themselves after death in the spiritual presence of Christ. In that sense perhaps, but only temporarily, they are indeed in paradise—or, if you must use that word, in "heaven."[19] In this pre-resurrection state, Wright argues, the saints may indeed be in communion with us and we can pray with them and even for them.[20] But even if in 2 Corinthians 5:1 it may look as if Paul thinks the future body is "in the heavens," nevertheless most certainly "it will not stay there."[21] And even though the apostle may say in verses 8-9 that to die would mean to be "at home with the Lord" (cf. Phil 1:23), Wright is sure that this situation can only be temporary and intermediate, not permanent. To suggest anything else would be "an unwarranted Platonizing of Christian hope,"[22] since "the use of the word 'heaven' to denote the ultimate goal of the redeemed . . . is severely misleading and does not begin to do justice to the Christian hope."[23] Declaring himself exasperated with his fellow Christians' failure to accept his view of this matter,[24] Wright invites us instead to rally to the task of rescuing the Christian tradition from its lamentable tendency "to drive a steamroller through what Paul actually says."[25]

So What *Did* Saint Paul Really Say?[26] In *Surprised by Hope*, Wright draws on his earlier work (*The Resurrection of the Son of God*) in documenting early Christianity's strongly continued affirmation of bodily resurrection, and he argues that this material at the same time establishes patristic support for a "two stage post-mortem future" involving an interim state followed by a bodily resurrection experienced not in heaven but on earth—or more specifically in "God's new world," which

---

[19]Wright, *Surprised by Hope*, pp. 183-87. Cf. Wright, *Simply Christian*, p. 187 ("Call it 'heaven' if you like").

[20]Unlike the book of Revelation and other Jewish and Christian texts, he does not believe they are in a position to intercede for us (e.g., Wright, *Surprised by Hope*, pp. 28-36; contrast, traditionally, 2 Macc 15:12-14; also Rev 5:8; 8:3-4; cf. Lk 16:19-31; Jn 11:25); and there can be no such thing as purgatory (ibid., pp. 184-85).

[21]Wright, *Resurrection of the Son of God*, p. 368—appealing (n. 154) to Col 1:5; 3:1-4; 1 Pet 1:4.

[22]Ibid., pp. 367, 369-70.

[23]Wright, *For All the Saints*, pp. 20-21, quoted earlier.

[24]Ibid., p. 21. "I am repeatedly frustrated by how hard it is to get this point through the thick wall of traditional thought and language that most Christians put up."

[25]Wright, *Resurrection of the Son of God*, pp. 367-68.

[26]Cf. N. T. Wright, *What Saint Paul Really Said: Was Paul of Tarsus the Real Founder of Christianity?* (Oxford: Lion, 1997).

is repeatedly and emphatically distinguished from "heaven."[27]

In relation to the parousia and resurrection hope more generally, *Surprised by Hope* takes the reader accessibly through a wide gamut of the relevant Pauline passages. Romans 8, 1 Corinthians 15, Philippians 3 and 1 Thessalonians 4 are all here; they are treated with characteristic exegetical competence, panache and forthrightness—and, for my money, unobjectionably. Romans 8, for example, is shown to illustrate Paul's vital interlinkage of creation and new creation, on which hangs a great deal of his eschatology—and indeed of his understanding of the Christian life and hope for the here and now. While appreciatively noting much agreement with Tom Wright on the theological posture and hermeneutical importance of these texts, I propose in what follows to single out two of them more specifically.

First, Tom Wright contends in 1 Thessalonians 4:14-17 with a puzzling eschatological passage that since at least the nineteenth century has led certain literally minded interpreters to imagine a scenario of abduction by extraterrestrial aliens—an idea that perhaps had its popular heyday in a late-twentieth-century series of well-known biblicistic sci-fi novels.[28] Their day may, one hopes, have come and gone; but it is perhaps not so hard to see how Paul's astonishingly complex symbolic language could have left him open to misunderstanding. At the parousia God through Jesus "will bring with him" (1 Thess 4:14) those who have in the meantime died in the faith, and yet they will "rise first"; but those still alive will, at the archangel's shout and the sound of the divine trumpet, follow the newly risen by (notoriously) being "caught up in the clouds together with them to meet the Lord in the air" and remain with him "always" (vv. 16-17).

Wright firmly rebukes literalistic speculations on this point as "grievously abusive" and indeed "Gnostic," suggesting instead that Paul here combines three metaphors: Moses coming down the mountain to the sound of trumpets and loud voices, Daniel's vision of the

---

[27]Cf. Wright, *Surprised by Hope*, pp. 169-71, citing *Resurrection of the Son of God*, chap 11; also *Simply Christian*, p. 186.

[28]Cf. Tim LaHaye and Jerry B. Jenkins, *Left Behind: A Novel of the Earth's Last Days* (Wheaton, Ill.: Tyndale House, 1995), with numerous sequels and movies in tow.

persecuted people of God raised up on the clouds to sit with God in glory, and (with echoes of Philippians) the Hellenistic ruler cult's image of a colony's people streaming out to welcome the emperor and escort him back to take possession of his rightful dominion. We will return to the colonial image soon, but for the moment it is worth noting a threefold paradox: (1) the dead are already with Christ, who "brings them" with him; (2) they then nevertheless "rise" and precede the living who are "caught up together with them" into the presence of Christ; and (3) the only explicit location of being "always with him" is said to be "in the clouds" or "in the air"—which does indeed allude to Daniel 7 and might be a way of denoting a quasi-celestial locus that comprises heaven and earth as one (rather than a mere stopover for a return from heaven to earth).[29]

Paul returns to partly similar themes a decade or so later in Philippians. The eschatological transformation of believers' bodies in Philippians 3:20-21 follows his earlier emphasis, reiterated in 1 Corinthians, on the parousia of Christ as the time when the dead will experience resurrection that is in some important sense bodily (1 Cor 15:23-27), while those who are still alive at that time will be dramatically "transformed" (1 Cor 15:51-54).[30] In Philippians more specifically, Wright identifies and employs an important imperial theme to support his view that believers' eternal destiny cannot be in heaven. Rejecting the idea that the heavenly domain of "citizenship" in Philippians 3:20 might denote a place to which one "will return and live there for ever," Wright finds Paul (unlike, say, Philo) envisioning Christians as outbound colonists, "leaving heaven for a new home." He reads this passage in close analogy to Roman citizenship, which in his view (p. 230)

> created neither an expectation that one would make the city one's eventual home nor an entitlement to do so. . . . Indeed, the colonists of Philippi a century before Paul's day had been placed there precisely because nobody wanted them back in Rome, or even in Italy: there was too much overcrowding, unemployment and shortage of food in Rome as it

---

[29]In Dan 7:13-14 the "clouds" of heaven conduct the Son of Man not to earth but to God's throne and to appointment as king over his eternal and all-encompassing kingdom.
[30]Wright, *Surprised by Hope*, p. 144.

was. . . . Their task was to live in the colony by the rules of the mother city, not to yearn to go home again.[31]

The trouble here seems to be that Wright's point about colonists is a half-truth that is again strong in its affirmative insight but misleading in what it denies. It is true that Philippi was in the first century markedly characterized by its status as a Roman colony, and that colonies were indeed (as already in ancient Greece) intended to project outward the virtues and values of citizenship that characterized the mother city.[32] The theologically compelling image of Christians civilizing and "colonizing" the world on behalf of heaven has good exegetical support.

Two corrections to Wright's analogy of Roman colonial citizenship are, however, required. First, Philippi's citizens belonged to Rome, not only in general legal terms but most were (whether by "fictive" or authentic kinship) inscribed into the specific ancient family line of the city's *tribus Voltinia*.[33] What is more, it was well understood that the fortunes especially of smaller colonies might ebb and flow. An old Republican law guaranteeing any Latin the right of citizenship by domicile (*ius migrationis*) had by the first century fallen out of use, but Roman citizens by definition had legal and settlement rights in Rome if they chose to move there.[34] It was certainly true that veterans and others tended to find their endowed lands and social status in the colonies economically and socially more advantageous, and that travel to the capital from far-flung colonies was expensive; but the idea that Roman citizens of Philippi had no entitlement or welcome in the mother city seems mistaken.

---

[31]Ibid.; Wright, *Resurrection of the Son of God*, pp. 229-30.

[32]For the following remarks see more fully Markus Bockmuehl, *The Epistle to the Philippians* (Peabody, Mass.: Hendrickson, 1998), pp. 2-19, with further literature cited there.

[33]See, e.g., Peter Pilhofer, *Philippi*, Wissenschaftliche Untersuchungen zum Neuen Testament 87, 119 (Tübingen: Mohr Siebeck, 1995-2000), 1:121-22; Joseph Hellerman, *Reconstructing Honor in Roman Philippi: Carmen Christi as Cursus Pudorum*, Society for New Testament Studes Monograph Series 132 (Cambridge: Cambridge University Press, 2005), pp. 115-16, 162.

[34]Pace *Resurrection of the Son of God*, p. 230. Cf., e.g., David Stockton, *The Gracchi* (Oxford: Oxford University Press; New York: Clarendon, 1979), p. 110. I am grateful for this reference and for confirmation of the general point to my colleague Dr. Teresa Morgan of Oxford's faculty of classics.

Second, it should perhaps also give us pause that Paul's political metaphors in Philippians do not in fact employ any colonial terminology (*apoikia*, *kolςnia*, etc.) at all. More particularly, the term *politeuma* in this context means not "citizenship" but rather "commonwealth"; indeed, theologically and politically it is in some ways analogous in meaning to the term *basileia*, "kingdom" or "empire."[35] While this does not indeed remove the effective political counterpoint, we do well to bear in mind that Christians at Philippi (as elsewhere) were of course overwhelmingly not Romans—but in this case Greek-speaking Macedonians, Thracians or immigrants. Inscriptions show that distinction to have been emphatic and important. Poignantly, Paul does not write to these Christians in Latin. In the end the theological and political point of passages like Philippians 1:27 and 3:20 is that Christians belong to another mother commonwealth: not Philippi, not Rome, but "heaven."

It seems therefore difficult to agree that the phrase "our commonwealth is in heaven" makes Christians earthly "colonists" who enjoy neither entitlement nor welcome "to go home again."[36] The image really does seem to concern where believers ultimately belong and have their identity ("Heaven is Home," indeed), not what they have left behind for good.

These debates aside, how then do we assess these Pauline texts about the Christian hope? Wright argues plausibly that when Paul's message is taken contextually and in its biblical and ancient Hellenistic idiom, what he means in 1 Thessalonians 4 is no different from 1 Corinthians 15 or Philippians 3. "Only when we put together the several different things that [Paul] says on the same topic does the truth emerge."[37] To understand the difficulty and diversity of Pauline eschatological expression one must heed the witness of the Pauline corpus as a whole, always recognizing that much may be adumbrated rather than spelled out in full.[38] For Wright, that exercise suggests a merely *interim* quasi-heavenly state followed by an ultimate destina-

---

[35]See, e.g., my discussion in Bockmuehl, *Epistle to the Philippians*, pp. 233-35.
[36]Wright, *Resurrection of the Son of God*, p. 230.
[37]Wright, *Surprised by Hope*, pp. 145-46.
[38]Cf. ibid., p. xiii, "signposts pointing into the fog"; p. 118 "into a bright mist" (similarly p. 144).

tion of resurrection life on a renewed earth that is emphatically distinguished from heaven. As we have seen, this is perhaps not the only way to understand these texts.[39]

WHAT SAINT PAUL REALLY SAID, ACCORDING TO HIS DISCIPLES

Wright's welcome principle of reading the Pauline part in light of the Pauline whole seems well worth applying more widely—not least to the question of the apostle's personal hopes for the afterlife. To understand what Paul meant, we will do well to listen to the apostle's disciples and earliest readers too—thus helping us understand the historical Paul in light of the emerging canonical Paul, indeed of the New Testament witness as a whole. Despite much diversity, for certain central convictions this does reveal, as Wright puts it, "a remarkably unanimous view spread throughout the early Christianity known to us."[40] Except in Gnostic circles, we do indeed find such unanimity on the resurrection of the body.[41]

But what did Paul's early Christian readers, both in and beyond the canon, understand him to be saying about his hope for life after death? And did they think he expected to go to heaven, to be forever in the presence of Christ?

Here too we do well to allow for a complex consistency to Paul's thought, which repeatedly comes to expression both in the so-called authentic Pauline letters and in the remembered profile of the apostle that emerges from the canonical corpus more generally. It is especially the contested letters of Paul that seem to show an enhanced interest in the heavenly realm as the believer's true home.

If we thus contextualize Paul's earlier reflections in 1 Thessalonians, Philippians and 2 Corinthians, it is particularly interesting to note the

---

[39]Contrast, e.g., the conservative construal of Harris, "New Testament View of Life After Death," p. 52: "In their teaching about life after death New Testament authors focus their attention . . . on the final destiny of resurrected saints: permanent residence in God's immediate presence, worshipping and serving him and the Lamb for ever, in spiritual bodies perfectly adapted to the ecology of heaven and totally responsive to the dictates of the Spirit."

[40]Wright, *Surprised by Hope*, p. 148.

[41]There is also, for example, a certain unanimity about an "epiphany" or "appearing" that neither the evangelists nor the second-century fathers hesitated to conceptualize in the Johannine terms of a personal return or second coming of Jesus (e.g., Jn 14:3).

imprint of the apostle's hopes and expectations in such texts as Colossians, Ephesians and 2 Timothy. As early as 1 Thessalonians, Paul had anticipated both that the coming Lord would bring the departed with him and that they would rise; all believers would thus (*houtes*) "be with the Lord forever" (1 Thess 4:17). If we join this to the equally early conviction that Christ's eternal rightful place is in exaltation to the right hand of God in heaven,[42] then to deny a heavenly locale for the eternal destiny of the saved would begin to strain the available spatial metaphors. More than one commentator has thought that what Paul on his visionary tour inexpressibly encounters in heaven (2 Cor 12:2-4) is in fact "what eye has not seen, nor ear heard, nor human heart imagined: what God has prepared for those who love him" (1 Cor 2:9).

By the time we reach Colossians, the Pauline hope is now explicitly "laid up in heaven" (Col 1:5), where Christ himself resides—seated at the right hand of God (Col 3:1-2; 4:1). It is there that the true life of Christians is already concealed and will in due course be revealed to all with Christ "in glory" (Col 3:4). Early Christian readers certainly assumed that this future revelation of their life "in glory" would not somehow entail a separation from where Christ is at the right hand of God, as if believers are only "in Christ with God" for an interim period but then move on to a different place—which (with Wright) one might call "down here" rather than "up there," "not heaven" rather than "heaven." Instead, it is precisely that polarity itself which disappears in the eschaton—and is therefore meaningless.

For Ephesians too, "the heavenly places" are where God is and where Christ is seated at his right hand, but they are also where Christians are blessed and indeed even now seated with Christ (Eph 1:3, 20; 2:6)—not in a provisional refuge or holding pattern, but rightfully by adoption. Such heavenly places clearly seem in these texts a permanent, not a temporary destination, however much it may be the case that the world to come will render these universally present and visible (as in, e.g., Col 3:4).

That same destination, indeed, is what the canonically remembered Paul anticipates as he contemplates his own imminent death and the

---

[42]E.g., in the traditional language of Phil 2:10-11.

abiding reward of his crown of righteousness: "The Lord will rescue me from every evil scheme and bring me safe into his heavenly kingdom" (2 Tim 4:18; cf. 2 Tim 4:8 with Phil 3:14).

ACCORDING TO OTHER EARLY CHRISTIAN READERS

But what might this Paul of Colossians, Ephesians or 2 Timothy actually mean to other ancient Christian readers? The church father Origen (c. 185-254) thought it was pretty clear:

> [Paul is therefore reminding us] that if you believe that God has raised Christ from the dead, believe also that he has raised you yourselves likewise with him. And if you believe that he sat down at the right hand of the Father in heaven, believe as well that you yourselves have been placed together with him no longer in earthly regions but in heavenly. And if you believe that you have died together with Christ, believe also that you will live together with him.[43]

Although Origen rightly understands the language of Ephesians 2:5-6 as applying to the believer's present life, he evidently sees here an abiding and permanent reality.

In a more explicitly future-oriented comment on 2 Corinthians 5:1 a century after Origen, Didymus the Blind (c. 313-398) similarly picks up on Paul's contrast between the earthly tent and the one not made with hands "in the heavens." He offers the following Pauline synthesis drawing on this passage along with Philippians 3:

> This scripture addresses two different "houses." One is the earthly, made by God's hands and visible. The other is invisible, made without hands and in heaven, the world beyond this one. . . . But once the visible world is left behind, the soul will move to the heavenly realm, where it will receive its body back, but one that has been transformed into a heavenly body.[44]

---

[43]Origen, *Commentary on the Epistle to the Romans*, Fathers of the Church, trans. Thomas Scheck (Washington: Catholic University of America Press, 2001), 1:275; for Rufinus's text see Hammond Bammel, *Der Römerbriefkommentar des Origenes: Kritische Ausgabe der Übersetzung Rufins*, Aus der Geschichte der lateinischen Bibel, 3 vols., ed. Caroline P. Hammond Bammel (Freiburg: Herder, 1990-1998).

[44]Fragments on 2 Corinthians in Karl Staab, ed., *Pauluskommentare aus der griechischen Kirche*, Neutestamentliche Abhandlungen (Münster: Aschendorff, 1933), p. 26; English translation

All the while, interpreters from Clement to Origen and Chrysostom to Theodoret make clear that this "heavenly body" is certainly a real resurrection body and not some sort of Platonizing or metaphorical idea. As all the major creeds insist, the resurrection of the body is a central tenet of orthodox Christianity, whether millenarian or nonmillenarian, Eastern or Western, Alexandrian or Antiochene.

It is well known that despite agreement in core ideas, early Christian eschatology is not reducible to a simple common denominator but remains diverse. There are those who believe that risen believers will share in a coming millennial rule of Christ on this earth, and there are those who believe this rule will take place in a wholly transcendent renewal of heaven and earth in the presence of the heavenly Christ, in which the departed participate without delay.

Nevertheless, and excepting only the Gnostics, resurrection of the body is never sacrificed, even by those who adopt a largely transcendental and nonmillenarian eschatology.[45] Despite their admittedly rather mixed record of appreciating the Jewishness of the New Testament gospel, the church fathers did not regard the expectation of "going to heaven" as a corruption of the hope of bodily resurrection (or vice versa), but firmly held on to both convictions without compromising either one.

For the sake of a relative proximity to the Pauline corpus, it is worth illustrating this point more specifically from second-century sources. One characteristic reader of Paul and the Gospels is Justin Martyr (c. 100-165). In his *Dialogue with Trypho* (80.4), set in Ephesus but written in Rome, he complains bitterly about certain believers (perhaps Valentinians?) "who are called Christians" but who "blaspheme" the God of Abraham, Isaac and Jacob by denying a bodily resurrection. Instead, they believe that when they die it is merely their souls that ascend straight to heaven: Justin writes, "do not imagine that these people are either Christians or Jews" (*Dial. Tryph.* 80.4). This is clearly an important tour de force supporting one aspect of Tom Wright's ar-

---

adapted from the Ancient Christian Commentary on Scripture.

[45]Charles E. Hill, *Regnum Caelorum: Patterns of Millennial Thought in Early Christianity*, 2nd ed. (Grand Rapids: Eerdmans, 2001); cf. Brian Daley, *The Hope of the Early Church: A Handbook of Patristic Eschatology*, rev. ed. (Peabody, Mass.: Hendrickson, 2003).

gument: Justin attacks those who affirm an escape to heaven at the expense of the "resurrection of the flesh" (*Dial. Tryph.* 80.5). What is more, he combines this with a concrete conviction about Christ's coming rule in a rebuilt Jerusalem and his ingathering of Gentile and Jewish believers to the Holy Land—even if earlier in the same passage he accepts somewhat vaguely that there are some "true" Christians who may not affirm all these things.

But the key point here is this: While he is uncompromising on the subject of the resurrection and of a concrete eschatological hope, elsewhere Justin finds this conviction happily compatible with the idea that Christian martyrs, like the Paul of 2 Timothy, immediately enter their true home in the permanent heavenly company of the Lord: they go "to the Father and King of the heavens."[46] In common with most other early readers of Paul, he refuses to choose between the destinations of "going to heaven when you die" and the resurrection of the body, or to subordinate one to the other.

Far from being quirky or eccentric, this combination of beliefs is widespread and uncontroversial in second-century Christianity, and even if they are not expressed with absolute unanimity, they are at least widely shared and regarded as compatible. The author of the *Shepherd of Hermas*, writing in Rome not long before Justin, similarly juxtaposes belief in the resurrection with the belief that the righteous are already "sheltered by the Lord forever," "dwelling with the son of God" and in the company of the angels.[47] In Asia Minor we find both Polycarp's (d. c. 155) *Letter to the Philippians* and the *Martyrdom of Polycarp* expressing the twin conviction that the martyrs will rise from the dead and also that they enjoy already "their due place in the presence of the Lord."[48]

---

[46]Justin Martyr *Apology II* 2.18-19. *Martyrdom of Justin* 4, though clearly from a different hand, also attributes to Justin acceptance of the belief that after decapitation he would ascend into heaven to receive a heavenly reward.

[47]See *Shepherd of Hermas, Similitude* 104 (9.27).3; also *Herm. Sim.* 101 (9.24).4; *Shepherd of Hermas, Vision* 6 (2.2).7; cf. more tentatively *Herm. Sim.* 60 (5.7).1-4 for resurrection of the flesh.

[48]Pol. *Phil.* 9:2; cf., *Mart. Pol.* 14.2; 19.2. Cf. Wright, *Resurrection of the Son of God*, pp. 486-88. He finds the *Martyrdom* uncharacteristic and "unclear" for failing to distinguish the two states more clearly. Contrast, e.g., L. Arik Greenberg, *"My Share of God's Reward": Exploring the Roles and Formulations of the Afterlife in Early Christian Martyrdom*, Studies in Biblical Litera-

We should note that the early and diverse authorship of these texts would certainly seem to rule out any easy dismissal of this twin conviction as somehow a "Gnostic" or "unwarranted Platonizing of the Christian hope," flawed by a concerted ideological misconstrual of Paul and the New Testament.

Nearer the end of the second century the same combination of beliefs persists even in a millenarian like Irenaeus (c. 130-200). Although he is fiercely anti-allegorical in his interpretation of the resurrection and expects Christ to rule an earthly kingdom from Jerusalem, he accepts that the present city is a mere "shadow" of the Jerusalem to come, which is the city of God. He cites the apostolic teaching of the Elders to affirm that Jesus' teaching about the eschatological "mansions" applies initially to different forms of believers' reward, according to the fruit they have borne. Significantly, some in fact do go straight to heaven, but all ascend in due course through the different stages by the Spirit to the Son and the Father (*Against Heresies* 5.36.1-2). Elsewhere the covenant of the gospel is said to recapitulate all things and to bear believers on its wings into the heavenly kingdom (*Against Heresies* 3.11.8). In the extant Latin translation, Irenaeus closes his great work *Against Heresies* with an echo of the famous Pauline "interchange" motif: Christ the firstborn Word came down into his creation so that "the creation should contain the Word, and ascend to Him, thus passing beyond the angels and coming to be in the image and likeness of God."[49]

In Egypt, finally, Clement of Alexandria (c. 150-215) famously concludes his homily "Can the Rich Man Be Saved?" with the somewhat stylized tale about a young man who had abandoned the faith, but whose repentance became

a trophy of the resurrection for which we hope; when at the end of the world, the angels, radiant with joy, hymning and opening the heavens,

---

ture 121 (New York: Peter Lang, 2009), on the widespread view of immortality as the martyrs' reward, beginning at least with Ignatius.

[49]For Pauline "interchange" (e.g., 2 Cor 5:21; Gal 3:13-14) see especially the classic essay of Morna Hooker, "Interchange in Christ," in *Journal of Theological Studies* 22, no. 2 (1971): 349-61. Cf. Morna Hooker, *From Adam to Christ: Essays on Paul* (Cambridge: Cambridge University Press, 1990), pp. 4-69.

shall receive into the celestial abodes those who truly repent; and before all, the Saviour Himself goes to meet them, welcoming them; holding forth the shadowless, ceaseless light; conducting them to the Father's bosom, to eternal life, to the kingdom of heaven.[50]

Doubtless there are important hermeneutical and theological shifts between Paul and Clement, some of them involving the intellectual appropriation of his message in a Greco-Roman context of thought. Nevertheless, the early readers of Paul do stand in a continuum of tradition in which the basic biblical convictions about life after death are not substantively questioned or revised.

For the fathers of the second and subsequent centuries it is clearly not the case, for example, that belief in a heavenly afterlife implies neglect of the resurrection of the body. These readers of Paul were uninterested in disaggregating the exegetical evidence for life after death from what Wright likes to call "life after life after death."[51] "Going to be with the Lord" was for them what the Christian departed experienced, not temporarily but forever: going to "heaven" was not a state they would then have to surrender for something that was "not heaven," "down here" rather than "up there." To resort briefly to a Johannine image, the early Christian writers believed the Lord had gone to heaven to prepare for believers an abiding place *(monē)* of joy among the many mansions of the Father's house; he would return and take them back with him "so that you may be with me where I am" (Jn 14:2-3). In other words, Jesus had gone to prepare a place for them to share his eternal home in the Father's house, rather than a temporary shelter en route to another destination.[52]

Some of these writers were chiliasts, perhaps especially in Asia

---

[50]Clement of Alexandria *Quis Dives Salvetur* 42.15-17.

[51]E.g., Wright, *Resurrection of the Son of God*, pp. 31, 86, 121, 123, 130, 153, 199, 201, 215, 218.

[52]More specifically, perhaps, the ultimate "abiding place" in heaven may be the same as the *monē* that the Son and his Father make with those who love him (Jn 14:23)—not temporarily, one assumes, but permanently. Replying to an earlier query on this matter, Wright prefers meanings like "hostel," "stopping place" or "stage of a journey" (Wright, "Incompleat (but Grateful) Response," p. 508). But John's context seems to assure Peter that where Jesus is gone he will follow later (Jn 13:36), and that the point of Jesus' departure is to prepare a place in which the disciples can be with him in his Father's house (Jn 14:2-3).

Minor;[53] others were not. Wherever hope for an earthly paradise or an earthly millennial kingdom does surface in the early sources (characteristically in Irenaeus, for instance), it is this earthly location, rather than the heavenly one, that tends to be a temporary or penultimate stopover en route to the ultimate destination.[54]

SAINT PAUL ON THE END, AND ON THE END OF SAINT PAUL

There is much more to be discussed here, and I am fully aware that a short essay can hardly begin to do justice to Tom Wright's extensive contribution to these challenging questions, let alone to engage with the wider scholarly debates.

The apostle and his early interpreters were at one in the belief that the object of creation is the object of redemption, that resurrection therefore must be bodily and located, and indeed that Christ's saving return to rule in his kingdom would not entail a Gnostic escape from the supposed prison of earthiness and materiality to some purely noumenal realm. The Christian believer's redemption is not complete without bodily resurrection. This is a conviction for whose learned clarification we owe Tom Wright a large debt of gratitude. His account rightly and eloquently rearticulates Scripture's vision for a future remaking of the earth, a resurrection, a new creation in which heaven and earth are fully engaged with each other. As key Pauline passages indicate, this conviction also lies at the heart of the apostle's eschatological hope.

The burden of this essay, however, has been to suggest that in certain pivotal denials Wright seems paradoxically to subvert a number of vital affirmations about the Pauline hope, appearing repeatedly to insist on the abiding importance of an earth-heaven distinction, and thus allowing for an ultimate eschatological space that is in some sense God's new

---

[53]Thus, e.g., Charles Hill, *Regnum Caelorum.*

[54]E.g., Irenaeus *Against Heresies* 5.35-36. Wright acknowledges this view of paradise as an interim destination (Wright, *For All the Saints*, p. 24). On paradise and its earthly location see my comments in Markus Bockmuehl, "Locating Paradise," in *Paradise in Antiquity: Jewish and Christian Views*, ed. M. Bockmuehl and G. G. Stroumsa (Cambridge: Cambridge University Press, 2010), pp. 192-209.

world but emphatically not "heaven."[55]

Wright affirms for departed believers an interim presence with Christ that may in some sense be heavenly, but the believer's ultimate destination is for him a different one, bodily and *not* heavenly. Here, by contrast, I hope to have demonstrated that the early Christians, from Paul via his disciples to the fathers, consistently affirm any intermediate state (whether chronological or merely logical, in an earthly paradise or in heaven) to be followed by an ultimate destination that is *both* heavenly and bodily. Beginning with the later New Testament itself, all known non-Gnostic early interpreters read Paul as affirming for the departed believer both a real, immediate and permanent presence with Christ in heaven and also a real bodily resurrection in the new creation in which any distinction between "earth" and "heaven" wholly disappears because God himself dwells in the city and illumines it (Rev 21:1-4). The church fathers see no need for either contradiction or compromise between these two basic beliefs.

Ever since antiquity, Paul's readers have seen in his letters "things that are hard to understand" and liable to distortion (2 Pet 3:15-16). This chapter's debate with Tom Wright should be seen not as a disagreement about theological fundamentals but rather as a discussion about how best to heed and assemble a few particularly subtle pieces of the Pauline hope as this is refracted through the canon and its earliest readers. I continue to suspect that what separates certain key denials in Tom Wright's theologically potent reading of the apostle's "hope of glory" from the Paul of traditional Christian belief may in the end be a matter more of rhetorical hyperbole and relative emphasis rather than of outright contradiction. In that case, clarification or restatement may move the discussion forward; other readers too have wondered if the denials may cloud a significant conviction of biblical and historic Christian faith.[56]

---

[55]See pp. 213-22 of this chapter. For a critique of Wright's demythologization of biblical and apocalyptic language about the physical end of the world, see Edward Adams, *The Stars Will Fall From Heaven: Cosmic Catastrophe in the New Testament and its World* (London and New York: T & T Clark, 2007), p. 347.

[56]Most cantankerously, see Neuhaus, "Possibilities and Perils" (with the reply by Wright, and Neuhaus' rejoinder). Analogous but more civil critiques are easily located on the Internet.

The biblical Paul believes, and was understood by his early readers to believe, that to die was to go "home" to the Lord and to enter safely—and permanently—into his heavenly kingdom (2 Cor 5:1, 8; 2 Tim 4:18). Paul believes just as firmly, and was understood to believe in the same Pauline and deutero-Pauline texts, that this assurance went hand in hand with the gospel's central conviction about "Jesus Christ risen from the dead." Christ indeed is the guarantee that "if we have died with him, then we shall live with him"—where he is, and in a resurrection like his (2 Tim 2:8, 11).

According to the New Testament, when St. Paul died he went to heaven.[57]

Response to Markus Bockmuehl
N. T. WRIGHT

I did not fully recognize the presentation of my views in Markus Bockmuehl's paper. I think there has been confusion caused by truncated sound bites in the popular media.

First, the word *heaven* itself. Markus, one of our foremost specialists on ancient Jewish thought, naturally thinks of heaven within that world of thought. I, however, have been reacting against the "heaven" of popular modern Western thought. Two things about this stand out and need correction. First, it is emphatically nonbodily: the ascension strikes most moderns, including many Christians, as an embarrassing category mistake. Second, it is the *final* destination for those who go there. Once you're in "heaven" in this sense, there is nowhere else to go; certainly no thought of a renewed body living on a renewed earth. This widespread modern view of heaven is firmly entrenched in popular imagination.

You could of course argue that it is better to keep the word *heaven* and fill it with new content, rather than try to wean people off the normal picture by speaking, as I have done, of heaven as the temporary, inter-

---

[57]I am grateful for comments received from Marianne Meye Thompson and David Lincicum, as well as for friendly engagement with Tom Wright and other participants at the 2010 Wheaton Theology Conference in his honor.

mediate state and "new heavens and new earth" as the final state. C. S. Lewis held a view of the ultimate future quite like my own, and he continued to call it heaven. A popular American writer, Randy Alcorn, has recently done the same. I have chosen the alternative route mainly for pedagogical reasons. If people go on using the word, the powerful modern meaning easily creeps back. That is a matter of tactics.

More importantly, I have never rejected, as Bockmuehl says I do, "the traditional Christian belief that the faithful 'go to heaven' when they die." I don't regard that expectation as a "corruption of the hope of bodily resurrection." I have said repeatedly that "going to heaven" is fine as a description of what happens when the faithful die. The point is that it isn't the final destination. It isn't the new heaven-and-earth reality. Bockmuehl's insertion of the word *permanent* makes the point: in terms of the normal modern Western picture, to stay permanently in heaven does indeed rule out the resurrection and the new earth (for many Christians today, "resurrection" is just a fancy way of saying "disembodied heaven"). By contrast, belief in resurrection actually entails (except for those who are transformed when the Lord returns) a period of nonbodily survival, requiring the gift of immortality. Immortality and resurrection are not, then, opposites, despite regular misunderstandings. When believers go to be "with the Lord" at death (Phil 1:23), they will never again be separated from him, but he will bring them with him when he comes to set up the further new reality, his new heaven-and-earth world. In this sense only are they "permanently in heaven," not in the sense normally imagined today.

I stand by my statement about the Gospels and Paul: they do not say "Jesus is raised, therefore we're going to heaven." John 3:14-15 links the *crucifixion* of Jesus to "eternal life," and (as Nick Perrin stresses in his paper) "eternal life" is not to be equated with the modern notion of heaven. John 14:2-3, 12, 23 is about the *monē*, the temporary dwelling place to which Jesus leads his people. The lexicons are quite clear about this meaning; to say "one assumes" that this is "permanent" again begs the question. Ephesians 2:6 is about the *present* heavenly session of those "in Christ," a very different point. Hebrews 12:22-24, again, is about present membership in the heavenly Jerusalem, and the writer does not link this causally with Jesus' resurrection. Second Corinthians 5, which I do discuss fully in *The Resurrection of the Son of God*, makes the point that the "house" is the new body. Its present existence "in the heavens" refers to its being kept safe until required. On Philippians 3:20, I am interested in the points about Roman colonials and citizenship rights, but overcrowded Rome neither expected nor wanted the colonials back, and the colonials themselves show (to my knowledge) no sign of making that their ultimate goal. The metaphor of citizenship cannot therefore be making that point; nor does Paul make it. Heaven is the place *from which* the Lord will come to transform us.

On William Wilberforce, I stand corrected. I do think, though, that the "heaven-as-ultimate-home" philosophy, as developed in the nineteenth century, did eventually cut the nerve of social justice and continues to do so. But the critical point for me is that I take Ephesians 1:10 very seriously as a Pauline statement of the ultimate goal: all things in heaven and earth are to be brought together in Christ. I have never suggested "the abiding importance of an earth-heaven distinction"; I have regularly insisted that heaven and earth overlap and interlock, and are designed eventually to be joined completely forever. Bockmuehl repeatedly says that I insist on the new reality being nonheavenly. I don't recognize that. Clearly I need to be more careful how I say things.

As for believers being already "seated in heavenly places in Christ," and their life being "hid with Christ in God": that is a premortem, not merely a postmortem reality. The ultimate destination, then, is the emphatically heavenly, but also emphatically earthly, reality of God's new world, as in Romans 8, ruled over by God's resurrected people.

On 2 Timothy 4:18 and similar passages ("God's heavenly kingdom"), I agree that the church has often read this in terms of "God's domain, namely heaven." But, as with "kingdom of heaven" in Matthew, that is by no means necessarily the meaning a first-century reader would understand. The point about God's kingdom is that it is to come "on earth as in heaven": heavenly, then, in character, earthly in location (again, an oversimplification to make the point).

The "continuum of tradition," though currently fashionable, is not

?/
 ?!

necessarily the best guide to what Paul meant in the first century. Clement of Alexandria, as Bockmuehl admits, was indeed making significant shifts. Paul himself, after all, was concerned about "the intellectual appropriation of his message in a Greco-Roman context," but that didn't make him slide, like Clement, toward Platonism.

9

Wrighting the Wrongs of the Reformation?

The State of the Union with Christ in St. Paul and Protestant Soteriology

Kevin J. Vanhoozer

When the conference organizers invited me to address the topic of justification, perhaps with the title "What St. Paul Might Say Back," I was happy enough to do so. I was minding my own business, blissfully unaware of John Piper's book critiquing Wright on the subject. What I *thought* I knew about justification was what Luther said: (1) it means being "declared" rather than "made" righteous; (2) its ground is the imputed righteousness of Christ; (3) it is the article by which the church stands or falls. Suffice it to say that I have been awakened, like Kant, from my dogmatic slumbers, not least by Wright's charge that Reformation theology has bowed the knee to tradition rather than Scripture on this issue. I see now that we need a new "critique of biblical reason": a reexamination of the ways we reason *from* and *with* the Bible *to* historical and theological conclusions.

Wright is an intriguing conversation partner for the systematic theologian. He is interested in the authors' worldviews, the big covenantal picture, and God. I was therefore taken by surprise by a question from the floor at the Renewing the Evangelical Mission conference at Gordon-Conwell Theological Seminary in autumn 2009. I had just led a pep rally for the integration of biblical studies and systematics when Dennis Hollinger asked about the elephant in the room: Wright's approach to justification. At the time I was still in my dogmatic slumbers; all I could do was stammer in reply "I think it's in *another* room." Well, the elephant—not the good bishop but the problem of biblical studies overturning received theological views—is indeed in the room. In fact, it is stampeding through our big evangelical tent, kicking up sawdust and overturning the tables of the doctrine changers.

I'm in no position as a systematic theologian to offer *ex cathedra* pronouncements about the true shape and substance of Second Temple Judaism. As one New Testament scholar kindly put it to me: "You might be right, but you won't be convincing." I therefore feel like a school-crossing guard—what the British call a lollipop man—charged with helping people navigate their way across the Berlin Wall separating biblical studies and dogmatics. My aim in what follows is to encourage peace talks between New Perspectives and old Protestants.

WHAT IS AT STAKE: PROTESTANT PAUL-BEARERS OR PALLBEARERS OF THE REFORMATION?

What is at stake in current debates over justification is nothing less than the legacy of the Protestant Reformation. Stated pointedly: Is Reformation soteriology something that we must recover or that we must recover from? Opinion is divided.

According to John Milbank, "a definitively Protestant theology is now extinct,"[1] and a "return to the reformers is not an option."[2] Calvin emphasized external realities (e.g., the alien righteousness of Christ) rather than more profound, nontransactional ontological matters. Milbank therefore proposes an "alternative Protestantism"—a more radical, orthodox Protestantism.[3]

Into this contested ground, previously known as the playground of

---

[1]John Milbank, "The New Divide Versus Classical Orthodoxy," in *Modern Theology* 26, no. 1 (2010): p. 26.
[2]Milbank, "Afterword," in *Radical Orthodoxy Reader* (London: Routledge, 2009).
[3]See Milbank, "Alternative Protestantism: Radical Orthodoxy and the Reformed Tradition," in *Radical Orthodoxy and the Reformed Tradition*, ed. James K. A. Smith and James H. Olthuis (Grand Rapids: Baker, 2005), pp. 25-42.

the theologians, Wright breathes a breath of first-century Palestinian air. The concluding paragraph of his book *Justification* asks, "Do we then overthrow the Reformation tradition by this theology?" and answers, "On the contrary, we establish it."[4] Not everyone is convinced. As I see it, Wright's work on Paul raises three concrete issues.

Recovering the voice of St. Paul. Who are the true Paul-bearers? We more or less know what St. Paul really said; we want to know what he really *meant*. What was his attitude toward Second Temple Judaism? Did he invent Christianity? There is a ready supply of Philips eager to climb into our chariots to guide us in our understanding.

The theologian's Paul. We're all acquainted with the Reformation theologians' Paul. He looks like Luther, only shorter.

The philosopher's Paul. Less familiar, perhaps, is the Paul of the contemporary Continental philosophers. Alain Badiou's *Saint Paul: The Foundation of Universalism* works a radical makeover on the apostle, turning him into the paradigm of a revolutionary post-Marxist subject who refuses to conform to any world order and embodies a universalism in which "there is neither Jew nor Greek, there is neither slave nor free, there is no male and female" (Gal 3:28).[5]

The historian's Paul. A conference at Syracuse University in 2005 brought Badiou together with several New Testament historians, including Paula Fredriksen, Dale Martin and Ed Sanders, the pioneer of the New Perspective on Paul. Fredriksen argued that the theological tradition is the product of strong misreading of New Testament texts by Reformation geniuses who inadvertently made Paul their contemporary. Martin said the philosophers got Paul's universalizing impulse right, but fail to see that, for Paul, it was a matter of grafting everybody else into the already existing ethnos of Israel: *extra Israel nulla salus est*. But it was Sanders who correctly identified the key issue: "The problem of interpretation is in part the problem of context: in the light of what views, events, and social structures shall we

---

[4]N. T. Wright, *Justification: God's Plan and Paul's Vision* (Downers Grove, Ill.: InterVarsity Press, 2009), p. 252.
[5]Alain Badiou, *Saint Paul: The Foundation of Universalism* (Stanford: Stanford University Press, 2003). Scripture quoted in this chapter is from the English Standard Version.

read X? The historian begins with the basic commitment either to read X in light of X's own day or to determine how X was understood during some subsequent period. But . . . people live simultaneously in multiple contexts."[6]

The exegete's Paul. Wright's self-stated goal is to think Paul's thoughts after him. I look forward to seeing how his worldview analysis approach displays Paul's Christ-centered thought as it borrows, confronts and improves the Jewish, Hellenistic and Roman contexts of his day. Of course, Wright wrote from a context too—twenty-first-century Durham—with its own complex set of concerns and interests. We must not despair of our situatedness, yet it is sobering. Here, for example, is what Sanders says about his own work as a historian: "Lots of people think that . . . somewhere in the pages of *Paul and Palestinian Judaism* there is a claim that Paul must be discussed only in the light of Jewish sources of Palestinian origin. There is no such claim: I merely compared him with the material that I had spent ten years studying. I thought that I had lots of ten-year periods left to study something else. But time has passed, and I am out of ten-year periods."[7]

Practicing sola scriptura. Wright's exegesis also raises questions about the meaning and function of *sola scriptura*. Conservative evangelicals are happy to profess the Protestant mantra "always reforming," at least as a theoretical principle. Yet in practice they often behave like people who are all for building homes until, having settled in a new neighborhood, they then want all further development to stop. So too with *doctrinal* development.

Scripture and tradition. The most provocative blurb for Wright's *Justification* comes from Scot McKnight: "Wright has out-Reformed America's newest religious zealots—the neo-Reformed—by taking them back to Scripture and to its meaning in its historical context. Wright reveals that the neo-Reformed are more committed to tradition than to the sacred text." I do not know whether the people McKnight has in mind are neo- or paleo-Reformed, but the challenge is the same. Wright puts it like this:

---

[6]Ed Sanders, "Paul Between Judaism and Hellenism," in *Saint Paul Among the Philosophers*, ed. Jack Caputo (Bloomington: Indiana University Press, 2009), p. 74.
[7]Ibid., p. 75.

"The formal principle which underlies all my reading not only of Paul but of the whole of scripture [is] . . . a total commitment to scripture itself, over against all human traditions."[8]

It is precisely because of the brilliance and doggedness with which Wright pursues this end that his work deserves our sustained attention. In this regard I was most intrigued by Piper's caution about categories of *biblical* theology controlling and distorting our exegesis. Wright is aware of the danger: "Here [specifically: the question of whether the Old Testament practice of laying hands on animals to be sacrificed is the functional equivalent of imputation] as elsewhere my main concern is lest we impose upon scripture a scheme of thought taken from somewhere else."[9] Indeed, his concern to think Paul's thoughts after him leads him to rank biblical studies higher than systematic theology: "Once we grasp the essentially Jewish categories of thought with which Paul is working, many problems in a de-Judaized systematic theology are transcended."[10]

What does it mean to be biblical? Wright has "lived with St. Paul as a more or less constant companion" for more than thirty years.[11] I have lived with the question "What does it mean to be biblical?" for almost as long. Wright addresses this important question in various places, most notably in the wonderful opening one hundred pages of *The New Testament and the People of God* and again in "Rules of Engagement," chapter 2 of *Justification*. Whereas some exegetes claim, on the grounds that they are closer to the particularities of the text, to be "Neue Testamentalischer than thou" ("thou" being the systematic theologian), Wright takes the hermeneutical high road, reading individual Pauline texts "as part of a single train of thought and discovering the meaning of its key terms within that."[12] A few critics worry that Paul's train of

---

[8]N. T. Wright, "Paul in Different Perspectives," a lecture given at Auburn Avenue Presbyterian Church, Monroe, Louisiana, January 3, 2005.

[9]N. T. Wright, "March 2004 Wrightsaid Q & A," NTWrightPage.com <www.ntwrightpage .com/Wrightsaid_March2004.htm>.

[10]Wright, *Justification*, p. 106.

[11]N. T. Wright, *What Saint Paul Really Said: Was Paul of Tarsus the Real Founder of Christianity* (Grand Rapids: Eerdmans, 1997), p. 7, with adjustments to math due to its publication in 1997.

[12]Wright, *Justification*, p. 49.

thought becomes in Wright's hands a freight train that carries an over-sized narrative load: a big picture that Paul nowhere explicitly states as such.[13] One wonders, for example, where or whether Paul actually says "that God called Abraham to deal with the problem of Adam as Wright claims."[14]

Does being biblical mean attending to the exegetical details or to the bigger picture? Yes. While many of us plod through the text word by word, phrase by phrase and paragraph by paragraph, Wright soars on the wings of narrative angles from Galatians to Genesis and back again, delighting his fans but sometimes occasioning interpretive motion sickness among his critics. For my own part, this is one of the features I most admire in his work. He is brilliant in connecting the textual and testamental dots, hitting home runs out of the park of theological interpretation with no need of allegorical steroids. I wonder, however, whether he may not sometimes commit on the hermeneutical level what James Barr terms, in regard to the lexical level, "illegitimate totality transfer."[15]

Wright correctly observes that "where first-century meanings are held at bay, concepts and debating points from completely other centuries come in to take their place."[16] This is a salutary reminder. However, though the past does not change, our grasp of it does. It is probably only a matter of time before our paradigm for understanding Second Temple Judaism shifts again. We may thus want to remember to remove the cultural beams out of our own twenty-first-century eyes before helping others to remove the speck from the Reformers' (Lk 6:42). The road to history is paved with fiduciary frameworks.

Theology is faith seeking understanding. This involves not only recovering the explicit meaning of the words the biblical authors used, but also a detailed conceptual elaboration of what they imply, and this is often what we get from attending to the history of interpretation that, at its best, is not a move away from but deeper into the text. In an age of rapidly shifting historical paradigms, it is important to re-

---

[13]I am indebted to Ross Wagner for this concern (though not for its metaphorical expression).
[14]Maico Michielin, "Bridging the Gulf Between Biblical Scholars and Theologians: Can Barth and Wright Provide an Answer?" *Scottish Journal of Theology* 61 (2008): 431.
[15]James Barr, *The Semantics of Biblical Language* (New York: Oxford University Press, 1961).
[16]Wright, *Justification*, p. 50.

member that the Bible is its own best normative context. So, yes: context, context, context—*including* the canonical context. It is for this reason that Brevard Childs's *The Church's Guide for Reading Paul: The Canonical Shaping of the Pauline Corpus*, in particular the section on "the historical and canonical Paul," is conspicuous by its absence from Wright's own books on Paul. Childs there says: "The historical Paul of the first century has been transmitted by Christian tradents who have received and shaped their testimony into the form of a canonical Paul. . . . This fusion . . . is most clearly reflected in the book of Acts."[17] It is precisely the voice of the canonical Paul that the Reformers and their successors strove so mightily to hear over the roar of ecclesial tradition.

In sum: Wright does not think the Reformers wrong in affirming *sola scriptura*. Indeed, what makes the contemporary debate over justification so disturbing is that, in appealing to Scripture to question the old perspective on justification, Wright is pressing the formal principle of the Reformation (biblical authority) into service against its material principle (justification by faith).[18] The question is whether in doing so he has merely bruised the (Achilles') heel of Protestantism or crushed the head of an ossified traditionalism (or both)?

Preserving the gospel's integrity. When we approach our third issue, the meaning of the gospel, we approach holy evangelical ground. Emotions run high. By and large the perceived problem with Wright's position is not what he affirms but what he denies. His affirmations are important and exciting: the gospel in Paul's context meant the proclamation that Yahweh was once again on the move, delivering Israel from the powers that oppressed it. The gospel is the good news of the covenant's climax: the news that Jesus, Israel's Messiah, has on the cross defeated the evil powers of this age, inaugurated with his resurrection a new age, and is thus Lord, the one true King of the world.[19] Paul's

---

[17]Brevard Childs, *The Church's Guide for Reading Paul: The Canonical Shaping of the Pauline Corpus* (Grand Rapids: Eerdmans, 2008), p. 256.

[18]The nomenclature of "formal" and "material" principles (*principium cognescendi* and *principium essendi*) comes from Philip Schaff, *The Principle of Protestantism* (1845; reprint, Eugene, Ore.: Wipf & Stock, 2004), pp. 80-98.

[19]See the section on the "fourfold gospel" in Wright, *What Saint Paul Really Said*, chap. 3.

gospel, then, is the "announcement of the person of Jesus," God's covenant faithfulness made flesh.[20]

Wright's emphasis on understanding Jesus' person and work in covenantal context is most welcome. So too is his recovery of the corporate dimension of salvation. Nor is he alone in bemoaning the tendency of many, especially in North America, to equate the gospel with the means by which we get to heaven when we die. For example, David Bentley Hart similarly observes the "rather feeble and formal way many Christians have habitually thought of [salvation] at various periods in the Church's history: as some sort of forensic exoneration accompanied by a ticket of entry into an Elysian aftermath of sun-soaked meadows and old friends."[21] What lands Wright in hot Reformed water are the denials: statements like "'the gospel' is not, for Paul, a message about 'how one gets saved,' in an individual and ahistorical sense."[22] Michael Horton calls Wright's definition of the gospel as "the narrative proclamation of King Jesus"[23] a terrific half-truth: "If the gospel is not 'how people get saved,' it is certainly the news of how *God has saved* people."[24] What Horton wants to hear is the message that God justifies the ungodly, apart from which "the news of God's kingship may legitimately evoke fear or despair."[25]

Piper shares a similar concern and minces no words in expressing it: "[Wright's] portrayal of the gospel . . . is so disfigured that it becomes difficult to recognize as biblically faithful."[26] This is strong language. What lies behind it is Piper's belief that Wright mistakenly identifies the basis of our final justification with *our* life lived, not Christ's: "[I]n my judgment, what he has written will lead to a kind of preaching that

---

[20]Ibid., p. 151.

[21]David Bentley Hart, "The Lively God of Robert Jenson," *First Things* 156 (2005): 30.

[22]Wright, *What Saint Paul Really Said*, p. 60.

[23]Ibid., p. 45.

[24]Michael Horton, *Covenant and Salvation: Union with Christ* (Louisville: Westminster John Knox Press, 2007), p. 33.

[25]Ibid., p. 34. So Michael Bird: "But merely stating that Jesus is king is an insufficient representation of the gospel if we do not point out how he has shown his kingly power in giving himself up for our sins and being raised by God for our acquittal" (*Introducing Paul: The Man, His Mission and His Message* [Downers Grove, Ill.: InterVarsity Press, 2009], p. 83).

[26]John Piper, *The Future of Justification: A Response to N. T. Wright* (Wheaton, Ill.: Crossway, 2007), p. 15.

will not announce clearly what makes the lordship of Christ good news for guilty sinners, or show those who are overwhelmed with sin how they may stand righteous in the presence of God."[27]

What Horton and Piper miss is a clear account of how individuals are reconciled to God. After all, they reason, the canonical Paul was not afraid to speak to the issue of individual salvation. When his jailer asks him, "What must *I* do to be saved?" (Acts 16:30), he did not respond by saying, "That's not the right question." On the contrary, he said, "Believe in the Lord Jesus, and you will be saved" (v. 31). It is true that the immediate context might suggest the jailer feared the prospect of temporal punishment, perhaps even execution, for letting his prisoners escape. Yet the way Luke shapes his narrative closes that interpretative door for, by the time the jailer asks his question, he already knows that his prisoners are all present and accounted for. It therefore makes no narrative sense for the jailer to contemplate suicide anew. Likewise, Paul's response and the subsequent baptism of the jailer and his entire household makes it clear that eternal salvation is what is in view.

Finally, if Childs is right, and the Pastoral Epistles play an important role in canonically shaping the reception of Paul's corpus as a whole, then we must not ignore such creedal-sounding statements as 1 Timothy 1:15: "The saying is trustworthy and deserving of full acceptance, that Christ Jesus came into the world to save sinners."

WRIGHTING THE WRONGS OF THE REFORMATION: THE STORY SO FAR

I am not able here to do justice to the whole sweep of Wright's thought. My focus will therefore be limited to considering the ways his recent work relates to the formal and material principles of the Reformation and their interrelation. To repeat: what makes Wright's work so controversial is his pitting one half of the Protestant principle (*sola scriptura*) against the other (God's gracious justification of sinners by the merit of Christ alone through faith alone). What the Rip van Winkles among us have missed in sleeping through the New Perspective on Paul is

---

[27]Ibid.

nothing short of an exegetical revolution, a massive shift of what
Thomas Kuhn calls, in relation to the history of science, an interpretive
paradigm.[28]

The structure of exegetical revolutions. "Wrighting" the wrongs of
the Reformation means not contradicting but *reframing* what the Reformers said. Wright makes a special point of saying things like "Nothing that the Reformation traditions at their best were anxious to stress
has been lost."[29] This may be, but the constellation of Pauline concepts
is all out of alignment: many Reformed no longer recognize the position of the doctrinal stars in Wright's theological night sky.

Consider, for example, Paul's notion of the righteousness of God.
This is often understood as God's determination to do what is right
and, in particular, to vindicate those who have been wronged, especially his covenant people. God's righteousness is his determination to
judge justly, to conform things to the norm of his own nature.[30] For
Wright and others, however, it is a technical term that means God's
covenant faithfulness. God's right doing is a function of *"God's single
plan to put the world to rights . . . through Israel."*[31] The righteousness of
God revealed in Jesus Christ means that God is making good on his
covenant promises to bless all nations through the seed of Abraham.

Wright makes the story of Israel's covenant the principal interpretive
framework—the main plot, as it were—through which to deal with the
story of the race of Adam. This is Wright's Copernican revolutionary
move: to install God's promise to Abraham in Genesis 12, and the narrative that it generates, as the sun around which the various Pauline
texts orbit. His Reformed interlocutors tend to see things differently:
"It is not . . . that the whole world is in Israel, but that even Israel is 'in
Adam.'"[32]

---

[28]Thomas S. Kuhn, *The Structure of Scientific Revolutions*, 3rd ed. (Chicago: University of Chicago Press, 1996).

[29]Wright, *Justification*, p. 247.

[30]See, for example, Herman Bavinck, *Reformed Dogmatics*, vol. 2, *God and Creation* (Grand Rapids: Baker, 2004), pp. 221-28. Interestingly, Bavinck anticipates Wright's position when he
comments that righteousness "is not the same as favor, mercy, or grace; neither is it something
like covenant faithfulness. . . . Righteousness is and remains a forensic term" (p. 225).

[31]Wright, *Justification*, p. 65.

[32]Horton, *Covenant and Salvation*, p. 61.

Wright and his critics express a mutual frustration at their apparent inability fairly to represent, or even understand, what the other is saying. His Reformed critics need something like a Rosetta Stone course that would help them to learn how to speak Wrightish. However, Wright is not the only one left scratching his head over the apparent incomprehension of those who do not read the lexical evidence as he does. Henri Blocher reviews what he takes to be decisive evidence for viewing God's righteousness in terms of his retributive justice and then says: "Textual facts are so clear-cut and so stubborn that only a tremendous pressure from the spiritual and intellectual environment explains their disregard by eminent theologians."[33] To cite but one example: Zechariah and Elizabeth "were both righteous before God, walking blamelessly in all the commandments and statutes of the Lord" (Lk 1:6). Of course, it takes more than a few pieces of recalcitrant linguistic data to overturn an interpretive paradigm. Yet we should not underestimate the evidence of such exegetical anomalies.

Paradigm change: "Ecclesiology is the new soteriology." Wright's exegetical revolution reframes how we view what Paul says about justification. Whereas for medieval Catholics justification meant "to make one righteous" and for Luther "to declare one righteous," for Wright it means "to declare one a covenant member." This is one of his main points of contention vis-à-vis the exegetical-industrial complex of old Pauline perspectives: "whenever Paul is talking about justification by faith he is also talking about the coming together of Jews and Gentiles into the single people of God."[34]

Justification "is not a matter of how someone enters the community of the true people of God, but of how you tell who belongs to that community."[35] It is the divine verdict, both present and future, that one is a member of God's covenant people, and thus forgiven. The connection with salvation does not disappear completely, for the covenant exists in large part to deal with sin. Being part of the family of Abraham

[33]Henri Blocher, "Justification of the Ungodly," in *Justification and Variegated Nomism*, ed. D. A. Carson, P. O'Brien, and M. Seifrid (Tübingen: Mohr Siebeck, 2004), p. 476.
[34]Wright, "Paul in Different Perspectives."
[35]Wright, *What Saint Paul Really Said*, p. 119.

"is not *opposed to* 'forgiveness of sins,' but is its proper and biblical context."[36] Hence, for Wright, the question of covenant membership precedes and frames the question of salvation.

Faith on Wright's view is the sign of covenant membership, not the instrument by which individuals acquire Christ's righteousness. Here we come to another bone of Reformed contention. If faith is not our entry ticket but the badge worn by those who are already in, then how does one gain admittance? What problem Wright's Reformed critics have is not so much with the affirmation ("faith is the badge of covenant membership") but rather with the denial ("faith is not the port of entry into the company of the saved").[37] The denial follows from Wright's commitment to what Douglas Harink calls the "massive theological construct" on which his every exegetical decision depends: the grand covenantal-historical metanarrative of God's covenant with Israel.[38] Wright's interpretative paradigm brings the theme of corporate inclusion into sharp relief yet risks obscuring the salvific experience of individuals like Paul's jailer and even Paul himself: "[Wright's] paradigm for justification does not fit well with the ordinary reading of many texts."[39] To be sure, all paradigms have rough edges. Yet, because of perceived lingering exegetical anomalies, we have not yet reached the stage that Kuhn calls "normal science." The revolution continues, its outcome uncertain.

A way forward? The state of the union and the sum of the gospel. I side with those who want to incorporate what they take to be the best aspects of Wright's work into the best of the Reformed tradition.[40] I do not put absolute confidence in the Calvinist tradition, though I myself have reason for confidence in confession also. If anyone else thinks he has reason for confidence in the 'fess, I have more: graduated on the 8th of May (1982), of the people of Geneva, of the tribe of Westminster, one formed of Reformed; as to the law, a Presbyterian; as to zeal, a doc-

---

[36]Wright, *Justification*, p. 134.
[37]For this contrast see Wright, *What Saint Paul Really Said*, p. 132.
[38]Douglas Harink, "The Wright Way to Read Paul," *Christian Century* 126, no. 24 (2009): 32.
[39]Piper, *Future of Justification*, p. 24.
[40]E.g., Michael F. Bird, *The Saving Righteousness of God: Studies on Paul, Justification, and the New Perspective* (Eugene, Ore.: Wipf & Stock, 2007).

tor of the church; as to righteousness under the law, blame*worthy*.

What fortuitously has been called the "new perspective" on Calvin's soteriology anticipates, though not always for the same exegetical reasons, some of what the New Perspective has claimed to discover about Paul's theology.[41] In particular, what Calvin does with Paul's notion of union with Christ provides fertile ground for a meeting of old and new perspective minds.[42] Reading Calvin read Paul on union with Christ illustrates what systematic theology at its best can contribute to the discussion: not an imposition of some foreign conceptual scheme onto the text *but rather a conceptual elaboration of what is implicit within it*. It may also show us that there is more truth and light yet to break forth out of the research program we know as Protestant soteriology.[43]

WHERE MUST WE *BE* TO BE SAVED? "IN HIM . . . THE RIGHTEOUSNESS OF GOD" (2 COR 5:21)

We turn now to consider the material principle of the Reformation: justification. In particular I want to raise two questions: What kind of divine declarative is it? How does it relate to union with Christ? To answer these questions we must move beyond exegesis to ontology, conceptually elaborating the reality and the logic of that about which Paul speaks. Such is the peculiar vocation and ministry of systematic theology: to advance the church, inch by conceptual inch, toward deeper understanding.

The declarative nature of justification: Communicating righteousness. We begin with justification itself. What happens when God declares someone righteous? This is well-trodden ground, but I want to

---

[41]Advocates of the new perspective on Calvin argue that he orders justification and sanctification under the more important rubric of union with Christ. For a critical account of this view see Thomas L. Wenger, "The New Perspective on Calvin: Responding to Recent Calvin Interpretations," *Journal of the Evangelical Theological Society* 50 (2007): 311-28. See also Marcus Johnson, "New or Nuanced Perspective on Calvin? A Reply to Thomas Wenger," *JETS* 51 (2008): 543-58.

[42]Wright thinks so too: "But I have often reflected that if it had been the Reformed view of Paul and the law . . . that had dominated biblical scholarship . . . the new perspective [would] not have been necessary" (*Justification*, p. 72).

[43]See J. Todd Billings, "John Calvin's Soteriology: On the Multifaceted 'Sum' of the Gospel," *International Journal of Systematic Theology* 11 (2009): 428-47.

focus on one aspect only: justification as a declarative speech act (after all, I have a stereotype to keep up).

What kind of declarative? Everyone agrees that justification involves God *saying* something about righteousness. Never mind imputed righteousness: the first thing to clarify is what, for lack of a better term, we may call *locuted* righteousness. According to Anthony Thiselton, *dikaioč* most frequently means "to account righteous": "It is not a descriptive locution, but an illo-cutionary speech-act of declaration and verdict."[44] Declaratives are one of the five basic types of things we do with words. Simply by virtue of being uttered, declaratives bring about changes in the world: "I now pronounce you man and wife"; "I declare the meeting adjourned"; "You're fired." To declare righteous is, similarly, a performative utterance.

Opinions diverge, however, over what kind of change God brings about in declaring someone righteous. On one extreme are those who say that justification is merely a conjuring trick with words, producing legal fictions. This position simply denies the existence of declarative speech acts. At the other end of the spectrum is Eberhard Jüngel, who claims that God's declaring righteous has ontological, transformational force: "This judgment has creative power because it is God's Word. . . . This is the Word . . . which calls into existence the things that do not exist [Rom 4:17]. . . . The forensic act *is* the effective act of making the ungodly righteous."[45] Justification is about God declaring us to *be* other than we presently are: it eschatologically constitutes us other than we empirically are (i.e., other than what we are by our "works").

According to Wright, "*dikaioč* is . . . a declarative word, declaring that something is the case, rather than a word for making something happen or changing the way something is."[46] It is "God's eschatological definition, both future and present, of who was, in fact, a member of

---

[44] Anthony Thiselton, *The First Epistle to the Corinthians: A Commentary on the Greek Text* (Grand Rapids: Eerdmans, 2000), p. 455. According to John Searle, a speaker in a position of authority "brings about a state of affairs specified in the propositional content by saying in effect, I declare the state of affairs to exist" (*Expression and Meaning* [Cambridge: Cambridge University Press, 1979], p. 26).

[45] Eberhard Jüngel, *Justification: The Heart of the Christian Faith* (Edinburgh: T & T Clark, 2001), pp. 210-11.

[46] N. T. Wright, "New Perspectives on Paul," in *Justification in Perspective*, ed. B. McCormack (Grand Rapids: Baker Academic, 2006), p. 258.

his people."[47] Simon Gathercole calls this a "minimalist" view because he thinks God's declaring righteous involves more than *recognizing* what is already the case.[48] Piper agrees: "The divine act of justification actually *establishes* the peace because in it God does not just declare but determines our new identity."[49]

Yet Wright can speak in these terms too: "When the judge in the law-court justifies someone . . . he *creates* the status the vindicated defendant now possesses, by an act of *declaration*, a 'speech-act' in our contemporary jargon."[50] Compare this with the Westminster Shorter Catechism: "Justification is an act of God's free grace, wherein he pardons all our sins, and accepts us as righteous in his sight, only for the righteousness of Christ imputed to us, and received by faith alone" (Q. 33). What is the difference between this "pardoning" and Wright's "creating the status the vindicated defendant now possesses"? Everything depends on the nature of the case, or rather, the *kind of law court* one takes to be the context for God's declarative utterance.

Civil or criminal court? Is God prosecuting a civil case between Israel and the nations over who has legitimate claim to the title "people of God," or a criminal case in which all humanity has been charged with "crimes against divinity"?[51] The opening chapters of Romans indicate that God has a case to prosecute against all humanity, for all have fallen short of the glory of God. Yet for Wright, to declare righteous is more like issuing a finding than an acquittal: it is to declare that one is a covenant member in good standing, not because one has achieved moral righteousness but because of one's faith in Christ Jesus as Lord. At least one Reformed critic—a pastor who desires God's glory above all things but who shall otherwise remain anonymous—thinks this gets things backward: "justification is part of the ground, not the declaration, of saving covenant membership."[52]

---

[47]Wright, *What Saint Paul Really Said*, p. 119.

[48]Simon Gathercole, "The Doctrine of Justification in Paul and Beyond: Some Proposals," in *Justification in Perspective*, ed. B. McCormack (Grand Rapids: Baker Academic, 2006), p. 229.

[49]Piper, *Future of Justification*, p. 42.

[50]Wright, *Justification*, p. 69.

[51]I owe this way of putting the matter to a conversation with Andrew Cowan.

[52]Piper, *Future of Justification*, p. 43.

Recall what Wright takes to be Paul's big idea: God's single plan to rescue the world through the seed of Abraham. To be declared a member of Abraham's offspring resolves the problem of Genesis 11, the disunity of the human race after Babel, and recalls the promise of Genesis 12: through Abraham's seed all nations will be blessed. Being declared a covenant member also deals with the more basic problem of Genesis 3 and the wrath of God, inasmuch as covenant members participate in the benefit of Christ's death. Sin has both horizontal (i.e., redemptive-historical) and vertical (i.e., properly theological) effects, alienating us from one another *and* from God: "the status of the individual before God and the status of individuals within a group setting are not mutually exclusive categories."[53] The only question is whether Wright has put these two axes together in what we may call, appropriately enough, a *right* angle.

What implications for imputed righteousness? Can we graft Wright's "newer perspective" onto a Reformed framework without bursting old wineskins? Both parties want to affirm a forensic dimension within a wider covenantal framework to justification. Where, then, is the problem? The disagreement concerns the nature of righteousness as a declared status. Is it the verdict to a civil or a criminal case? Does it mean *in* or *innocent?* What is God *doing* in locuting righteousness? Neither Wright nor Reformed theologians would say that God's declaring someone righteous is a matter of describing that person as being morally upright. Declaring righteous pertains to one's status, not one's actual state.

According to Wright, to be deemed righteous has nothing to do with the imputation of righteousness to the defendant. It makes no sense, he thinks, for the judge to impute, impart or convey his own righteousness to someone else. Nor does God transfer what Christ has accumulated in his "treasury of merit"—Christ's moral standing—to sinners' accounts. Wright is rightly concerned not to encourage legalism. But why need we construe Christ's obedience in terms of "morality" rather than covenant faithfulness? Could we not say

---

[53]Bird, *Saving Righteousness of God*, p. 34.

that in justification God reckons Christ's "right covenantal related-ness" ours? Calvin himself was quite clear in his refutation of Osian-der that to be declared righteous is not to participate in one of God's essential attributes but rather of being the beneficiaries of Christ's mediating, messianic work. Christ does everything that Israel (and Adam) was supposed to do. He suffers the covenant sanction and fulfills the covenant law, including its summary command "to love God and your neighbor as oneself." In counting us righteous, then, God both pardons us ("there is therefore now no condemnation" [Rom 8:1]) and gives us the positive *status* of rectitude, a down pay-ment, as it were, sealed with the Spirit, on our eventually achieving an actual righteous *state* (i.e., sanctification).

How many things does God do in declaring someone righteous? At least four: justification is "the act whereby God creates a new people, with a new status, in a new covenant, as a foretaste of the new age."[54] The question is whether imputation too is part and parcel of this pro-digious declarative speech act: "[Imputation] ascribes to one what be-longs properly to another."[55] Can such an attribution ever be proper? With this question we come to the heart of my constructive proposal. To declare someone righteous is to declare that person *incorporated* into Christ's righteousness: "I now pronounce you man in Christ."

To incorporate means both "to include as part of a whole" (in this case, the body of Christ) and "to constitute as a legal corporation." In-corporated righteousness thus includes the forensic, covenantal and es-chatological dimensions that Wright associates with justification, yet orders them in such a way as to make possible a rapprochement with Reformed theology.[56] "Incorporated righteousness" may not yet be the

---

[54]Bird, *Introducing Paul*, p. 96.

[55]Mark A. Garcia, "Imputation as Attribution: Union with Christ, Reification and Justification as Declarative Word," *International Journal of Systematic Theology* 11 (2009): 419.

[56]What we need is a new formulation that would do to present-day discussions what the Regens-burg Colloquy (almost) did in the sixteenth century for Protestant-Roman Catholic relations. Article 5, which posited a twofold righteousness, imputed and inherent, was affirmed by both sides and was approved by Calvin (Anthony N. S. Lane, "Twofold Righteousness: A Key to the Doctrine of Justification?" in *Justification: What's at Stake in the Current Debates*, ed. Mark Husbands and Daniel J. Treier [Downers Grove, Ill.: InterVarsity Press, 2004], pp. 205-24). According to Lane the only concession required of Protestants at Regensburg was termino-logical.

formula to reconcile old and new perspectives, but I continue to hope that some such formula of concord may yet be possible.[57] For this to be the case, however, both sides may need to give more prominence to the theme of union with Christ.

The state of our union with Christ: forensic, ontological and/or covenantal? Calvin's—and more importantly, Paul's—notion of union with Christ combines the forensic and participationist elements to which the concept of incorporated righteousness attempts to do justice. God declares us to be "in the clear" and thus "in the covenant"; Paul declares us to be "in Christ." Is there room in this latter "in" for the two others, and if so, how do they relate? Are we in the covenant and in the right because we are in Christ? Are we in Christ and in the right because we are in the covenant? Or are we in Christ and the covenant because we are in the right, and if so, how did we get to be there? Amid the complexity, one truth stands clear: *outside the Christ there is no salvation*. Nor does it make much sense to speak of the *body* of Christ outside Christ. To be "in Christ" involves soteriology and ecclesiology alike. Hence my working hypothesis: to be declared righteous ("in the right") is one dimension of being found "in him."

The dogmatic location of justification. John Webster gives us his own version of the big picture in the course of reflecting on the place of the doctrine of justification in dogmatics. It concerns the way in which the God who has life in himself gives life in its fullness to sinful creatures. The form this divine self-giving takes is redemptive history, and "no one moment of the history can bear the weight of the whole."[58] Webster here reminds us that justification is but one soteriological moment among others. Each has a vital contribution to make. It is the task of systematic theology "to restrain the capacity of a confessional focus upon one particular aspect of Christian teaching from deforming or reducing the scope of the church's apprehension of the gospel as a whole."[59] It is precisely for this reason, and to mediate Wright's debate

---

[57]I owe the basic idea in this paragraph to Bird, *Saving Righteousness of God*, esp. chap. 4.

[58]John Webster, *"Rector et iudex super omnia genera doctrinarum?* The Place of the Doctrine of Justification," in *What Is Justification About? Reformed Contributions to an Ecumenical Theme,* ed. Michael Weinrich and John P. Burgess (Grand Rapids: Eerdmans, 2009), p. 41.

[59]Ibid., p. 47.

with the Reformed, that I propose thinking about justification and union with Christ *together*.

Union with Christ. The expression "in Christ" occurs some 150 times in Paul's letters. To be "in Christ" means, for Wright, "belonging to the people of God as redefined around the Messiah."[60] To be counted a "family member" is the "fuller meaning" of justification by faith,[61] and may be another way of talking about imputed righteousness: "the accomplishment of Jesus Christ is *reckoned* to all those who are 'in him.'"[62]

The key question, however, concerns precisely what is reckoned to us. It has something to do with Christ's status, but opinions diverge over whether it is his status as the vindicated one, the one whom God raised from the dead, or the faithful one, the one who set things to right in part by *doing* right. The Reformed concern is that Wright deemphasizes Jesus' obedience to the Father, thus raising questions about the ground of our right standing before God.

It is just here that Calvin may have a genuinely Pauline insight, even if his exegesis did not always get Paul's historical situation right, and even though his followers may have compartmentalized his soteriology more than he did. Calvin asks: "Do you wish to attain righteousness in Christ? You must first possess Christ; but you cannot possess him without being made partaker in his sanctification, because he cannot be divided into pieces."[63] Calvin here anticipates and guards against the very dangers that Wright sees in contemporary evangelicalism.

According to Calvin both justification and sanctification flow from our union with Christ.[64] There is no contradiction between the forensic

---

[60]Wright, *What Saint Paul Really Said,* p. 152.

[61]Wright, *Justification,* p. 134.

[62]Wright, "Paul in Different Perspectives," cited in Piper, *Future of Justification,* p. 121.

[63]John Calvin *Institutes of the Christian Religion* 3.16.1 (John McNeill, ed., Library of Christian Classics, 2 vols. [Philadelphia: Westminster Press, 1960]).

[64]Cf. Lane G. Tipton's comment: "Union with Christ furnishes the organizing structure in terms of which the Spirit applies to believers all of the realized redemptive benefits in Christ distinctly, inseparably, simultaneously, and eschatologically" ("Union with Christ and Justification," in *Justified in Christ,* ed. K. Scott Oliphant [Tain, U.K.: Christian Focus, 2007], p. 24). See also Richard B. Gaffin, "Biblical Theology and the Westminster Standards," *Westminster Theological Journal* 65 (2003): 165-79; and Mark A. Garcia, *Life in Christ: Union with Christ and Twofold Grace in Calvin's Theology* (Milton Keynes, U.K., and Colorado Springs: Paternoster, 2008).

and the formational: through Christ's blamelessness we have a gracious Father in heaven rather than a judge; through his Spirit we may cultivate blamelessness and purity of life.[65] Nor is there a temporal gap between the two graces, though justification (God's gift) is the context and condition of the other (our gratitude).[66] Calvin does not say that we ought to love others and do good works, but rather that, as renewed in Christ, we *will* love others and do good works. I submit that this may be what Wright is getting at when he says that our present justification anticipates our future justification. If so, then he might have appealed to Calvin's analogy: the two graces are like sunlight, in which "the brightness cannot be separated from its heat." This language echoes Chalcedon's formula of "distinct, though not separated." Calvin here works a Copernican revolution of his own, complete with solar reference.

The word and Spirit of adoption: a declaration that does what it says. Calvin's "double grace" of union with Christ approaches what I mean by "incorporated righteousness." We need to take one more step, however, in order to see that union with Christ is an apt place for Wright's lion to lie down in peace with the lion of Reformed theology (neither is particularly lamb-like). I submit that adoption, first cousin as it were to union with Christ, is the perfect mediating category inasmuch as it pertains both to the question of covenant membership (i.e., who is in God's family) *and* of legal standing before God (i.e., rights of inheritance). Hear again the word of Calvin: "as soon as you become engrafted into Christ through faith, you are made a son of God, an heir of heaven, a partaker in righteousness."[67] Son, heir, partaker: we have now to speak of a *triple* grace that flows from union with Christ.

Just as Paul needs many metaphors to do justice to what Jesus accomplished on the cross, so he needs multiple models for articulating what it means to be "in Christ." Adoption is an especially rich metaphor that involves both confessing family membership and conferring

---

[65]Calvin *Institutes* 3.11.1.

[66]So Billings, "John Calvin's Soteriology," p. 446. See also J. Todd Billings, *Calvin, Participation, and the Gift: The Activity of Believers in Union with Christ* (Oxford: Oxford University Press, 2007).

[67]Calvin *Institutes* 3.15.6.

legal status.[68] Indeed, it is a lens through which one can view the whole history of salvation: "In love he predestined us for adoption as sons through Jesus Christ" (Eph 1:4-5); "They are Israelites, and to them belong the adoption" (Rom 9:4); "God sent forth his Son . . . to redeem those who were under the law, so that we might receive adoption as sons" (Gal 4:4); "For you did not receive the spirit of slavery to fall back into fear, but you have received the Spirit of adoption as sons. . . . The Spirit himself bears witness with our spirit that we are children of God" (Rom 8:15).

Wright does not say much about adoption in Paul's thought, at least not in the context of justification. Neither do most Reformed systematicians, more's the pity.[69] The etymology of the Greek term, though not a semantic norm, is nonetheless intriguing: *huiothesia* = *huios* (son) + *thesia* (from *tith™mi* = to place).[70] To be united with Christ is to be in the Son's place. Adoption—receiving sonship—is thus a powerful statement of the gospel. The good news is that God the Father counts us his children "in Christ."

Here we do well to recall Paul's first statement of the gospel: "the gospel of God . . . concerning his Son, who . . . was declared to be the Son of God in power according to the Spirit of holiness by his resurrection from the dead" (Rom 1:1, 3-4). This same Spirit, who Calvin names the "bond of our union" with Christ, is also the Spirit of adoption. *Bond* is an apt term, carrying both objective and subjective connotations, for our union with Christ is both forensic *and* filial. Adoption adds to justification the notion of familial status and to union with Christ the note of legal status.[71] For, unlike being "born again," adop-

---

[68]See Tim J. R. Trumper, "The Metaphorical Import of Adoption: A Plea for Realisation. I: The Adoption Metaphor in Biblical Usage," *Scottish Bulletin of Evangelical Theology* 14 (1996): 129-45.

[69]For a survey of this history of omission, see Tim J. R. Trumper, "The Theological History of Adoption. I: An Account," *Scottish Bulletin of Evangelical Theology* 20 (2002): 4-28.

[70]It is also noteworthy that the term is "conspicuously absent from the corpus of classical Greek writers and from other Jewish literature of the period" (Trevor J. Burke, *Adopted into God's Family: Exploring a Pauline Metaphor* [Downers Grove, Ill.: InterVarsity Press, 2007], p. 22).

[71]For a helpful account of the soteriological gains to be had from recovering the metaphor of adoption, not least for the doctrine of justification, see Tim J. R. Trumper, "A Fresh Exposition of Adoption. II: Some Implications," *Scottish Bulletin of Evangelical Theology* 23 (2005): 194-215, esp. pp. 206-11.

tion refers to a forensic act.[72] One might even say that adoption *imputes* filial status.[73]

And this is precisely what we are looking for: something in Paul's thought that links what Wright says about covenant membership to what the Reformed say about imputed righteousness.[74] Might it be that the law court in which the justifying verdict is read out is also an *adoption* court, such that in declaring men and women his children God assigns them all the rights appertaining thereunto, including the incalculable privilege of calling God "Father" and the concomitant eschatological privilege of having the Spirit of the Father's Son dwell in our hearts (Gal 4:6)? The salient point is that adoption is one way of expressing what it is to be "in Christ" that bridges present and future, the forensic and the familial.

Christians become members of God's covenant family by receiving the Son's status: *righteous sonship*. Jesus Christ was the righteous Son the Father always wanted Israel, and Adam, to be. (I note in passing that some Roman emperors, most famously Augustus Caesar, were also adopted sons.) Adoption is a way of spelling out the nature of our union with Christ in trinitarian fashion in ways that account for both the individual and corporate aspects of soteriology and ecclesiology. Sons and daughters in Christ, we have Christ's righteousness standing before God *and* unity with one another as members of Christ's one body. Adoption "in Christ" puts biblical flesh on the bare conceptual bones of "incorporated righteousness."

In sum: the *state of the union* and the *status of imputation* come together in the *sonship of adoption*. Putting it this ways reminds us that justification is ultimately a trinitarian communication of righteousness: the Father adopts strangers by uniting them to Christ by the Spirit through faith. The Father declares, the Son enables, and the

---

[72]"Sonship by adoption should be carefully distinguished from . . . sonship by regeneration" (Louis Berkhof, *Systematic Theology* [Edinburgh: Banner of Truth, 1976], p. 516).

[73]Cf. L. O. Yarbrough: "for . . . Paul . . . adoption into the family of God is a key metaphor for the new status believers have obtained" ("Parents and Children in the Letters of Paul," in *The Social World of the First Christians: Essays in Honor of Wayne A. Meeks*, ed. L. M. White and O. L. Yarbrough [Minneapolis: Fortress, 1995], p. 140).

[74]The operative term is *link*, not *collapse*. I agree with Trevor J. Burke that neither justification nor adoption should be subsumed under the other (*Adopted into God's Family*, pp. 23-25).

Spirit effects the sinner's right standing.[75] In justifying or declaring righteousness, then, God rectifies the status of his people, declaring sinners sons and daughters of God, heirs of heaven, and partakers in righteousness.

By tying together justification, union with Christ and adoption, I have tried to bridge the ugly ditch that divides Wright's view from the Reformed tradition. Observers disagree as to the ditch's width; what is important is to keep building the bridge from both sides. For no one idea, whether imputation or "filiation," should take Pauline center stage to the neglect of others. The wisdom of Solomon in this case consists not in dividing but dialoguing. In this regard the saddest line in Wright's book on justification is his comment about the present moment in the justification debate: "We are not in dialogue."[76] Let me therefore conclude with a call to all parties to beat their diatribic swords into dialogic plowshares (Mic 4:3).

CONCLUDING UNVITRIOLIC POSTSCRIPT

The English theologian F. D. Maurice was right: "people are more likely to be right in what they affirm than in what they deny."[77] The truth of the principle pertains not to logic but psychology: people are more likely to assert something that they have experienced or found out themselves. C. S. Lewis explains: "A negative proposition is harder to establish than a positive. One glance may enable us to say there is a spider in the room; we should need a spring-cleaning (at least) before

---

[75]The act of declaring righteous thus involves locution, illocution and perlocution alike.

[76]Wright, *Justification*, p. 20.

[77]I am not the first to think this. Cf. I. Howard Marshall, *New Testament Theology: Many Witnesses, One Gospel* (Downers Grove, Ill.: InterVarsity Press, 2004), p. 446; John Frame: "I tend to applaud this and other movements for what they affirm but not for what they deny" (*Speaking the Truth in Love* [Phillipsburg, N.J.: P & R, 2009], p. 80); Robert H. Gundry: "It is popular nowadays to interpret biblical righteousness not as behavior according to a moral norm but as behavior according to the terms of a covenant. This view is correct in what it affirms but wrong in what it denies; for at least where God is concerned, the terms of a covenant are rooted in his moral character" ("The Nonimputation of Christ's Righteousness," in *Justification: What's at Stake in the Current Debates*, ed. Mark Husbands and Daniel J. Treier [Downers Grove, Ill.: InterVarsity Press, 2004], p. 35 n. 40); cf. Michael Bird: "Ultimately the NPP [New Perspective on Paul] is correct in what it affirms but wrong in what it denies" (*Saving Righteousness of God*, p. 182).

we could say with certainty that there wasn't."[78]

Wright's clarion call to return to Scripture and to the big covenantal picture we discover therein is to be welcomed, as are his emphases on God's single plan for the whole world and the corporate implications of justification. However, do these affirmations require the controversial denials, for example, that justification is *not* about how one becomes a Christian? I applaud Wright's recognition "that the accomplishment of Jesus Christ . . . reckoned to all those who are 'in him'" is "one of the great truths of the gospel,"[79] but when he says, apparently with equal conviction, that "it makes no sense whatever to say that the judge imputes . . . his righteousness,"[80] I clap with only one hand, since, as we have seen, the Reformers were talking about the *status* of *Christ's* covenant faithfulness.

No single voice can speak the whole truth. If no one Evangelist could say everything that needed to be said about Jesus Christ, then it should come as no surprise that no one New Testament scholar can do so either. Yes, Scripture is the supreme authority for the church's life and thought. But Wright is not the first to attend to its meaning. No one person, even one with Wright's energy and prodigious intellectual gifts, can work a paradigm revolution single-handedly. He needs to win not more battles, but more allies.

Is it not possible that the Reformers and their successors, despite their ignorance of the first-century Palestinian context, were nevertheless able to penetrate to the heart of Paul's concerns because they believed that Scripture interprets Scripture, attended to the canonical context (as well as to orthodox tradition), and were illumined by the Holy Spirit? Sometimes it takes two different but complementary perspectives to say what is. Might this be the case with Wright and the Reformed tradition? I do not hear blatant contradictions between their respective affirmations. Yet each side probably needs to stop denying certain things and soften the polemics. The Reformed need to accept the ecclesiological implications of being declared in Christ; Wright needs to retool his understanding of the law court and develop a fuller

---

[78]C. S. Lewis, *An Experiment in Criticism* (Cambridge: Cambridge University Press, 1961), p. 117.
[79]Wright, "Paul in Different Perspectives," cited in Piper, *The Future of Justification*, p. 21.
[80]Wright, *What Saint Paul Really Said*, p. 98.

understanding of our union with Christ. And both sides need to work harder to incorporate Paul's metaphor of adoption into their respective soteriologies.

Finally, both sides of the discussion need to keep working on the dialogical virtues: those habits of discourse that are conducive to understanding others and to making oneself understood. Among dialogical virtues such as honesty, fairness and clarity, one stands out: humility, the opposite of pride or self-righteousness. The dialogical virtues, first cousins to the intellectual virtues, aim to inculcate right communication and right thinking, especially when the topic is God's setting things to right.[81] What I am calling the dialogical virtues are ultimately the fruit of the Spirit. With this thought in mind, I can perhaps guess what St. Paul might say back, not only to Wright, but to us all: "love, joy, peace, patience, kindness, goodness, faithfulness, gentleness, self-control; against such things there is no law" (Gal 5:22).

Response to Kevin Vanhoozer
N. T. WRIGHT

It is always encouraging for an exegete to find that the systematicians are engaging creatively with his proposals without telling him to forget the first-century detail. Kevin clearly enjoys the same sort of things as I do in the area where our disciplines overlap. His concluding call for the dialogical virtues is wonderful—though we should beware: our culture regularly assumes that *humility* means "not pressing your point." Kevin, of course, doesn't go that route, and I agree that we need to work at the challenge of humble confrontation. Much like Miroslav Volf's "exclusion and embrace": we need both.

To the detail. To a big-picture person such as myself, the protests of James Barr about "illegitimate totality transfer," while relevant, always sound like the protest of someone who has forgotten, in analyzing the individual trees, that there is such a thing as a forest. Actually, when

---

[81]See Robert C. Roberts and W. Jay Wood, *Intellectual Virtues: An Essay in Regulative Epistemology* (Oxford: Clarendon Press, 2007).

reflecting on the Reformers and their supposed canonical context, we must remind ourselves that theirs was a highly selective canonical context. It privileged a reading of Romans and Galatians which, arguably, does not do full justice to either of those texts; it began the long, slow process of pushing Ephesians and Colossians toward the margins; and it paid remarkably little attention to the four Gospels and their deep theology of God's kingdom coming on earth as in heaven. There is no space here to engage with Brevard Childs's book on Paul, but I would suggest that there is more to the "canonical Paul" than he allows.

This point needs to be emphasized when we are discussing how to preserve the gospel's integrity. The message that God justifies the ungodly simply *was*, for Paul in Romans 4:4-5, the message that God would bring Gentiles into Abraham's family. Of course it has wider application. But cutting off the Pauline root of meaning won't produce the fruit of an integrated gospel. And here I don't understand why Kevin has suggested that, for me, the covenant with Abraham is the main plot and the Adam story the subplot. I would suggest, on the contrary, that the story of God and creation is the main plot; the story of God, Adam and creation is the subplot; and the story of God, Abraham and Israel is the sub-subplot which, through Israel's representative Messiah, drives and resolves the subplot so that the main plot can at last be restored (Rom 8). Within this, so far from "salvation" being a minor concern, it is highlighted all through. But that happens *within*, not apart from, the question of God's people on the one hand and restoring creation on the other. Gathercole's comment that my reading is "minimalist" balances the more regular objection that my picture is too maximalist. We piped, and you didn't dance; we wailed, and you didn't mourn.

So to Kevin's proposal about a larger Reformed framework within which what he calls my "newer perspective" can be maintained. That, indeed, is what I have hoped to achieve all along, and I am very grateful for Kevin's help in articulating it. "Incorporated righteousness" may not quite catch the Pauline meaning of *dikaiosyn*™, but it certainly moves in the right direction. It has been my contention all along that the forensic and participationist elements in Paul's thought are two aspects of his covenantal, that is, Israel-as-the-means-of-rescuing-Adam, theology. To speak of justification as "one metaphor for salvation among others" misses this point and reduces the particularities of Paul's argument— and his larger theology!—to the status of various pictorial musings around a central theme. Granted, Paul uses many metaphors and multiple models, but there is a clear single narrative within which the metaphors and models make their distinctive and appropriate contribution. There is regular metonymy as well as metaphor.

Within that narrative, as Kevin stresses, "adoption" is a vital and central idea, expressed particularly in Romans 8 and Galatians 3–4. I am surprised he hasn't seen this as central to my work; perhaps I need to find ways of highlighting it further. Certainly I have long seen it as vital. Here again, of course, "adoption" brings one into the status of "child of God," which is precisely an Israel category.

What is so splendid in Vanhoozer's discussion—apart from his brilliant writing—is that he draws Romans 5–8 into the argument about justification in a way that many in the Reformed camp fail to do. Thus adoption-plus-incorporated-righteousness strikes me as a major step in the right (Wright?) direction. We still then need to tease out the way in which, when Paul wants to declare that what is true of Jesus the Messiah is now true of his people, it is the *death and resurrection of the Messiah*, not his "righteousness," that is front and center. That, of course, brings us back to Romans 6 and the question of baptism. I suspect that in many post-Reformation circles the embarrassment at Paul's solidly realistic language about baptism and its effects has encouraged people to tiptoe around the chapter rather than integrating it into their justification theology. That is one area for further work; the other would be how to integrate Paul's view of the law into the Vanhoozer-Wright picture. Plenty to ponder, plenty to celebrate.

10

Whence and Whither Pauline Studies in the Life of the Church?

N. T. WRIGHT

I AM UNCOMFORTABLY AWARE of the bishop who said, "Everywhere St. Paul went there was a riot; everywhere I go they serve tea." It's a good question as to why we don't have riots about St. Paul today (the "riots" on certain blogsites don't count, and anyway they are usually for the wrong reason). What is Paul about? Why did he cause such trouble in his own day, and what might he mean for ours?

Let me begin with a word of autobiography. On June 2, 1953, I was four and a half years old. It was my mother's birthday; it was the day the Queen of England was crowned; and my parents gave to my sister and me a Bible each. It was a small but fat King James Version; that's all we knew in our church at that time. My sister, a year older than me, could read reasonably well; I had just learned to do so. I remember the two of us sitting on the floor, leafing through this great fat book and being rather appalled at the size of it. (It was quite a step up from *Thomas the Tank Engine.*) We had a feeling we should read something from it but didn't really know what. So, having searched through the apparently endless books of Kings and Chronicles, and the Gospels and Acts, we came to one much shorter book, and we decided we'd read that. It was the first time I'd ever read anything in the Bible, let alone a whole book right through; and the book we chose was the letter to Philemon.

Philemon is a great place to start. Few Pauline theologies, I think, start with Philemon. But perhaps we should; I am doing so in the book I'm trying to write at the moment. The little letter to Philemon gives us a bird's-eye view of what's going on throughout Paul.

Consider the situation. Here we have a slave and a master, who in anybody else's worldview in the first century would be pulled apart by the social and cultural forces which insisted that they remain in separate compartments. And Paul brokers a new kind of deal, the vulnerable deal by which the relationship between Onesimus and Philemon is to be restored. Onesimus has to go back to Philemon, not unlike the prodigal son going back to face his father. Paul is sending him back to where the trouble had happened. But Onesimus will not go back jauntily, with his head held high and a smirk on his face, saying "Paul says you've got to set me free—ha, ha, ha!" No; this is a deeply serious and vulnerable moment, and Paul wants Philemon to know just how serious this is for both of them. And the way Paul writes that letter is magnificent as a piece of practical theology. He stretches out one hand and embraces Onesimus: "Here he is, he's my child, my very heart, I've begotten him in my imprisonment. I'd much rather keep him with me, but I really have to send him back." And then he stretches out the other hand and embraces Philemon: "You are my partner, my fellow worker, we're in this together—and by the way, remember you owe me everything." Then, standing there with outstretched arms, he says to Philemon: "If he owes you anything, put it down on my account."

You see what's going on. Paul does not mention, in this letter, the crucifixion of Jesus Christ. But it is the cross of Jesus Christ, exemplified and embodied in Paul's ministry, which is bringing the master and slave together. Paul is doing the unthinkable, bringing about what he says in Galatians 3, close-up, sharp and personal: in Christ there is neither Jew nor Greek, slave nor free, no male and female. This is what it means in practice. The cross is the place where the irreconcilable can be reconciled.

And if you start there, you have to ask, as a historian: what on earth is going on? Nobody else in the ancient world thought you could do that kind of thing. There are hints throughout the letter of the answer:

there is a special, different God at work, not like the gods of the empire who dominated the horizon and believed in keeping the social structure of the world exactly as it was, so that slaves had to stay as slaves, and if they tried to have it otherwise they might get crucified. Rather, this is the God who sets slaves free; this is the God of the exodus, at work in a new way. This is the God who says, "I have heard the cry of my people, and I've come to do what I promised to Abraham, Isaac and Jacob, to set the slaves free." And he does it through—being crucified. If you want the theology underneath the letter to Philemon, look at 2 Corinthians 5:11-21, climaxing in that final verse: God made him to be sin for us, who knew no sin, so that in him we might become, might embody, the covenant faithfulness of God.

So the question presses: What is this new worldview? How do we describe the worldview of Paul the apostle? It clearly isn't the worldview of Second Temple Judaism, yet in another way it clearly is. My friend Professor John Barclay wrote a book about Second Temple Judaism a few years ago (*Jews in the Mediterranean Diaspora*) in which, in the final chapter, he wrestles with the puzzle of Paul. Paul looks so much like a classic Jew, quite strict and orthodox in many ways, and yet in other ways disturbingly free from his tradition: he sits light to the Sabbath, to the food laws and so on. Barclay, I think, sets this up as a tease; he wants to provoke fresh thought on the question of where Paul fits, of how to categorize him. He hasn't yet written the subsequent volume, which he has promised, to show how it all works out. But I think the answer is clear. Paul's worldview has shifted dramatically because of Jesus the Messiah. From one point of view the story has been fulfilled. From another point of view, the symbols have been relativized. It's the same story—the story of how the one God is fulfilling his promises to Abraham, Isaac and Jacob, so that through that fulfillment he might accomplish the wider purpose of rescuing the whole world. That's where the story was going. But precisely because it is now for the benefit of the whole world, it cannot be contained or captured within the enclosed world of Judaism. It cannot be defined in terms of Judaism's ethnic symbols. It is not the case, then, that Paul is cavalierly seeking to overthrow tradition for the sake of it. He is not just some kind of a liberal, thinking, *Well, we're doing something new, let's forget some of those old scriptural requirements, they're a bit out of date after all*. It's nothing whatever to do with that. It is rooted in a theologically worked through principle: "Through the law I died to the law, so that I might live to God" (Gal 2:19).[1] The Torah itself is both fulfilled and, in its fulfillment, set aside; not because the Torah was a second-rate, shabby system and we were glad to get rid of it, but because it was a gift for a purpose, and the purpose has now been accomplished. The Torah wasn't a strange, stupid first attempt of God to save people, enticing them to try to keep it and earn their own salvation, so that only after a millennium and more of unsuccessful attempts God would decide to wave it away and try a different plan. No: the Torah was a wonderful, glorious thing, as far superior to the codes of other peoples as the sun is to the moon. It was holy, just and good, given for a purpose, for a time; and with the Messiah the time was up. All that was there in Torah that God intended to be of permanent value and intention has been transformed into the life of Messiah and Spirit.

What then are the symbols of Paul's own worldview? They are the symbols which speak of Jesus Christ. They include the acted symbols of baptism and the Lord's Supper. But I have come to the conclusion that the central symbol of Paul's worldview is the united community: Jew-Greek, slave-free, male-female: the one family of Abraham, the family for the world, the single family created anew in Jesus Christ from people of every kind. I begin here as a kind of thought experiment; I am trying to work through Paul in the same way that I worked through questions about Jesus in *Jesus and the Victory of God*, analyzing worldviews not least in terms of symbols and stories.

THE CENTRAL SYMBOL: THE UNITED FAMILY

When you go to the shelves and pick a volume on Pauline theology, the chances are there will be a chapter on the church, but it will probably come some way toward the back of the book. When the writer has exhausted the topics of God, humans, sin, salvation, Jesus Christ and his

---

[1]Scripture quoted in this chapter is the author's translation.

death and resurrection, the Spirit, and so on—finally they may get to a
chapter on the church. And within that, as one subsection among many,
you will find, perhaps "the unity of the church," with an exploration of
Paul's different metaphors, the body of Christ, the new temple and so
on. I think that is just the projection onto Paul of certain types of Western Protestant thinking. When we read Paul in his own terms, we find
that for him the one, single community is absolutely central. The community of Christ, in Christ, by the Spirit, is at the very heart of it all.

I love the doctrine of justification. It is hugely important. But it only
really occurs in Romans and Galatians, with little flickers elsewhere.
But wherever you look in Paul, you see him arguing for and passionately working for the unity of the church. We've seen it, up close and
personal, in Philemon. In Galatians the real thrust of the whole letter
is that Jewish Christians and Gentile Christians should sit at the same
table together. That's not incidental; it's the main point of the argument. And in 1 Corinthians, of course, the unity of the church is one
of the main themes of the letter, all through, not just in chapter 12. "Is
Christ divided? Of course not." The exposition builds all the way to the
picture of the single body with many members in chapter 12. And then,
in case you wondered how that could happen, Paul writes that majestic
poem on *agap*™, love. Then, in 1 Corinthians 14, we see what that must
look like in the worshiping life of the church; God is not the God of
chaos but of order. And then, in chapter 15, all of this is rooted in the
gospel which speaks of new creation, of the kingdom of God, because
of the resurrection of Jesus himself from the dead.

Then, in Philippians, the question is raised: How are you going to
"let your public life be worthy of the gospel of Christ" (Phil 1:27)? Answer, in chapter 2: "make my joy complete: be of the same mind, having
the same love, being in full accord and of one mind" (v. 2). Have you
ever tried that in a group of three or four? Have you ever tried it in a
group of fifteen or twenty? In a group of a thousand or more? It is very
difficult. Don't imagine it was any easier in the first century. But don't
imagine that just because we all find it difficult we can go soft on this
central imperative. Rather, recognize that the only way to do it is
through what Paul says next.

Let this mind be in you, which you have in the Messiah, Jesus: he was in the form of God, but didn't regard his equality with God as something to exploit, but emptied himself, becoming obedient to death, even the death of the cross. Therefore God highly exalted him, and bestowed on him the name above every name, that at the name of Jesus every knee should bow, and every tongue confess Jesus Christ as Lord, to the glory of God the father. (Phil 2:5-11).

There's the secret, the living heart of this new, revolutionary way of being human. That's why Paul can at once go on to urge: "Do all things without grumbling or questioning, so that you may be blameless and innocent, children of God without blemish in a dark world among whom you shine like lights" (Phil 2:14-15). You see the point: the unity of the church, the new way of humble unity lived out by the followers of Jesus, is to be the sign to the church that there is a different way of being human.

Or we could consider the letter to the Ephesians. The unity of Jew and Gentile in Christ (Eph 2:11-21) is the direct outflowing of that exposition of justification in verses 1-10. And then in chapter 3 this explodes in the glorious truth that *through the church*, the multicolored, many-tongued family, the manifold wisdom of God might be made known to the principalities and powers in the heavenly places. It is the fact of a new family that declares to Caesar that he doesn't run the show any more, because Jesus Christ runs it instead. It is the fact of a new, single, united family that tells the powers of the world that Israel's God is God, that Jesus is Lord and Caesar is not. As long as we continue to collude with things that no Paulinist should ever collude with—fragmentation, petty squabbles, divisions over this or that small point of doctrine—the powers can fold their arms and watch us having our little fun while they really still run the show. But when there actually is one body, one spirit, one hope, one Lord, one faith, one baptism (Eph 4), then the powers are called to account, and they will know it. Something new has happened, and the gates of hell shall not shall prevail against it.

And there's a cost, the cost of being different. That's why we have the challenge of marriage in Ephesians 5, in which the coming together of male and female—and what a challenge that always has been, and still is—symbolizes once more the coming together of Jew and Gentile, which symbolizes again the coming together of heaven and earth. That is why it's so important that in our generation we struggle again for the sanctity and vitality of marriage, not for the sake of maintaining a few outmoded ethical concepts and taboos, but because this is built deep into creation itself, now to be renewed in Christ and the Spirit.

Then consider the ecumenical imperative in Romans itself. Many of you have lectured or preached on Romans, and you will know what happens. You have the schedule organized, you know how you want it to go, and somehow the exposition of the first eight chapters eats up the time allotted for chapters 9-11, and then when you've dealt with those chapters in turn you hardly have any time left for chapters 12-16. But actually in chapters 14-15 we have some of the most profound teaching anywhere in Scripture on the unity of the church and how to maintain it. It isn't a detached topic; it grows directly out of all that has gone before in this most majestic of letters. The hard-won, complex unity of the church, which results in the church glorifying the God and Father of our Lord Jesus Christ with one heart and voice: that's what it's all about. Romans 15:7-13 is the climax of the theological exposition of the whole letter, and it insists on the *united* worship of the multicultural church as the ultimate aim of the gospel. That is the heart of Paul's ecclesiology.

And it's a new-temple ecclesiology. You are the temple of the living God; that's there in 1 Corinthians 3 and 6, and it's there in Romans 8 too, where the indwelling of the Spirit has the same temple resonance, though it's not usually noticed. So, similarly, in Colossians 1:27: where Paul says, "Christ in you, the hope of glory," he doesn't just mean my individual hope of glory and your individual hope of glory. The "you" is plural, in any case, but the point goes further than simply stressing that this is more than a sum total of individuals. Look at it like this. God intends to flood the whole cosmos with his glory. There is coming a time when the most Spirit-filled person in this room will be just a pale shadow of what God intends to do for the entire world. But that is anticipated when a room full of people in Colossae, a dozen or two in Ephesus, maybe fifty or so in Rome, are worshiping and praying in the Spirit: this is a sign of the time that is to come when the earth will be filled with the glory of God as the waters cover the sea. The Messiah is in *you*, *now*, as the sign of the hope of glory for all creation. That is the point which flows directly from Romans 1:15-20 and that remarkable verse 23, where every creature under heaven has already heard the word.

We are therefore the people of the renewed covenant, the line that runs from Deuteronomy and Jeremiah in to the New Testament. Deuteronomy has a forward look; the covenant is not an abstract, steady-state constitution. You are a people whose story is going somewhere—but where? If you disobey the covenant, you will go into exile; that's the warning of Deuteronomy 28–29. But then, when you're in exile, if you return to the Lord with all your heart and your soul, he will circumcise your heart so that you can love him with all your heart. And then will come to pass the promise that the "word" will be not far from you, up in heaven or across the sea, but "very near" to you, on your lips and in your heart, so that you can do it. People won't say, "This covenant is so difficult for us to keep; how can we possibly do it?" No: the word will be near you, in you and with you, so that you can do it. And Paul picks up exactly that: not just in Romans 10, where he quotes Deuteronomy 30 explicitly, but by implication in Galatians 3, in Romans 2, 7 and 8: again and again, his message can be summed up as "You, the people of God in the Messiah, are the people of the renewed covenant." The long story of Israel, of Abraham and his family, has found its goal, its *telos*, at last. It has had its explosive fulfillment in Jesus as Messiah, the *Christos:* take away the idea of Jesus as Messiah, as some readers of Paul still try to do, as though "Christ" was simply a proper name, not a title—do that and you will never get the point. The Messiah is the one who sums up Israel in himself, so that what was true of Israel is true of him. And now the new covenant has been inaugurated, and the people who are in Christ discover that when they confess with their lips that Jesus is Lord and believe in their heart that God raised him from the dead, they are wearing the badges which say, "We are the people of this renewed covenant." They are in fact "doing the Torah" in the deepest sense that God always intended, that Deuteronomy always held out.

And therefore they are also the renewed humanity through whom God is now rescuing and ruling the world and putting it to rights. We often screen out this stuff, but have you noticed that odd little bit at the start of 1 Corinthians 6? When Paul is saying that you shouldn't have lawsuits among yourselves, he challenges them: Don't you know that we are to judge angels? Our response to this will probably be, "Er, no, Paul, actually we didn't know that; where do you get that idea from?" I think he gets it from the apocalyptic traditions in Daniel and elsewhere, which have God's people exalted to a place of sovereignty over the world, sharing God's rule through which justice comes to the world at last. They are to be under God and over the world. That's what "reigning with Christ" actually means; we talk about it, we sing about it, but we too infrequently reflect on the reality of it. It comes again in Romans 5:17. Just when you expect Paul to say "as death reigned through the one man, so grace reigns through the one man," he says something different: "those who receive the gift of righteousness *will reign in life [basileusou-sin]* through the one man Jesus Christ." They will be *kings*. Paul lived in a world where there was already a *basileus*, a king. But no: *we* shall be "kings." And so in 1 Corinthians 15: the kingdom of God, which is over all the powers of the world, will be established not only *for* God's people but *through* God's people. We are the human beings who are designed to play the key role in God's renewal of all things. Don't so stress the doctrine of your own salvation that you fail to see what we are saved *for*.

In and through all of this, we are the people of God *in the Messiah*. We have been radically redefined and reformed through our incorporation into his death and resurrection. "I am crucified with the Messiah; nevertheless I live; yet not I but the Messiah lives in me; and the life I now life in the flesh I live by the faithfulness of the Son of God, who loved me and gave himself for me." The "faithfulness" of the Messiah? I know this has been controversial, so let me just explain very briefly how I see it. In Romans 3 Paul says that it looks as though God's plan for Israel and through Israel has gone totally wrong. God has promised to save the world through his people Israel, but Israel as a whole has gone off the rails, has failed to be faithful to God's commission. Israel has not failed simply at believing; no, Israel was given a commission.

You understand what a commission is. Supposing I give you a letter and ask you to deliver this letter to such-and-such a professor. If you were to be faithful to that commission, you would deliver the letter to the right person. You wouldn't keep the letter for yourself. Paul says that Israel is greatly privileged to be God's messenger, the nation through whom God has promised blessing for the world, but Israel, despite that privilege, has failed to be faithful. They were *entrusted* with the "oracles of God," for the sake of the world, not given them for themselves. So when Paul says that Israel has been faith*less*, he doesn't just mean that they haven't had faith in the sense of "believing in him"; he means they have been faithless *to that commission*. They haven't done what they were supposed to do. I have orthodox Jewish friends who will admit, with real humility, that ethnic Israel has indeed failed to bring the news of the true God and his covenant to the Gentile nations. And of course that is said without an ounce of anti-Jewish feeling, rather the reverse. It is simply the case that, if Israel's vocation was to be the light of the world, Israel has failed in that vocation.

So what is God going to do? Is God going to scrap the whole Israel idea altogether? There's a whole swath of Western thought which has said that, has said, in effect, that since the first plan has gone wrong, God has decided to do something quite different, to send his own Son to die for sinners, so we can forget about all that Israel stuff. Not a bit of it. That is the way to misread Romans and to misunderstand Paul at his very heart. Instead, Paul declares in Romans 3:21 that God's covenant faithfulness has now been revealed *through the faithfulness of the Messiah for the benefit of all those who are faithful*. He, the Messiah, is "Israel in person." That's why faith is not an arbitrary badge of membership in the Messiah's people. We are to be the people marked out by *pistis*, "faith" or "faithfulness" or, better, both, because he himself is the faithful One, the one who embodied the covenant faithfulness of God by offering to God the covenant faithfulness of Israel. And we, in him, are to be known by our own answering *pistis*, faith, faithfulness.

So we return to Galatians, where all this comes back full circle. In Galatians 2, all who believe in Jesus the Messiah belong at the same table. This, then and now, is the challenge to the powers.

This is the full context of the doctrine of justification. God will put the world right one day. He has promised to do so. He has launched that project in Jesus Christ; he is going to do it. How? Through human beings. Creation is longing for the revelation of the sons and daughters of God. Why? Because creation was subjected to futility, not of its own will but of the will of him who created it; because creation itself will be set free from its bondage to decay, to share the liberty of the glory of the children of God. When the children of God are glorified, creation will give a huge sigh of relief and say, "I'm so glad you lot have finally got your act together." Creation is longing to be wisely stewarded by the gentle, wise governance of human beings.

And therefore God puts human beings right, against the day when he will put the world right. Justification is not designed to take us out of the world but to qualify us to be God's putting-right people for the world. That's why between present justification and future justification comes the entire theology of justice. Unless we make those connections, we're not thinking Paul's thoughts after him. But how does that happen? It happens because then he sends his Son, as the faithful Israelite, who takes the weight of the world's sin on himself, in order then, once it's been defeated and dealt with, to launch his new creation. That is how it works.

 So the center of Paul's worldview, in terms of symbolism, is this community. It is about Philemon and Onesimus getting it together. It's about Euodia and Syntyche getting it together in Philippi. It's about Jew and Gentile learning to sit at the same table in Antioch or Galatia. That is the center: the united community. But how can that community be generated and sustained? How can such a fellowship keep going, when living in a world from which the normal symbols that define the various constituent communities have been taken away? The only way this community can be sustained, I believe, is through what we call *theology*. I believe when we are reading Paul we are seeing the birth of a discipline, which we now call Christian theology.

THE NEW TASK: A NEW KIND OF THEOLOGY

If you force Jews to do theology, these are the three things they will come up with: monotheism, election, eschatology.

1. Monotheism revised. You see, if you asked Jews of Paul's day what they believed about God and the world, about the future hope, about humankind and so on, they could give you answers. But that wasn't their central discipline. That wasn't what they habitually did. These things were not in dispute, and they were not primary community boundary markers. Jews will tell you to this day that theology isn't a characteristically Jewish subject of study. It's a Christian discipline. But if you take away the worldview markers of Paul's original Jewish setting—circumcision, Sabbath and food laws in particular—then you are left with a vacuum. Or, changing the metaphor, you will be left with a tent without ropes to hold it up in the winds of cultural, social and political pressures and challenges. Theology plays the key role within Paul's worldview. Theology has to grow from its previous size and role, to take on a new size and role, to be a new sort of task. The prayerful, wise contemplation of *who God really is*, and the reflection on and invocation of this God, has to be undertaken in quite a new way, in order that the united community, through its own worship and prayer and witness, can be rooted in this God and so sustained in its common life. That's why Paul says in Romans 12, as he summons people to obedient worship, that we have to be transformed by the renewal of our *mind*. It's not enough to coast along, doing this and that and hoping it will all work out.

Christians have always been in the forefront of education, within world history. There's a reason for this. Christians have always wanted to teach people to read. There's a reason for this. Christians have always wanted to love God with the *mind*, as well as with heart, soul and strength. There's a reason for this. God wants us to be, in Christ, people who can *think through* who he is and what therefore it means to worship and serve him. Unless every generation is doing this, the church will divide, the church will go soft in the middle, and the principalities and powers will say, "Oh good; we were worried for a minute, but now they're in disarray again, and we can go on running the world the way we want."

Who is this God of whom Paul speaks, and why does believing in this God have this effect?

He is the one God of Abraham. Jewish monotheism is absolutely basic for Paul. But it's a monotheism that has been radically redefined around Christ and the Spirit. Paul in several passages takes the Jewish statements of monotheism themselves and discovers Jesus in the middle of them. First Corinthians 8:6 is perhaps the best known example. Paul has taken the Jewish daily prayer, "Hear, O Israel, the Lord our God, the Lord is one," and has rephrased that prayer so that by "God" we mean "the Father," and by "Lord" (*kyrios*, YHWH) he means "Jesus Christ." "For us there is one God, the Father, . . . and one Lord, Jesus Christ."

Notice what this means. When I was younger, people used to say that the early Christians were all Jewish-style monotheists, who couldn't possibly think of Jesus too as in some sense divine. Incarnation couldn't have been envisioned until the church moved away from its early Jewish roots. That's absolute rubbish, and here is the evidence, and in other passages too. Jesus is, for Paul, at the heart of reenvisioned Jewish-style monotheism. And the Spirit, too: in 1 Corinthians 12, just at the point where Paul is saying that all Christian life is basically one, that there are many varieties of Christian life and expression but the same divine force behind it all—at the very point where he wants to say that it's all one, he says it in three different ways: varieties of gifts, but the same Spirit; varieties of service, but the same Lord; varieties of working, but the same God who works it all in all. It's all one; but it's Spirit, Lord and God.

The same point emerges in Galatians 4:6-9. God sends the Son and the Spirit of the Son. And then he says, "Now that you have come to know God, or rather to be known by God"—in other words, with this Son-and-Spirit dispensation, we see clearly for the first time who the true God really is. The passage is a piece of exodus theology, rooted in the narrative through which the slaves are freed by the redeeming power of God. But the exodus was the time at which, and the event through which, Israel came to know in a fresh way who the God of Abraham actually was. And Paul makes exactly the same claim. "Now, with the Messiah and the Spirit, you have come to know God—so how can you turn back to what are in effect pagan idols once more?" If the doctrine of the Trinity hadn't existed, it would be necessary, on the basis of these passages, to invent it.

The result of having this God for our God is—renewed humanness. You are remade in the image of God, and one of the basic spiritual laws is that you become like what you worship. You've got to serve somebody, and when you worship *this* God, a new, genuine humanness emerges. A humanness which knows what resources are there for and how to deal wisely with them. A humanness that knows what relationships are all about and how to handle them; difficult though they are, in Christ they can be healed. A humanness that knows about responsibility and how to shoulder it wisely for the good of all. A humanness, in other words, which isn't going to do what people normally do, and diminish resources, relationships and responsibilities into money, sex and power. We talk about those three because we live in a shrunken world. And our vocation is so to worship the creator God, so to reflect his image, that we are to grasp afresh the meaning of resources, relationships and responsibilities.

All this takes place within Caesar's world. There are "many gods, many lords," but you'd better watch out because Caesar is a pretty powerful one. And in that world money, sex and power are rampant.

2. Election revisited. Who are Israel? They are the circumcision; they are the family of Abraham, the seed of Abraham. And now they are refocused on the Messiah. The Jewish doctrine of election is rethought around the Messiah. This is new covenant theology.

This is difficult to state, because these days if you get anywhere near what I've just said somebody will use the *S* word: Supersession. "The church has superseded Israel"; that's what people will say I am saying. Actually, this is completely wrong, and the charge frequently rebounds onto the heads of the accusers. (Notoriously, those who claim to be reading Paul as an apocalyptic theologian, who imagines that God has swept away everything in the past and launched something totally new. This is not how apocalyptic Judaism functions, and such a scheme is worryingly close to that of Ernst Käsemann, who allowed himself to speak of "the hidden Jew in all of us.") But to discuss this in any detail we would need a full treatment of Romans 9–11, for which there is no time here. But let me just say this. In Romans 9:6–10:13 Paul tells the covenant story of Israel, the two-thousand-year story of the people of God, all heading on to the arrival of the King, the anointed One (Rom 10:4). He is the goal, the *telos*, the climax of the whole narrative. That is the point. How can it be anti-Jewish to celebrate the coming of Messiah at the climax of Israel's long history and the fulfillment of its ancient prophecies?

But Paul tells this story in a letter to Rome—precisely at the time when the Roman story was being told in a new way. The court poets and historians had been telling the story of Rome as a seven-hundred-year saga, which had now at last exploded into new life through the arrival of the king, the emperor, the savior, the son of God, the one who had brought justice, peace and prosperity to the world. From the beginning, from Romulus and Remus, there was a hidden purpose moving forward through the time of the Republic, but now the new day had arrived. Through this man, Augustus, a new age had dawned, an age they announced with the word *euangelion*, "gospel." Paul knows exactly what he's doing when he writes this particular letter to Augustus's capital city.

So, just as monotheism confronts the idols of the world in a new way when redefined in Jesus Christ and by the Spirit, so it is with the redefined doctrine of election. Perhaps it's because our world is afraid of this challenge that whenever we get anywhere near this point the world shouts "Supersession!" Caesar is quite happy with that move. It removes the church, at a stroke, from being a *political* challenge.

Because, as in Ephesians 3, the task of the church, to be the united community in Christ, is meant to be the standing rebuke to the powers. We are to be the people of reconciliation, the people of responsibility— and so the people who look at the powers of the world, who carve up the world and ill-treat it, and we hold them to account. Not because we're anarchists. Not because we are a Christian version of eighteenth-century left-wing philosophy. Far from it. God wants the world to be ordered. All the powers and principalities are created in and through and for Christ (Col 1). God is the God of order, not of chaos. This is the foundation of a Christian political theology. But as soon as you give anyone any power or responsibility you give them the temptation to abuse that for their own privilege, prestige and so on. Not least in the church. And when that happens they need to be dethroned, not so that there can then be a holy anarchy but so that there can be wise order. We go round this cycle again and again. Politics is the constant to-ing and fro-ing between tyranny and chaos. But we believe in Jesus Christ and in the sovereign, saving rule he exercises through his cross, resurrection and spirit. And we have the task of modeling before the world what that sort of *polis* would look like.

This challenge can never be undertaken as an independent thing, where we hide away from the world, keeping the light to ourselves, saying how dark the rest of the world is. Well, of course it is, if we're not shining our light into it! Paul says we've got to shine the light into the world, and we've got to hold the powers to account by what we *are*, and then and then only by what we *say*. That is the context for the apostolic task of mission.

3. Eschatology reimagined. After monotheism and election, there is eschatology. The great Jewish hope, that one day God would flood the world with his knowledge and love and glory, so that the wolf will lie down with the lamb, and a little child will lead them, because the earth will be full of *da'ath 'adonai*, "knowing YHWH." There will be a deep knowing of the Creator from every blade of grass, from every whale and every waterfall.

That's the Jewish hope. And to serve that Jewish hope there is the promise of the land. There is the hope that the land will be fruitful and prosperous. The land will turn out to be an advance metaphor for the renewal of the whole world. Then there is the hope of the rebuilding of the temple, but actually the hope is that one day God is going to do for the whole world what he was going to do for the temple. The temple is already a cosmic image. And all this will involve the rescue of Israel from its enemies, and this will involve the defeat of tyranny and the devil in every form. And this means ultimately the defeat of death itself. And that means resurrection. And it will involve, above all, the return of YHWH to Zion. He will come back and dwell in his world and with his people forever.

This is the Jewish hope, and Paul sees every bit of that Jewish hope fulfilled in Jesus the Messiah and implemented by the Spirit. And again, he articulates this over against the rather hope-less philosophies of his day.

Stoicism believed that the world did have a narrative, but that in that narrative the world would go on and on, and then one day it would dissolve into fire, and then be reborn and everything would happen all over again.

Epicureans believed in random process. They were the Darwinians of the first century, if you like, believing that the world consists of molecules doing their own thing, and if there is a god, he's so far away he's not really worth bothering about. Not much hope there unless you have money, land and slaves and can have a comfortable life.

But this eschatology is to be articulated in particular in the face of Caesar, and the imperial hope of his arrival. *Parousia* ("second coming" or "appearing") is not an Old Testament technical term. It is an imperial technical term. It's what happens (for instance) when Caesar has been away from Rome and comes back, and his royal and perhaps divine appearing is expected (by this time, some of the Caesars started to give themselves divine honors), and everyone goes out to meet him, to welcome him back into the city.

That's what is going on in 1 Thessalonians 4 and Philippians 3. Jesus is coming back, and it is at *his* name that every knee shall bow. In Philippians 3, Paul invites his readers to give up their privileges as he has given up his. How? They are not Jews. But at least some of them are Roman citizens, and all the city benefits from Roman patronage. And Paul says, "I want you to sit loose to your privileges." He upstages their Roman status by pointing to the true coming King. Please note, when Paul then says "our citizenship is in heaven" (Phil 3:20), he does not mean "that's our real home and one day we'll be going there." This ignores the way in which the whole logic of citizenship actually works. Rome had founded colonies all round the Greek world, partly at least to cope with the fact of thousands of veteran soldiers who had fought Rome's battles, especially in the civil wars of the first century B.C., but for whom there wasn't anything like enough room back in Italy, let alone in Rome itself. The last thing Rome wanted, in fact, was all those old soldiers returning to the mother country or city. So they founded colonies, whose inhabitants were to be citizens of Rome, but colonizing Greece (or wherever) with Roman culture. So what Paul means by saying "you are citizens of heaven," he means, "you are the people who are bringing the civilization of heaven into the world." And he doesn't say "one day you will be going away from here to the mother city," but "*from* heaven we expect the Savior, the Lord, Jesus the King"—those are all Caesar words, by the way—and he will come *here*, not to snatch us away but to change our humiliated state and body to be like his own. Paul, as often, quotes Psalm 8: "You crown him with glory and honor, putting all things in subjection under his feet." That is the Adam picture and also the Jesus picture. It's because of that—the biblical picture of human sovereignty over creation, fulfilled now in Jesus the Messiah—that we know that Jesus is Lord and Caesar isn't.

And within that eschatology, as in Romans 8, prayer is that bit of anticipated eschatology which we do even though we don't understand it, but which holds heaven and earth tightly together with the struggle and the groaning of creation. When we pray at the places where the world is in pain, we sense its pain in ourselves; and then, if we have faith, we sense the Spirit groaning within us. Where is God in all of this? God is not outside the pain, outside the mess. God is there at the heart of the mess. That's why Paul says we are chosen so that we might be "conformed to the image of his son" (Rom 8:29). Back to Philemon or to 2 Corinthians 5:21. Prayer stands cruciform at the place of the world's pain, to hold together Jew and Greek, slave and free, male and female, to hold together a battered and bleeding world, and say, "No. There is a different way to be human." Think of Desmond Tutu in South Africa with the "Commission for Truth and Reconciliation," and think of the enormous suffering this has cost Desmond personally. That is gospel work.

We need theology, then. We need it, not because it's a nice thing to get our ideas sorted out and our heads organized so that we can do the jigsaw of all these wonderful ideas. We need it because without prayerful reflective investigation of who God is, who the people of God are and what is the hope that belongs to our calling, without that prayerful, wise investigation the worldview whose central symbol is the one church of Jesus Christ will not be sustainable. Think of churches that have given up theology, and you'll see what I mean.

CONCLUSION

The aim is, as Paul says in Romans 15, "that you may with one heart and voice glorify the God and Father of our Lord Jesus Christ." Paul comes back at the end of his argument, in Romans 15:12, to Isaiah 11, to the Messianic portrait, the great eschatological scene. But this is how he leads up to it, from verse 7: "Therefore welcome one another, as the Messiah welcomed you, to the glory of God." There is the ecumenical imperative: shared worship, across traditional ethnic divisions. This is then at once explained by verses 8-9, which together form quite a complete summary of Paul's gospel: "The Messiah became a servant to the circumcised, because of the truthfulness of God, to confirm the promises to the patriarchs, and so that the Gentiles should glorify God for his mercy." There is an enormous amount of central Pauline teaching packed into those clauses.

Then Paul quotes from the Psalms, again urging the united praise which arises from the world. But he finishes with Isaiah 11. (If you've ever written anything careful and structured, you will know that you put your strongest points at the beginning and the end. That's exactly what Paul does here.) At the start of Romans, he describes his gospel in terms of Jesus as the risen, powerful Son of God and Lord (Rom 1:3-5), and he contrasts this, by strong implication, with the "son of god" who lives just up the street from where his Roman audience live. That "son of god," Caesar, demands your complete allegiance, and Paul says, "No. It's Jesus who does that."

So he reaches his final emphasis, making a huge circle around the whole argument of Romans, to the Messianic point: "the root of Jesse, who rises to rule the nations; and in him the nations shall hope."

But I don't want to end there. I want to end with the longest short journey in the world. We come back where we started: the journey home for a runaway slave. All that theology has to be focused, now on this church, now on these two people who are having such a difficult time, now on the crisis where Jews and Gentiles are separating at table, and now, perhaps, on the great political questions of the day and the challenge of the church to navigate its way through and bear witness to the light of Christ in a darkened world.

When you're working at these Philemon-type tasks (and most of us probably spend most of our lives working at that kind of task rather than the big, flashy, grandiose things that look so much fun), we are to be people who put into effect the exodus which Jesus Christ has achieved through his death. We are to be people who stand there between the Philemons and the Onesimuses of the world and say, "In Christ you are reconciled, and here's how it might work out. *This* life, *this* community, here, now, is where it matters."

May God give us grace so to study Paul prayerfully and wisely, that this worldview symbol of the united church will say to the principalities and powers of the world of our own day that Jesus is Lord and they are not. And may God give us courage to face whatever riots may come as a result.

Contributors

Jeremy Begbie is the Thomas A. Langford Research Professor in Theology at Duke Divinity School. He is also Senior Member at Wolfson College, Cambridge, and an Affiliated Lecturer in the Faculties of Divinity and Music at the University of Cambridge. Previously he has been Honorary Professor at the University of St. Andrews. He has authored numerous books, including *Voicing Creation's Praise: Towards a Theology of the Arts* (T & T Clark, 1991), *Theology, Music and Time* (Cambridge University Press, 2000) and *Resounding Truth: Christian Wisdom in the World of Music* (Baker, 2007).

Markus Bockmuehl is a Fellow of Keble College and Professor of Biblical and Early Christian Studies at the University of Oxford, having previously held professorships at the Universities of Cambridge and St. Andrews. Among the books he has authored or coedited are *Seeing the Word: Refocusing New Testament Study* (Baker Academic, 2006), *Scripture's Doctrine and Theology's Bible: How the New Testament Shapes Christian Dogmatics* (Baker Academic, 2008) and *Paradise in Antiquity: Jewish and Christian Views* (Cambridge University Press, 2010).

Richard B. Hays is the Dean and George Washington Ivey Professor of New Testament at Duke Divinity School. His book *The Moral Vision of the New Testament: Community, Cross, New Creation* (HarperSanFrancisco, 1996) was included among *Christianity Today's* list of the 100 most important religious books of the twentieth century. Among his recent publications are *The Conversion of the Imagination* (Eerdmans, 2005), *Seeking the Identity of Jesus: A Pilgrimage* (Eerdmans, 2008) and *Reading the Bible Intertextually* (Baylor University Press, 2009).

Edith M. Humphrey is the William F. Orr Professor of New Testament at Pittsburgh Theological Seminary. Her most recent books include *Ecstasy and Intimacy: When the Holy Spirit Meets the Human Spirit* (Eerdmans, 2005), *And I Turned to See the Voice* (Baker Academic, 2007) and *Grand Entrance: Worship on Earth as in Heaven* (Brazos, 2011).

Sylvia C. Keesmaat is an adjunct professor at the Institute for Christian Studies and the Toronto School of Theology as well as an instructor in the Creation Care Studies Program in Belize. Dr. Keesmaat has written, along with her husband Brian Walsh, *Colossians Remixed: Subverting the Empire* (IVP Academic, 2004). She is also author of *Paul and His Story: (Re)Interpreting the Exodus Tradition* (Sheffield Academic Press, 1999) and editor of *The Advent of Justice* (Dordt College Press, 1994).

Nicholas Perrin holds the Franklin S. Dyrness Chair of Biblical Studies at the Wheaton College Graduate School. Between 2000 and 2003, he was research assistant for N. T. Wright. He is the author and editor of numerous articles and books, including *Thomas: The Other Gospel* (Westminster John Knox, 2007), *Lost in Transmission: What We Can Know About the Words of Jesus* (Thomas Nelson, 2007) and most recently *Jesus the Temple* (Baker Academic, 2010). He is coeditor of *Questioning Q: A Multidimensional Critique* (IVP Academic, 2004).

Marianne Meye Thompson is the George Eldon Ladd Professor of New Testament at Fuller Theological Seminary. She is coauthor of *Introducing the New Testament: Its Literature and Theology* (Eerdmans, 2001). Among her other books are *1–3 John* (IVP Academic, 1992), *The God of the Gospel of John* (Eerdmans, 2001) and *A Commentary on Colossians and Philemon* (Eerdmans, 2005).

Kevin J. Vanhoozer is Blanchard Professor of Theology at the Wheaton College Graduate School. Previously he was Research Professor of Systematic Theology at Trinity Evangelical Divinity School and Senior Lecturer in Theology and Religious Studies at the University of Edinburgh. He is the author of numerous books, including *First Theology: God, Scripture & Hermeneutics* (IVP Academic, 2002) and *The Drama of Doctrine: A Canonical-Linguistic Approach to Christian Theology* (Westminster John Knox, 2005), which was named best theology book of 2006 by *Christianity Today*. He has also edited *The Dictionary for Theological Interpretation of the Bible* (Baker, 2005) and most recently authored *Remythologizing Theology: Divine Action, Passion, and Authorship* (Cambridge University Press, 2010).

Brian J. Walsh is a Christian Reformed campus minister at the University of Toronto. He is author of *Truth Is Stranger Than It Used to Be: Biblical Faith in a Postmodern Age* (IVP Academic, 1995). He has also coauthored *Colossians Remixed: Subverting the Empire* (IVP Academic, 2004) with his wife, Sylvia Keesmaat, and *Beyond Homelessness: Christian Faith in a Culture of Dislocation* (Eerdmans, 2008) with Steve Bouma-Prediger.

N. T. Wright has recently been appointed to a Chair in New Testament and Early Christianity at the University of St. Andrews after serving seven years as Bishop of Durham and previously as Canon of Westminster. He also formerly taught New Testament studies at Cambridge, McGill and Oxford Universities. Dr. Wright has written over 40 books and hundreds of articles at both scholarly and popular levels, including three volumes in the acclaimed series *Christian Origins and the Question of God* (Fortress Press, 1992, 1997 and 2003). Other works include *Justification: God's Plan and Paul's Vision* (IVP Academic, 2009) and most recently *After You Believe: Why Christian Character Matters* (HarperOne, 2010).

Subject Index

Scripture Index